For Jim _____
who helped make
it possible for
this book to
be written.

Hadley Read

Communication: Methods for All Media

Communication: Methods for All Media

HADLEY READ

UNIVERSITY OF ILLINOIS PRESS

URBANA : CHICAGO : LONDON

TO PHILLIP NATHAN READ

*for reasons we both knew
without having to say*

Contents

About This Book

Throughout history man's progress has been related to his ability to communicate with other men. His failures and frustrations have often resulted from his inability to communicate.

Of all human experiences, few are as contradictory as communicating with others. Communication is both simple and complex. The results can be rewarding or disappointing, exciting or frustrating, important or trivial. It is the process we use most in our daily lives and perhaps understand least.

We have developed communication systems to permit man on earth to talk with man on the moon. Yet mother often cannot talk with daughter, father with son, black with white, labor with management, or democracy with communism.

Communication science has given us cameras that transmit color television from outer space, computers that "think," machines that reduce the printed page to dots of film, and devices that listen over vast distances. Yet we are still trying to master the communication principles that will help us teach all mankind how to live in peace and how to stop polluting the environment in which we live.

While we all communicate in the business of living, we tend to assign the communication business to professional writers, editors, broadcasters, advertisers, public relations experts, composers, artists, and others with specialized talents. The ability to communicate is obviously essential to men and women in these professions.

But the ability to communicate is equally important if you are now, or intend to be, a teacher, social worker, farm leader, labor leader, extension agent, conservationist, or a representative of business and industry. It is important whenever you must help people learn something they didn't know before. In such professions, you are the transmitter of information, knowledge, facts, opinions, and attitudes. You are in the business of saying something in some way to someone for some purpose. Your success depends upon your ability to communicate—to know and to understand the process of communication—and to use the necessary skills.

That is what this book is about—the process of communication, the environment in which communication takes place, and the skills needed to make the process work. The book attempts to blend theory with practice, because theory without practice contributes little, and practice unsupported by theory may only represent a repetition of errors. This book is not intended for the professionals in the various communication fields; rather, it is indebted to them for their contributions. But it is written for you and for others in professions in which your success and satisfaction are related to your ability to communicate effectively.

A wise man once observed that any person who claims originality for his ideas or views either has a short memory or is telling an untruth. In truth, then, I cannot claim originality for the material in this book. But neither can I accurately or adequately identify and credit all those who influenced my thinking about communication or who helped bridge the gap between theory and practice.

I have learned from many teachers and associates throughout a long period of time. Special mention, though, must be made of those who helped design and teach a series of communication workshops sponsored by the National Association of State Universities and Land-Grant Colleges through its National Project in Agricultural Communications. I have borrowed liberally from references used during the workshops and from notes of the discussion sessions. I want especially to acknowledge the contributions of George Axinn, David Berlo, A. Conrad Posz, Russell Jenkins, Joseph Bohlen, George Beal, William E. Bright, Jr., and Ralph Nichols.

I have gained much, too, from association and discussion with present and former staff members of the University of Illinois Office of Agricultural Communications and owe special thanks to John Behrens, Glen Broom, Jim Evans, Jack Everly, Joseph Harris, Donald Schild, and Victor Stephen.

In a special way, one learns from observing the interplay of communication within the family. In my family, my wife Margaret, sons Gregory and Phillip, and daughter Mary have each enriched my understanding of the mysteries of communication.

A unique category of personal and professional appreciation is reserved for colleagues Helen Fry and Delbert Dahl who, during the manuscript's final stages of delivery, served as sympathetic critics, consultants, editors, and cheerleaders.

While my debts are many, I must accept final responsibility, of course, for filtering knowledge through my mental processes and matching it against my experiences and observations in the field of communication. In relating the contributions of social scientists to the practical assignment of getting information to people, I have at times only sketched outlines of concepts without filling in the shades of meaning or the details of application and exception. I trust that you, in turn, will match my views against your experiences and observations.

You will notice that I have divided the book into two unequal parts. The first seven chapters, roughly one-third of the book, make up Part I and deal with the process and environment of communication. The remainder of the book, Part II, deals with the skills of communication.

The material is presented in this way because the perfection of any communication skill—writing, speaking, visualizing—depends upon an understanding of the communication environment and an application of the communication process. If, in your haste to learn more about newspaper writing, radio and television broadcasting, or exhibit building, you skip Part I, neither of us will have achieved his purpose.

HADLEY READ
Champaign, Illinois
October 1, 1971

Part I

THE PROCESS AND
ENVIRONMENT OF
COMMUNICATION

All of us will be better listeners, writers, speakers, editors, artists, and broadcasters when we more fully understand what takes place when people communicate with one another.

CHAPTER I

The Process and
the Purpose

A group of leaders were in a meeting at the University of Illinois. Some were teachers, some were administrators, and some were industry representatives. Each was asked to describe or define the term "communication." Here are some of their answers:

It is our method of teaching and giving information to our students—which should encourage active exchange of ideas rather than passive acceptance.

The transfer of ideas, enthusiasm, information, and understanding among individuals.

Communication is the transmitting of messages from one source to another by whatever means is available or seems desirable.

To impart or express knowledge, thoughts, or opinions and feelings to another person in such a manner that he understands.

To express oneself clearly and effectively in both writing and oral communication, to understand the ideas of others, and to acquire cer-

3

tain skills and habits required for critical and constructive thinking, including the proper use of the English language.

The ability to transcend all physical, mental, and emotional blocks to transmit an idea so that it moves from mind to mind.

Any means of expression by which we get ideas or knowledge across to others.

Each definition touches the essence of communication. Any one could serve as the starting point for this discussion. Communication does involve the "transfer of ideas, information, and understanding." Communication may not be a "method of teaching," but it is involved in all teaching. We communicate "by whatever means is available." And for communication to take place, we must "transcend all physical, mental, and emotional blocks."

COMMUNICATION—A PROCESS

Beginning with the 1950s, it has become increasingly common to define and discuss communication as "a process." There is a reason. The term "process" suggests an activity going on all of the time in a continually changing environment. Communication between two people changes as their relationship changes from strangers to friends. It changes as they go from being fresh and wide awake in the morning to tired and sleepy at night.

But even though we know that communication is a continuing process, we can "stop the action" and look at the essential parts. The popular approach is to design and describe a model of the process that helps us to understand how the process works.

In 1947 Claude Shannon and Warren Weaver of the Bell Telephone Laboratory suggested a model for the process of electronic communication. They said that for communication to take place there must be (1) a message source, (2) a transmitter, (3) a signal, (4) a receiver, and (5) a destination.

Later, communication scholars adapted the Shannon-Weaver model for electronic communication, using different terms and modifying some of the various parts. One of the most popular was designed by David Berlo, then of Michigan State University, and labeled the "S-M-C-R Model." For communication to take place there must be a *sender* of communication, a *message* to be sent, a *channel* for carrying the message, and a *receiver* of the message.

Two other terms help explain the process—encoding and decoding. In other words, before a message can be sent the sender must encode the message—translate it into words, signals, or some sort of symbols that the channel can carry. The telephone instrument encodes spoken words into electrical impulses that can be sent over the telephone wire. Or, to use another example, a message for a pretty girl might be encoded into an appreciative whistle.

The receiver must decode the message. The telephone instrument at the receiving end of the line decodes the electrical impulses into spoken words for the receiver of the message. In the case of the pretty girl, her mental processes decode the whistle into the thought phrase, "He finds me attractive." A word of caution here. Perfect communication takes place when the message is decoded by the receiver as an exact reproduction of the message sent by the sender. Unfortunately the pretty girl may decode the whistle message into the thought phrase, "He is a wolf and he insults me."

While Berlo and others do not include the purpose of communication as a part of their models, they agree that all communication has a purpose. Purpose is the functional reason for communication. It is always there, and we will talk more about its importance later.

When translating any model of the communication process into everyday terms we may say, *"The process of communication takes place when someone says something in some way to someone else for a purpose."* The *someone* is the sender; *something* is the message; *some way* is the channel; *someone else* is the receiver; and *purpose* is the reason for communicating in the first place.

The intriguing aspect of the process of communication is that we use it practically every moment of our waking hours. We either send messages or receive them. The process is in operation when we say "good morning" to a friend, stop for a red light at an intersection, have a bull session, write a news story, read the newspaper, perform on radio, listen to the radio, speak to a group at a meeting, or show slides of our recent vacation. Someone is saying something in some way to someone else for a purpose. There is a sender, a message, a channel, and a receiver. Messages are encoded and decoded.

But if that is all there is to the communication process, why is it so complicated? Why are there so many failures? Why can't mother talk with daughter, father with son, or black with white? Why do two people read the same news story, listen to the same speech, or watch the same movie, and come away with distinctly different impressions? Why does your friend meet you *on* the corner *by* the drugstore when you distinctly told him to meet you *in* the drugstore *on* the corner?

One of the participants at the Illinois workshop mentioned earlier came close to the answer when he observed that communication must "transcend all physical, mental, and emotional blocks to transmit an idea so that it moves from mind to mind." Communication fails because physical, mental, and emotional blocks get in the way. When Shannon and Weaver discussed their electronic communication model they spoke of interference from "noise" in the system. We've all had the experience of trying to talk on the telephone with a jackhammer pounding outside the window. The jackhammer noise interfered not only with what we were saying but also with what the receiver was receiving. The signal was garbled and distorted. The message went into the system as *Thursday* and came out as *thirsty*.

We can analyze why communication succeeds or fails by taking the communication model apart and looking at each of the elements, even though we appreciate that all elements are related and interdependent.

We logically plan an automobile trip by first identifying our destination. We just as logically examine the process of communication by first considering purpose, because purpose is the *destination* of our communication effort. In Chapters 2 and 3 we will look at the other elements of the process—audience, message, sender, and channel.

A PROCESS WITH A PURPOSE

If a friend thinks or asks, "Why are you telling me this?" you can be fairly sure you are experiencing a failure in communication. The friend didn't understand the purpose of the message, and there is a good chance you did not fully understand or identify the purpose either.

To communicate effectively we must understand and appreciate the role of purpose in the communication process. We must know exactly why we are communicating. What do we expect to accomplish? What is our intent? What do we want the receiver to think or do?

We may say that we communicate for a wide variety of reasons. We communicate to inform, to teach, to report facts, to entertain, or just to pass the time of day. These are handy, everyday labels for explaining why we communicate, but they may not clearly identify the root purpose of communication. Why inform? Why teach? Why entertain?

When we inform, teach, or entertain we are actually trying to influence someone in some way—to produce a specific response from the receiver of the message. In discussing his model, Berlo says flatly that all communication intends to *persuade* the receiver in some specific way.

Newspapers "inform" their readers about the rising level of crime in the streets. In so doing they influence or persuade their readers in a variety of ways—to take personal precautions, to vote for stiffer crime laws, or to pay closer attention to their children.

A play in the theater or on television may "entertain," but the writer of the play intended to influence his audience. He wanted his message to produce a specific kind of response. He did, in fact, intend to persuade.

If we agree that the purpose of communication is to influence or persuade someone, then we must take the next step and clearly identify the someone. Specifically, what person or persons do we want to persuade with the message?

The county extension agent who says he is writing a news story for "farmers" to help them "raise better cattle" is falling short of precisely identifying the purpose of his communication effort. The receivers of his message—the "who" of his purpose —are not *all* of the farmers in the county but only those *who raise cattle*. His real purpose is to influence those cattle growers to *adopt certain practices* that will permit them to produce more pounds of beef with less feed or at less cost.

Once we clearly identify the receiver of the message and agree that the intent is to influence his behavior, there is a final step in refining the purpose of communication. When and how will the receiver benefit if he does change his behavior? Immediately? At some specific time in the future? Gradually, during a long period of time? A combination of all three ways? The sellers of headache remedies promise "immediate relief from aches and pains." They say "you will feel better fast" or "your headache will disappear in minutes." The sellers of retirement life insurance policies set a goal at some time in the future for reaping the benefits of responding to their message. The man who sells air conditioners tells us that a favorable response to his message will bring immediate benefits that will last all during the "long, hot months of summer."

The county extension agent, writing the news story about better production practices, will communicate most effectively if his message makes clear when and how farmers will benefit by responding to his message.

Regardless of communication method, we help eliminate communication failure when we define our purpose by asking this question: "What person or persons do I want to influence with my message, in what way, for what reason?"

THE OBLIGATION OF RESPONSIBILITY

Having established his belief that the ultimate purpose of communication is to persuade, Berlo stresses the importance of responsibility on the part of all who communicate. These are his observations on responsibility:

We are manipulators. We are agents of effect. Whenever we communicate, we want our audiences to know that some things are true, and some things are not—as we see it. We want our audiences to understand that some interpretations are adequate, and others are not —as we see them. We want our audiences to be convinced that some courses of action are desirable, and some are not—as we believe them to be. We communicate to manipulate. We communicate to change. He who says that he has no intention of manipulating— persuading—changing—altering his audience either hides his real goals or demonstrates an unawareness of the nature of the communication process. To teach is to manipulate; to write is to manipulate; to broadcast is to manipulate.

We have a responsibility to:

1. Recognize that we are manipulators—agents of change. We can not duck our responsibility by looking on ourselves as agents of "truth," or presenters of information. We must recognize what we are about when we select and present information, make inferences, and draw conclusions.

2. Know whereof we speak. We must not only experience the subject matter which we report. We must be aware of the principles of verification, the methods ascertaining truth. If we are to communicate what we believe to be the truth, we must know it when we see it.

3. Understand the principles of inference. If we are to contribute interpretations, we must know what we are about. What do we mean by deductive validity—inferential probability? These are not academic concepts. We operate daily as if we understood them. Understand them we must.

4. Predict the effect of the variables of the communication process. We must know how people learn, how social action occurs, what are the processes of communication, how people behave in groups, etc. We must understand this not only to

improve our effectiveness, but to assess what we are doing—responsibility.

5. Utilize language adequately. When we intend to report, we must understand the structure of the language of reporting. When we intend to interpret, we must understand the language of interpretation. When we intend to judge, we must understand the language of judgment. We must not confuse these functions of language, or we shall risk manipulating our audiences unintentionally. It is not manipulation which is irresponsible; it is casual, unintentional, capricious manipulation which is evil.

6. Possess faith in man. Without this, adherence to my first five principles will produce psychosis, indecision, equivocation. We must realize that we are deficient in the skills that are necessary for effective and responsible communication. We must realize that we will err—and live with it. Our faith in man can not be blind, mystical, or all embracing. We must recognize the limitations of man: his tendency to judge character and sentiment, not issues; his tendency to be irrational; his tendency to operate on limited, short-sighted, and selfish goals. We must recognize all these things. Nevertheless, if we have not faith in the potential of man, communication is not worth the effort.

These are just a few possible criteria of responsibility. Some are debatable. The list is far from conclusive. My real position on responsibility is this: We can never be sure that we are responsible, that we are wise, that we speak the truth, that we analyze validly, that we conclude beneficially. All we can do is worry about it. All we can do is think about it, whenever we communicate. My faith in man is this: If he can be convinced that responsibility is his personal concern, that he must manipulate, but that he must strive to do this responsibly, if he is frustrated continually, and always faced with self-doubt and self-criticism, WE WILL COME OUT ALL RIGHT.

CHAPTER 2

The Audience and the Message

To communicate effectively we must know and understand our audiences. We can't define audiences simply by putting people in occupation categories—farmers, housewives, carpenters, doctors, businessmen, and so on. Such a breakdown helps, but it is not enough.

We must know more about the fellow we are speaking to, writing for, or showing pictures to. What kind of person is he? What does he know? How does he think? What does he read, watch, and listen to? The closer we come to answering such questions, the less chance we have of communication failure.

KNOWLEDGE—WHAT DOES HE KNOW?

As receivers of messages we use two expressions to signal a communication breakdown. We may say, "The guy is talking over my head." We become irritated. The speaker or writer has assumed that we know more about the subject than we do. Either he does not understand *our* level of knowledge, or he is trying to impress us with *his* knowledge. If his purpose is to influence our understanding of the subject, he has failed. If his purpose is to impress us with his authority, he may have succeeded. More likely he has failed in this case, too, because his purpose and our purpose contradict each other. He wastes his time and ours. There is "noise" in the system, and the message does not get through.

A comparable breakdown occurs when we say, "The guy is talking down to me." That means the sender of the message doesn't think we know as much about the subject as we actually do. The speaker or writer insults our intelligence, and we tune him out.

Regardless of channel, we cannot select the right message or present it effectively unless we know how much the audience knows about the subject. With a large audience there will be a range of knowledge levels, of course. Ideally, we will be aware of the range and will select and present our message to "fit" the middle group. We can use words and phrases to let the audience know we are aware that some know more about the subject than others. We can say, "Many of you probably know this, but . . ." and then go on and cover the material for those who don't know. Or we can say, "For those of you who have not had this experience, let me point out. . . ."

Defining the audience includes knowing what the receiver knows and doesn't know about the messages we are sending to him.

ATTITUDES—WHAT DOES HE BELIEVE?

Attitudes, while more difficult to determine, may be even more important than level of knowledge. Attitudes include the way people think about and respond to other people, ideas, concepts, and philosophies.

A person has all kinds of attitudes, of course, but there are three categories that apply directly to the process of communication—attitudes about the source of the message, about the message itself, and about the receiver himself.

The receiver's attitude toward the source of a message may determine whether communication succeeds or fails. If the receiver likes us, trusts us, and has confidence in our judgment, the chances for our success are obviously much better than if he doesn't like us or has doubts about our knowledge or judgment.

The audience may have favorable or unfavorable attitudes— favorable, it is to be hoped—because of previous experiences. Attitudes may also be influenced by identification and association of the message source. Being a "university professor" may help create favorable attitudes with some audiences and unfavorable attitudes with others. Good and bad attitudes may be associated with our identification with the medical profession, the legal profession, or with farmers, labor leaders, or government officials.

The audience, whether a single person or a large group, has attitudes toward the message itself in addition to the source of the message. For years farmers judged other farmers by whether corn rows were straight and true. When soil conservationists first tried to get farmers to plant corn on the contour—around the hill instead of up and down—attitudes toward the message were negative. Contoured rows were not straight.

Many messages carry built-in attitudes, either favorable or unfavorable. Most of us react negatively to messages that cost more money without giving added pleasure—higher rents, higher taxes, or higher food costs. We react positively to messages that give us pleasure with little or no additional cost.

Finally, the receiver of our messages has attitudes about himself. He thinks of himself as a winner or a loser, successful or unsuccessful, informed or uninformed, secure or insecure. And the way he thinks about himself affects the way he responds to every message.

Most school dropouts, for example, think of themselves as failures or potential failures. Messages intended to influence them to return to school recognize this self-attitude. Charles

Atlas built a multi-million-dollar body-building business by directing his sales messages to people who thought of themselves as frail, unattractive, and unimpressive. Fortunes have been made in the cosmetic industry by developing products and directing messages that take advantage of a woman's image of herself—attitudes about herself as she is and as she would like to be.

We cannot give a simple formula—or a complicated one, for that matter—that assures success in measuring audience attitudes. Industry spends millions of dollars annually on attitude research to learn what people "think" about automobiles, air travel, life insurance, breakfast food, perfume, and hundreds of other items.

You may not be in the big business of attitude determination, but you face a similar task if you are a county agent trying to get farmers to adopt new practices, a social worker trying to persuade low-income families to spend money more wisely, or a school representative hoping to convince local citizens to support a bond issue.

COMMUNICATION BEHAVIOR—WHAT DOES HE READ, WATCH, OR LISTEN TO?

We must know a great deal about the audience's communication behavior before we can encode messages in the right way and send them over the right channels.

We should know, obviously, whether the people in our audience can read, how well they read, and how much they read. When writing, we must use a level of language that the audience can receive, decode, and understand.

Many audiences spend little time reading but a lot of time listening to the radio and watching television. To reach such audiences we will be wasting our time writing news stories, sending bulletins and leaflets, or maybe even sending letters. Our best channel will be the spoken word—person-to-person or on radio or television.

We often hear the expression "he doesn't speak my language"

or "that's sure Greek to me." The sender speaks or writes English but his language differs completely from that of the receiver. The expression "it's cool, man" means something quite specific to members of the younger generation, but it may not have the same meaning to those who are older.

Effective communication does not start with knowing your subject. It starts with knowing your audience and the reason or reasons for communicating with them.

We have talked about knowledge, attitudes, and communication behavior as separate characteristics of audiences. Actually, these characteristics are all related and intermixed. A person's skill with language affects both what he knows and how he thinks. What a person knows and thinks affects his communication behavior. Knowledge affects our attitudes toward people, things, and social systems. Attitudes affect our search for knowledge and our acceptance of the new and the different.

MOTIVATION

When we speak about what a person knows, how he thinks, and how he communicates with others, we are talking about the nature of man. The "nature of man" also includes an array of human motivations.

Some social scientists suggest that four basic needs motivate every human being, and that man's life is directed toward priority efforts to satisfy these needs. These needs have been identified as (1) security, (2) response, (3) recognition, and (4) new experiences. Every person attaches a different value to each of these needs.

The wish for *security* has many interpretations. Money and wealth mean security to some. Spiritual beliefs mean security to others. Some people think of security in terms of good health, protection from physical harm, freedom from debt, a nice home, acceptance by friends and neighbors, or a suitable role in society.

When strong enough, the wish for security motivates some people to accumulate great wealth. Others become misers and hide their "security" under the mattress.

When we have a strong urge to have people "like us," we are attempting to satisfy our need for *response*. We want people to extend themselves to us, to need us, to appreciate us, and to love us.

Such motivation leads us to do the "acceptable"—actions that will please our friends, neighbors, parents, and professional associates.

Children, especially, have a strong need for response. They want to be loved, admired, praised. They want people to be aware of them and would rather be scolded than ignored.

The fellow who wants the flashiest car, the biggest house, the fattest cattle, or the cleanest wheat fields may be seeking security. More likely, he is motivated by the need for *recognition*. This fellow strives to be "better" than his neighbors down the road. He wants status. He wants to be somebody. He wants people to know his name, look up to his position, and acknowledge his place in society.

The need for recognition may, and often does, oppose the need for response. Being at the top of the heap may bring recognition, but it may not win friends.

For some people the most compelling need calls for them to sample life's *new experiences*. They are attracted to the untried and the unknown. To satisfy this need they climb mountains, take trips, try new foods, and adopt new life styles. Often, but not always, the desire for new experiences relates to the desire for recognition. It generally conflicts with the need for security.

All of us, especially as we grow older, experience conflicts in the needs that motivate us. We want to belong and to be accepted by the group (response), but we want to protect our individual personality, to speak our piece, and to be looked up to (recognition). We think we should play it safe (security), but we suspect it would be more fun to try something new and different (new experiences).

The better we understand the needs of people in our audiences, the better we can direct our messages to satisfy those needs. We can also code our messages with the most effective appeal.

Too often we use the appeal of goodness or worthwhileness of a practice or an activity to get people to change their behavior. It is not the practice or the activity itself that is good or worthwhile. The real issue is whether the change in behavior satisfies one of the receiver's needs.

Most people do not react to a message because such action is good for them. They react because they are convinced that such action will bring them response, security, recognition, or a new experience.

Even with the purpose defined and the audience known, communication can fail if we don't select the correct message or if we handle the correct message in the wrong way. The message is the "something" that someone says to someone else for some purpose.

We can analyze messages in terms of three somewhat independent but closely related characteristics: (1) content, (2) code, and (3) appeal.

MESSAGE CONTENT

Content is the substance of a message. It is the "thing" or the combination of "things" we select to send to the receiver to achieve our purpose. Communication success depends partly upon how wisely and carefully we select and combine the things that make up the content of our message.

Message content usually relates to the question-words who, what, when, where, why, and how. It should answer questions the receiver might ask before deciding upon his response to the message. Who said that? What proof? When did it happen? Where should the action take place? How do I do it? Why?

We also can think of content in terms of simple, everyday words we use all the time—facts, opinions, rumors, gossip, distortions, assertions, interpretations. But in using these words to describe content we identify one of the basic truths about communication and human behavior. Messages by themselves have no meaning. The meaning is in the mind of the sender and the receiver. What constitutes facts to us as the source may be considered only opinion by the receiver. The message intended to convey an opinion may be translated and interpreted by the receiver as a fact—or as a distortion.

As the source or sender, we determine and structure the content of messages. We decide what "bits" to include and what to leave out, what to play up and what to play down, what to put first and what to put last. We choose between available facts if there are such facts, weigh the value of opinions, and decide between too much and too little. We accomplish this task best when we know the audience and anticipate the questions the message must answer.

What message content should a wife select who wants her husband to take his umbrella to work this morning?

Her content might be a simple suggestion: "I think you should take your umbrella to work this morning." If the husband has a high regard for the source and his previous experience with her advice has been good, the simple content may produce the desired response. But it may not, since the question *why* has not been answered.

So the wife might say, "The weather report says yesterday's rain will continue today, so I think you should take your umbrella to work this morning." The *why* question has been answered but the content may still fail to get response because the receiver's dislike of umbrellas is greater than his concern about getting wet.

The wife may achieve her purpose by adding one more bit of content to her message ". . . and then you won't get your suit all wet and wrinkled before your important meeting with the president of the board."

MESSAGE CODE

Message code may be defined as any symbol or combination of symbols capable of expressing the message, being transmitted, being received, and then being translated by the receiver. We may group codes into two broad categories—verbal and nonverbal. Most messages are coded in a combination of verbal and nonverbal symbols.

We fail to communicate when we lack skill in coding our message, when we use the wrong code, or when the receiver lacks skill in translating the code we have used.

Verbal Codes

Most of our communicating is done by writing or speaking, so we code our messages into language symbols, either written or spoken. We select words, put them together in sentences, arrange the sentences into paragraphs, and structure the paragraphs into some logical start-to-finish order. Our success, then, depends upon how well we select and use words (code symbols) that can be correctly translated and understood by the receiver.

Written codes are translated (decoded) through the eye and the sense of sight. Spoken codes are translated by the ear and the sense of sound. People vary in their abilities to translate either the written language or the spoken language. Physical condition, education, habits—all affect a person's skill in receiving and interpreting written or spoken words.

Nonverbal Codes

Much of our communication—perhaps more than we think—is accomplished through the use of nonverbal symbols. We communicate when we smile, frown, squint, raise a hand, point a finger, clench a fist, rub our faces. We communicate when we whistle a tune, wear perfume, or enter a room.

Nonverbal codes most often carry emotional messages—fear, hate, love, happiness, sadness, concern, envy, elation, despair.

Often, but not always, we use verbal and nonverbal codes in

combination. We raise our hand and say "stop." We beckon and say "come." We smile and say "thank you." We draw a picture and say "here's how it works."

Cosmetic manufacturers send out their sales letters on scented paper. Radio combines music with words to sell soap, cigarettes, new cars, and a host of other products. Motion pictures use theme music to support the messages conveyed by the scenes and dialogue. Some parts of messages are even coded in silence or white space.

Given a purpose, an audience, and message content, communication succeeds or fails, depending upon our ability to choose and use the proper code or combination of codes. This is one of the communication skills we will discuss in Part II.

MESSAGE APPEAL

People respond to satisfy one or more of their basic needs—security, response, recognition, and new experiences. There may be others, and there may be different ways to express those four. But we can agree that people do have wishes or needs that motivate them, and communication will fail unless the receiver believes the message will help him satisfy one or more of his needs.

The task, then, is to treat the message with a motivational appeal. What is our bargain? What are we offering in order to achieve the purpose of our message? Do we suggest that by responding the audience will achieve security? Response? Recognition? A new experience? If he takes the action we propose, will he be wiser, richer, more successful, more attractive, more important, less afraid?

People's needs often are in conflict. Our message urges the receiver to have the "new experience" of a trip to Hawaii, but that appeal must overcome his need for "security" associated with staying in the familiar environment of home. Our message urges a school dropout to return to school in order to "be somebody" (recognition). But freedom from school satisfies the dropout's need for new experiences and for the response of associates who are also dropouts.

Appeals fall short if they only suggest higher crop yields, more milk in the pail, greater returns on investment, higher profits. Higher returns for what purpose? More milk in the pail to satisfy what basic needs?

We make mistakes when we assign motives to people. We also fail to communicate when our messages appeal to false motives. The farmer who wants more than anything else to be liked by his neighbors may not want his yields to be too much higher than everyone else's—as strange as that may seem. The youngster who climbs the highest tree doesn't respond to an assigned motive of safety and security when asked to come down. He has his own motives, thank you.

Unfortunately there is no easy way to be certain we are treating our message with the right appeal. Choosing appeals is another phase of communication skill. Our skill can be sharpened by observing people; by noting how they think, speak, and act; by asking questions; by learning from trial and error. If our messages consistently fail to achieve their purpose, we can suspect that we have selected the wrong content, used a poor code, or treated the message with the wrong appeal.

CHAPTER 3

The Sender and
the Channel

As the sender of a message, we make all initial communication decisions. We decide whether to speak or be silent, whether to dial the telephone, send the letter, write the news story, make the radio announcement. We decide message purpose, identify receivers, determine message content, select codes, choose appeals, and pick the channel for transmitting the message. The questions asked and answered in the preceding chapter to help us understand audiences can also be asked and answered to help us understand ourselves better as message senders in the communication process.

KNOWLEDGE—WHAT DO WE KNOW?

Much time is wasted debating the question of who makes the best teacher. One side says the best teacher is the man who is the world's authority in his field—students will learn from him regardless of how he teaches. The other side argues that the best

22

teacher is the man who knows students and knows how to teach —he can teach any subject. The ideal teacher, of course, is the man who knows his subject and also knows how to teach.

As the sender we may be either the originating source or the interpretive source. As the originating source, we base message content upon personal knowledge gained from experience, observations, and formal study and research. We must be aware. We may know so much that we may have trouble adjusting our knowledge level to the knowledge level of the audience. If so, we may speak or write "over the heads" of the audience without knowing it. We may code our message in the special language of our technical field and learn later that the language was "foreign" to the audience.

There is an equal danger in knowing too little. We may have wide knowledge about agriculture but find ourselves speaking or writing "down" to a group of farmers about their business of raising beef cattle. We have *general* knowledge about their business. Their knowledge is *specialized*.

In many cases, perhaps most, we will be the interpretive source of the message. We select and interpret messages from other sources. This is the traditional role of the editor, reporter, and newscaster. We may play this role as a county extension agent quoting a university specialist, or as the public-information person for the school system quoting the members of the school board.

In this role we must know the subject and the language of the authority in order to interpret the original information accurately. We must also know the audience in order to translate the message into the language of the receiver. We use substitute words and phrases for the technical words and phrases that the authority uses, or we explain those words and phrases for the receiver.

The interpretive source-sender often runs the danger of "mixing" his own knowledge with that of the originating source without separating the two for the reader or listener. Most of the time, though, the two can and should be separated.

On the other hand we may be the primary source but use

other sources to add to or support the content of the message. In writing we use quotation marks around the material attributed to another source. In speaking we say, "I would like to quote what so and so says about this."

When all of the content comes from another source, we remind the receiver of the source at various times during the entire message. Many phrases help do this. We say, "Jones also points out . . ." and a little later we use another signpost that says, "At the same time, Jones takes the position that. . . ."

ATTITUDES—WHAT DO WE THINK?

We analyze the receiver in terms of attitudes toward the source, toward the message, and toward himself. We use the same approach in thinking about our own attitudes.

About the Audience

We asked a talented associate to head a program designed to reach low-income urban families with educational information. He declined. When asked why, he said he didn't want to go into the "social welfare business." He was, in fact, expressing an attitude toward an intended audience. He believed that too many people with low incomes lacked desire to help themselves. He was not interested in trying to help them with educational information.

At about the same time, another colleague asked for a change in assignments. He said he didn't "feel comfortable" communicating information that helped successful farmers become more successful. He wanted to direct his efforts toward helping people "who really need help."

It is difficult to disguise attitudes toward people. Attitudes show in the way we code a message—in the way we speak and write. We have all used versions of the expression, "I think he knows what he is talking about, but I just don't like the way he says it." We are really saying that we don't like the fellow's attitude toward us.

If we think the audience is stupid, uninformed, and uneducated, we will inevitably project this attitude when we communicate. Our attitude will also show if we think the audience is better educated and more sophisticated than we are.

About the Message

With some unfortunate exceptions, most good salesmen believe in what they are selling, most writers in what they are writing about, and most speakers in what they are speaking about.

The salesman may not believe he is selling the "best" automobile on the market, but he had better believe it is the best automobile for his customer if he intends to make the sale. Unless you truly believe the school system will suffer if the bond issue fails to pass, you will have difficulty convincing the voters to vote "yes." If you are not convinced that improved farming and homemaking practices will help farm families satisfy their wants and needs, your success in the Cooperative Extension Service will be limited. The huckster who can "sell anything" believes in only the first part of the Lincoln quotation, "You may fool all the people some of the time; you can even fool some of the people all the time; but you can't fool all of the people all the time."

If you find yourself in the communication business with a message you don't believe in, change the message or get out of the business.

About Ourselves

Someone has said that every individual represents the sum total of his experiences. We are products of inherited capabilities and the way those capabilities have been shaped and influenced by our experiences. In short, we have attitudes toward other people and the world around us, and we have attitudes about ourselves. Both our outward and inward attitudes affect the way we communicate and the success of our communication effort.

We cannot communicate effectively if we think we lack knowledge of the subject, or do not make a good impression, or cannot express ourselves in writing or speaking. Nor can we communicate well if we think people don't like us or don't respect our authority in the field.

On the other hand, attitudes of over self-confidence can get in the way of effective communication. The fellow who thinks he is always right, always has the correct answers, always speaks with authority, may write and speak for a diminishing audience.

COMMUNICATION SKILLS—HOW WELL DO WE WRITE, SPEAK, LISTEN?

Honest appraisal of our communication abilities will guide us in selecting the most effective message code and the most appropriate channel. Many leaders who write excellent personal columns for their local newspapers do a miserable job when they perform on radio. They have poor voice quality, stumble over words, and talk too fast or too slowly. Speaking, especially on radio, is not their special skill. Writing is. Unless they can improve their radio skills they should stick with writing.

Some people who make excellent person-to-person presentations seem to assume a completely different personality on television. They do not look, sound, or act the same as they do when talking with a friend or speaking before an audience at a meeting.

Our actual communication skills often relate to our self-attitudes about such skills. If we think of ourselves as poor speakers the chances are we will speak poorly. If we think of ourselves as poor writers we must overcome the barrier in order to write well. Communication skills combine knowledge of techniques with self-confidence. We reveal our appraisal of our communication skill when we select a channel for writing or speaking.

The channel is the connecting link between sender and receiver—the carrier of the coded message. It is the telephone line that connects the encoding telephone with the decoding telephone; the airwaves over which radio signals travel from the station to receiving sets; the newspaper combined with the carrier boy or mail service that brings the newspaper to the door; the line of sight between you and the pretty girl or handsome man smiling at you.

We may classify channels by the kinds of coded messages carried most efficiently, and we may further refine the classifications by audience size. For each breakdown and sub-breakdown, we may analyze the channel's strengths and weaknesses for carrying coded messages.

CHANNELS FOR WRITTEN COMMUNICATION

Choice of channels for written communication is almost endless. Each channel is designed to reach one of three audiences—a single-person, select-group, or mass audience.

Single-Person Audience

Every time we write a letter, drop a postcard in the mailbox, or send a memorandum to a friend, we use the single-person channel for written communication. The channel is highly selective. It provides the greatest opportunity to "fit" the content, code, and appeal of the message to the receiver's needs. If mother writes to ask why her son got such low marks on his report card, the teacher can write a specific reply.

If a farmer wants to know what kind of pasture-seeding mixture to use, the county agent can send him a letter that is highly specific for his unique situation—size of farm, soil type, kind of livestock, and so on.

If the audience consists of many mothers with questions about the progress of their children, or many farmers who have questions about seeding mixtures, the single-person channel is inefficient. Other channels are available.

Select-Group Audience

If 50 or 100 people have a common problem it is more efficient to write one letter, have it mimeographed or printed, and mail a copy to each person.

When we change from the single-person channel to the select-group channel, the basic process is the same but we change message content, code, and appeal. Usually the content must be more general. Words and expressions (code) must have meaning for the poorest reader, and the appeal must attract the audience majority.

Mass Audience

To reach large numbers of people we use newspapers, magazines, trade journals, and other "mass-media" channels that reach mass audiences.

The mass-media channels can be effective and efficient. We can contact large numbers of people at a relatively low cost in time and money. Again, the process is the same, but we adjust the content and appeal of the message.

With a larger audience we are less sure of knowledge levels and needs that must be satisfied. Ideally we anticipate the upper and lower levels of knowledge and direct the message toward the middle ground.

People are selective about what they read in their newspaper, magazine, or other printed mass media. Some concentrate on sports, some on the front page, others on the local news. Farmers read the stories that affect their business of farming. Businessmen read the financial page and the stories that affect their businesses. More women than men read the society pages.

When using a mass-audience channel we should assume selective readership. Not everyone who subscribes to the paper or magazine will receive our message.

When writing a story about the learning problems of children we assume that more parents than nonparents will read the story. The most attentive readers will be parents with children who have learning problems. Such self-selectivity permits a degree of freedom in the way we present the message.

There are dangers, however, in assuming too much selectivity. We have an "intended" audience for our message, but it also is received by an "unintended" audience.

A news story intended to tell farmers how they can take advantage of the new farm program may be read by an unintended audience of city people who already blame farmers for the high cost of meat and bread.

We might use overcrowding in the city's schools as an appeal to taxpayers for approval of a school-tax hike. The unintended effect may be to alarm parents over the quality of education for their children.

Any time you use the mass-media channel for written communication, consider the degree of selectivity of your intended audience and the possible negative effects on your unintended audience.

CHANNELS FOR SPOKEN COMMUNICATION

We may also classify channels for spoken communication by audience size.

Single-Person Audience

We use this channel every day in social, professional, and business situations. We talk with a friend over coffee, visit with a neighbor across the back fence, call an associate on the telephone. We may even visit with a person in another state or another country by shortwave radio. We are using single-person channels for spoken communication.

But this simple and most used of all communication channels is noted for its share of failures. The channel fails because of its very simplicity and familiarity. We don't take the time or trouble to consider purpose. We just talk. We assume the receiver has knowledge that he may not have. We often use verbal shorthand, leaving out important parts of the message.

We say to a friend, "Fred thinks it will go up a quarter in a month." Who is Fred? What will go up a quarter? In which month? Oh, I thought you knew. "Fred Trader, stockbroker, thinks the price of General Motors stock will go up a quarter before this month is over." Why didn't you say so?

Faulty communication may be saved by one important characteristic of person-to-person channels of spoken communication. There is a facility for immediate "feedback." The receiver can let us know whether he is receiving and understanding. By nodding, frowning, smiling, or a dozen other nonverbal signals he can give instant response. He can also reverse the process of communication and ask us to repeat the message, to change the code, to "speak his language."

The big problem is that we may miss the signals. The receiver doesn't understand, but he smiles to be agreeable. He doesn't know our language, but doesn't like to admit it. He is irritated by our appeal, but too polite to tell us so.

Select-Group Audience

Because man is a social animal he likes to be with other people. So he goes to meetings, listens to lectures, attends conferences, and participates in workshops and seminars. And because we are social animals we like to "see" the people we communicate with. So we invite people to our meeting, agree to speak to the PTA, or arrange a conference to discuss our proposal. We expand our channel for spoken communication from a single person to a select audience. What have we gained, and what have we lost?

Obviously we are able to reach more people with a single expenditure of time and money. If we want to tell 100 homeowners how to landscape their lawns, it is less costly and time-consuming to have them attend a meeting than to meet with each one individually.

We hope that there will be some feedback because then we can observe the reactions of the audience. Are they attentive? Restless? Asleep? We can call for questions to clear up points or make new ones.

There may be opportunities for our messages to be "amplified" by other sources in the audience. The fellow who had experience with that grass, or tree, or shrub may contribute a supporting message.

But again we must make adjustments in the content of our

message, our code, and our appeals. Some members of our audience may be experts in landscape design. Others may not know a shrub from a tree. We will probably deal with principles rather than specifics. We may talk over the heads of most of our audience because of the favorable response signals coming from a few.

Mass Audience

Once more we are back to mass-media channels. Instead of using newspapers and magazines that carry the written language, we deal with radio and television that carry the spoken language. There are both similarities and differences.

While radio and television are both mass-audience channels, they are even more audience-selective than are the print media. Most people can listen to only one radio program or watch one television show at a time. (There are those, of course, who listen to radio music while watching a ball game on television.)

Again, this characteristic of selectivity has advantages and disadvantages. On one hand, we can assume that the audience listening to us on radio or watching on television has chosen to listen or watch. They have selected us in preference to other programs available to them at the same time. To a degree, we can assume that the audience will keep on watching or listening so long as the message satisfies them. This characteristic permits us to use the mass-media channel to reach a select audience, and our content, code, and appeal can be directed toward that select audience. But there are disadvantages.

The newspaper audience doesn't have to read our story *now*. The reader can turn to the sports page first, then to the front page, and finally to our story. He can read the story before dinner or after dinner. If he misses it today he may even catch it tomorrow. Not so with the channels of radio and television. Except for repeat shows, the listener or viewer must catch us now or not at all.

If an audience of businessmen is interested in both financial news and baseball and we are reporting financial news in competition with a baseball game on another station, we will have a hard time knowing whether the selection characteristic of the channel worked for us or against us.

CHANNELS FOR NONVERBAL COMMUNICATION

As mentioned earlier, nonverbal codes of communication are usually, though not always, associated with verbal codes and they ride along on the same channels.

People smile or frown when they talk person-to-person, or they illustrate their circular letters and put them on scented paper, or they include pictures to illustrate their news stories.

A good meeting combines an array of "visual aids" to support the talk or lecture. Television uses both verbal and nonverbal language to convey messages.

THE DIFFICULTY OF CHOICE

How do you, then, as a person with a message, choose the channel you will use to reach your intended receivers? There are no easy answers but you can analyze choices by asking and answering some specific questions.

How big is the audience—how many people do you want to reach? The answer to this question, coupled with the amount of time you have, should tell you whether to use the single-person channel, the select audience, or the mass-audience channel.

How complicated is your message? As a rule, complicated, detailed, or instructional messages are best carried by written communication channels.

How timely is the message? Of the mass media, radio and television can present information faster than newspapers and magazines.

What are your communication skills? If you speak well but write poorly, your choice of channels is partly decided.

What is the communication behavior of your audience? You

obviously cannot use news stories to reach people who don't read, or radio for people who only listen to rock music, or meetings to reach people who would rather stay home and watch television.

CHAPTER 4

Communication and Learning

Whether we communicate in the formal atmosphere of the classroom, by participating in a meeting, by writing a news story, or by appearing on television, we use the communication process to facilitate learning. One purpose of communication is to help the receiver learn something. If we accept that premise we can sharpen our communication sensitivity and, we hope, our skills by knowing something about how people learn.

In fact, communication and learning are so intimately related that it is almost impossible to consider one process without considering the other. And the two processes are remarkably similar. Man's special ability to communicate and his unusual capacity to learn are the dominant characteristics of human nature.

While each of us has the capacity to learn, our capacities are not alike. We learn at different rates and in different amounts but in roughly the same ways. Learning takes place when we acquire knowledge, attitudes, habits, skills—any new way of responding to messages that come to us via our senses. Our ability to communicate determines how fully we use our capacity to learn.

We *learn* to like certain foods, symphony music, a sauna bath.

34

We *learn* to believe that skin color doesn't determine whether man is good or bad, competent or incompetent. We *learn* to tie our shoelaces, dance, play the piano, climb a tree. We have acquired new knowledge, new beliefs, new skills, new ways of responding. But exactly how did this learning take place?

THE LEARNING PROCESS

Someone hands us a new variety of apple and says, "Take a bite; it tastes good." Two of our senses have received a stimulus. We see an apple that looks similar to other apples we have seen and tasted. We *hear* a voice transmitting a message that suggests a positive response on our part if we "take a bite." There has been communication, but there has not yet been learning with respect to our response to a particular variety of apple.

So we take a bite, and a third sense, taste, receives a stimulus. Our particular taste mechanism responds with the sensation that the apple is sweet, sour, bitter, bland, or something else. We take several more bites to confirm the sensation, compare it with our taste preferences, and then conclude that the apple does taste good. In this simple illustration, we have *learned* to like a new apple variety.

Stimulus-Response

While there are different theories of learning and different versions of particular theories, there is strong support for the stimulus-response concept of learning. This concept suggests that we learn through the process of receiving, interpreting, and responding to messages (stimuli) transmitted to our brain and central nervous system by one or more of our senses. We then interpret the consequences of our response as favorable or unfavorable and develop habits or patterns of behavior to maximize the favorable consequences or to minimize the unfavorable consequences.

This concept suggests several obvious conditions. Before learning takes place there must be a stimulus, and there must be a sense mechanism to receive the stimulus. So far so good. But is there learning when the response to a stimulus is automatic or built-in? Learning theorists say probably not. We respond automatically to certain stimuli, and the response does not have to be learned. The response is simply there. Our eyes dilate when we enter a dark room; we get "goose pimples" when we are chilled; our mouths water when we are hungry and smell good food—or even when we think of the smell and taste of good food.

Learning takes place when the brain and central nervous system interpret the stimulus, suggest a response, and then interpret the consequence of the response. Over time, as we repeat the stimulus-interpretation-response-interpretation process, we try to enhance the rewards or to reduce the penalties. We then acquire (learn) behavior patterns or habits, and we tend to repeat such patterns and habits unless we discover a new response that offers greater rewards.

Because each person has his own particular set of sense organs, each person receives stimuli in a different way. We hear differently, see differently, and taste differently. Some people have a high threshold of pain; some a low threshold. A food that may taste bland to us may taste slightly sweet, sour, or salty to others. What looks red or green to you looks neutral to the person who is colorblind. To a degree, therefore, learning is related to the ability of our sense organs to accurately receive and interpret stimuli.

Learning is also influenced by other factors, including the attitude and interests of the learner.

When the consequences of our response are favorable—when we are rewarded—we learn by frequent repetition of the stimulus-response-reward experience. There is truth in the adage "practice makes perfect."

In general, the more favorable the consequences of our response, or the greater the reward, the more likely we are to maintain a behavior pattern once learned. We also are more likely to establish a behavior pattern and to maintain it if we experience immediate rather than postponed rewards.

As most of us know, there is a relationship between learning and effort. We tend to learn those things that will give us the greatest reward for the least effort.

Perception

When we relate one sensation to another and understand the meaning of the relationship, we say we learn by perception. A simple example: We *touch* a hot stove and respond by jerking our hands away. We also *see* that there is a source of heat—a flame, hot coals, or a glowing rod. We associate the sensations of touch and sight, relate the two, and come up with the perception that flames, hot coals, or glowing rods produce heat that can hurt if touched. So we learn not to touch things that look hot.

In much the same way, we perceive that things that smell sour usually taste sour; silk-like fabrics are less scratchy than wool-like fabrics. Learning progresses as we acquire new percepts, relate them to previously learned percepts, and attach new or different meanings to both the old and the new.

Sensations and perceptions are combined when we learn new physical skills such as climbing a tree, threading a needle, or typing on a typewriter. We use both when we go through the trial-and-error process of learning, although the process wastes both time and energy. We resort to trial and error when we are unable or unwilling to relate previous learning experiences to the current problem.

We also learn by association—by making connections and establishing relationships among ideas, perceptions, and different learning experiences. We learned to run after we learned to walk by associating the sensations of running with the sensations of walking. Each new bit of learning is associated with and tempered by all previous bits of learning.

THE ROLE OF COMMUNICATION

Even with this brief glimpse of the learning process it should be apparent that communication and learning are interdependent. Communication must be involved in the learning process, and learning is one of the results of communication.

We communicate most effectively when we understand the learning process and make use of established principles of learning. Through communication we help receivers interpret sensations and establish percepts by relating one sensation to another. Through communication we relate new ideas and concepts to previously learned ideas and concepts.

Advertisers code their messages to appeal to the senses and to relate favorable sense responses to the product for sale. We are told, for example, that the new detergent will not only get clothes clean but also make them "smell as fresh as a spring breeze." We have learned, the advertiser assumes, that fresh smells are good and stale smells are bad.

There are untold numbers of products on the market today that "melt in your mouth," or are "softer to the touch," or "taste cool and refreshing." Others "get rid of unsightly dirt and scum," "remove that itching and burning sensation," or "brighten your day."

By studying how people learn, social scientists have suggested a number of learning principles. These principles can and should guide our communication effort.

1. *People have different learning capacities.* This principle underscores the need for knowing the audience. By study and observation we will find clues to learning capacities. In general, young people learn more quickly and more easily than older people. Bright people understand a complex message more easily than less-bright people. Years of schooling completed, however, may or may not be an indication of learning capacity.

2. *Learning is related to the strength of the emotional response.* We said earlier that the message must "offer something" to encourage a favorable message response from the receiver. His response should satisfy one of his basic motivational needs. Usually rewards are more effective than penalties in encouraging response and learning. But penalties, either real or im-

plied, can encourage learning if they arouse a strong emotional response. We often learn by getting hurt.

3. *Order of presentation affects learning.* For any given message, points made at the beginning and end are remembered better than those in the middle. That's one reason for concentrating the essential information at the beginning of a news story in the "lead." (We will discuss other reasons later.) Speakers are often advised to tell the audience what they are going to tell them, then to tell them, and finally to tell them what they have been told.

4. *It is better to show how to do things than to tell how to do them.* Demonstrations or television are better than news stories for communicating complex how-to-do-it instructions. It is best to show the process or skill from the same angle the receiver would see if he were doing the job himself. For some demonstrations on television, for example, have the camera look over your shoulder rather than straight at you.

5. *Attitudes toward source affect attitudes toward message.* Sometimes the "who said" may be as important as the "what said" in determining immediate response to a message. However, in the long run it's the message that counts.

6. *Memory is related to recency.* We remember the most immediately after receiving and responding to a message. We begin to forget soon after exposure. If the purpose of communication is to encourage action, aim for immediate action—today, not tomorrow; this week, not next week. Message repetition encourages message retention.

7. *Participation assists learning.* We learn better when we do than when we merely see and hear. The 4-H Club motto "Learn by Doing" makes a direct application of this principle. So far in this book you have been merely reading. In later sections we will suggest that you participate by practicing skills.

8. *Unusualness of presentation affects learning.* The way we package and present a message helps determine the level of attention and the strength of the emotional response. That is why

an effective communicator combines language codes for his message. He shows and tells. He uses words, visuals, and sounds. Too much variety or novelty in a presentation, though, can hide or destroy the message. We say of a speaker, "Yes, he put on a good show, but what did he say?"

When we combine learning principles with communication principles, we also come up with practical and important considerations for effective use of the communication process.

We have said that people learn and develop attitudes over a long period of time based upon many different kinds of learning experiences. But once a person has an attitude or has learned something he is reluctant to change. Communication that reinforces attitudes already held will therefore be better received and more successful than communication that conflicts with such established attitudes.

Conflicts in attitudes tend to be resolved, and the resolution is normally in the direction of least change. Communication, therefore, should help the receiver resolve conflicts in the behavioral direction we want him to take.

Communication scientists also speak of the concept of *selective exposure*. Audiences tend to see and hear signals and messages that interest them and to block out signals and messages that don't interest them. Three people walking down the same street at the same time may see different things. The first may see the clock on the corner, because he is late for an important conference. The second may see the sign for a dress shop, because she intends to buy a dress. The third may see the bank sign in the middle of the block, because he needs to cash a check.

The concept of *selective perception* is related to the concept of selective exposure. This concept simply explains that each of us perceives messages and attaches meanings to experiences in terms of individual wants and needs. We believe what we want to believe. We select and interpret the message that promises us the greatest reward or the least penalty.

In communication we can also make use of the concept of *expectation*. Past experiences guide expectations for the future. If the receiver's response to a message has consistently satisfied his needs he will expect a similar response to a similar message to bring similar satisfaction. A message that reminds a receiver of past favorable experiences has the best chance for favorable reception and response.

There is also the concept of *image reinforcement*. Each of us has an image of himself. We tend to respond and pay the most attention to those messages that reinforce our self-image. If we think of ourselves as the hardest-working individuals in the community, we may reject a message that encourages us to "take it easy" or to "save labor."

This chapter was intended to influence the way you think about the process of communication as it relates to learning. We hope that you have known about and believed in many of the ideas before. If so, we may have reinforced your previous knowledge and attitudes.

CHAPTER 5

Communication within Groups

Much communication takes place between a single sender and a single receiver. This is true even though we use a mass-media channel. While the mass-media message reaches an audience of thousands or even millions, each individual may be reading, listening, or watching alone. In this environment of oneness the receiver's response depends upon his level of knowledge, his understanding of language codes, his attitudes, and his capacity for learning.

Communication also takes place within groups, and the group environment affects the communication process.

Our response to a motion picture is different when we watch it on television alone in our living room than when we watch the same picture in a theater filled with people. A funny movie is funnier when other people are laughing. Suspense is more gripping when we sense that those around us are tense. Nearly all emotional responses are tempered, usually heightened, when shared with others. (This may not be true of the emotion of terror as we watch a horror movie in a lonely house late at night, when we may wish for the company of the theater audience to diminish the terror level.)

Radio and television producers recognize the influence of group response by staging presentations before live audiences or by dubbing in laughter, applause, and other clues of audience reactions. Such artificial stimulation, of course, can produce unwanted or unexpected response from the intended audience and the message gets lost. The canned laughter or applause may remind us that we are being manipulated, and our response is irritation rather than enjoyment.

Often the group environment is incidental to the process of communication. It is simply there, and its effect, either positive or negative, must be taken into account. We can't avoid the group environment when we go to the theater, listen to concerts, or attend lectures. The group is incidental to our purpose as a receiver.

Many groups exist, however, to provide an environment for communication. It is such an environment that we will discuss now as we consider the characteristics of a group, the ways people communicate in the group setting, and the reasons why communication succeeds or fails.

REASONS FOR BELONGING

We belong to some groups automatically, without choice and without prior decision. Such groups include our family and the associates with whom we work. Communication takes place within such groups but perhaps not as a primary function.

We belong to other groups because of choice. We desire to associate with other people, to belong, and to communicate. Belonging to a group may, in fact, satisfy one of our emotional needs. The group environment may provide security, response, recognition, or a new experience. We join business clubs, professional associations, or the local PTA. We volunteer for committees, join fund drives, or sign up for educational seminars and workshops.

But regardless of why or how we happened to join a particular group, we are part of that group's structure and environment. We have a particular status, play an identifiable role, and accept or reject assigned or implied duties and responsibilities.

ENVIRONMENT AFFECTS BEHAVIOR

The group environment often has strange effects upon an individual's communication behavior. "Joe is one of the most interesting people I know until he gets in a group, and then he doesn't say a word." "You can talk with Fred for an hour without having any idea where he really stands. But get him in a group, and he will fight everyone to win his point." "Mary has a lot of ideas of her own, but she always seems to agree with the majority. She never says what she really thinks."

We may belong to, or even create, a group for the purpose of participation and communication and then find that the group members neither participate nor communicate. If we are in charge, our task is to find out why and to do something about it. We start looking for "blocks" that stand in the way of the nonparticipating member and see if we can eliminate them. Here is a partial list:

Fear. The group member believes that everyone else is smarter and more knowledgeable than he is. He thinks his actions will reveal his ignorance, so he doesn't respond.

Insecurity. The member feels insecure because of a lack of experience, unfavorable past experiences, or a negative self-attitude.

Lack of knowledge. The individual assumes that everyone else knows more than he does so his participation consists of passive listening.

Value rejection. Having joined the group, the member can't agree with the group objectives, the methods used to gain the objectives, or the priorities of effort.

Time commitments. The individual thinks he is already too busy and is concerned that the group will demand too much of his time. He belongs for reasons other than participation. If he participates he may be assigned unwanted responsibility.

Adjustments to Frustrations

An individual may or may not be aware of why he is unable to communicate in a group environment, but his actions often provide clues to his reasons and his frustrations. He may adjust his behavior in one or more of the following ways:

Aggression. He overcompensates for feelings of fear or insecurity by vigorously striking back at everyone and everything. He may avoid the idea and attack the motive. Or he may withdraw and refuse to say another word during the whole evening.

Compensation. He avoids participating by doing chores— arranging the chairs, making the coffee, or taking minutes.

Rationalization. He says the purpose of the group is foolish in the first place, so why bother.

Identification. He associates his views with some other member of the group and lets the other fellow participate for him. "Joe speaks for me."

Projection. He finds a cause outside himself for his lack of participation. "The government is going to tell everyone how to do things anyway, so what difference does this group make?"

Regression. He is an agreeable fellow so he just goes along with the crowd.

Meaningful communication cannot take place within a group unless the members participate. A first step is to recognize and eliminate as many of the participation blocks as possible to avoid the resulting frustrations and adjustments. Think of groups as having personalities and a communication behavior similar to that of an individual. Group action results from continuous and related communication among the members of the group.

GROUP GOALS EXPRESS NEEDS

The individual has wants and needs and often seeks satisfaction through communication. Similarly, the group has wants and needs, expressed as goals. Goals guide the activities of the group and serve as the base for measuring success or failure of the group's actions.

For success, the group's goals need to be as precisely defined as the sender's purpose in the communication process. Lack of definition results in off-target communication: no two people talk about the same thing; people listen with different expectations; messages are miscoded and poorly translated; means are confused with ends.

It is extremely difficult, if not impossible, to establish a goal for a group of people. Each group member should have the opportunity to help set the group's goals. Only then will he have a personal, motivating reason for achieving the goal.

For example: The president of the PTA announces one evening that the group plans to sponsor a tax referendum to raise more money for schools in the community. He asks for a discussion on ways to get the job done and wonders why the meeting seems to fall apart. Joe talks about how high property taxes are already. Margaret has the opinion that lunches in the school cafeteria are not as good as they should be. Max can't understand why the basketball team needed new uniforms. The discussion finally focuses on the problems of finding well-qualified teachers.

The group did not have an opportunity to decide whether "more money for the schools" was really the problem or whether there were other alternatives to solving the problem. The individuals in the group had purposes different from the one proposed for the group by the PTA president.

The group should establish goals after thorough discussion of the situation, the needs, and the alternatives for meeting needs. In the above example such discussion might have produced two goals: a plan to raise more money and a plan to cut expenses.

"ROLES" IN GROUP COMMUNICATION

Group action depends almost entirely upon effective communication among group members. Each individual alternates between being a sender and a receiver—a talker and a listener. If the talking is done by only one or a few, with the rest listening, there is little chance of arriving at a mutual goal and even less chance of accomplishing it.

Too often we think of a group as being composed of two sides, with the chairman on one side and the members on the other. The chairman initiates; the members respond. Ideally there are no sides at all. The group members play a variety of roles in the continuing processes of communication. The next time you are involved in group communication, note which members play one or more of the following roles that help the group accomplish its purpose.

The *initiator,* often the chairman but not always, suggests or proposes new ideas or a changed way to consider the problems or the proposed alternatives for action. He is the fellow who says, "Let's think about this."

The *information-seeker* asks for clarification of discussion points in terms of their factual adequacy, for authoritative information, and for facts pertinent to the problem being discussed. He is the fellow who says, "How much of our taxes go for schools now?" or "How much do we spend now for basketball uniforms?"

The *information-giver* is the man with the answers or the man who knows where the answers can be found. He may be an authority in his own right, or he can provide the facts from other authorities.

The *opinion-seeker* doesn't ask primarily for the facts but for clarification of values related to goals or proposed alternatives for action. He may say, "Are we sure that cutting school expenses now won't hurt the quality of education in the long run?"

Such opinion questions are answered by the *opinion-giver.* He may suggest a point of view based upon previous personal experiences or the experiences of others in different situations. He may offer an opinion as a means of encouraging opinion responses from others in the group.

Some member may play the role of an *elaborator,* who relates the facts given and the opinions expressed by others in the group. He may project an idea or a suggestion and consider how it would work if adopted. He may point out that the decision to postpone remodeling the chemistry laboratory will cost more money three years from now.

If the discussion tends to stray from its central direction, a member may play the role of *orientor* by reviewing the discussion that has taken place, pointing out how it is straying, and reminding other members of the agreed purpose and direction of the meeting.

There is often an *evaluator* in the group. He assumes or accepts the task of measuring the group's actions, accomplishments, or progress against some standard. He may also serve as the critic of methods and procedures.

The *energizer,* on the other hand, prods the group toward action or decision. He says, "Let's decide what we want to do. We have talked about it long enough."

You will notice that in most groups some member plays the role of *technician.* He attends to the environmental needs of the group and takes care of seating arrangements, ventilation, coffee breaks, and sound systems.

Whether requested to or not, another member usually plays the role of *recorder* and serves as the group's "memory" by keeping track of suggestions, writing down decisions, and providing minutes if minutes are needed.

By playing these roles, regardless of nametags, the various group members contribute to the effective and continuing flow of communication. These are somewhat technical roles that relate to the group's objectives.

Other Roles

In an ideal environment, members will assume or accept other kinds of roles designed to help the group function as a group. These roles help eliminate "noise" from the communication process and assure high fidelity in the communication system. In your group you may notice some or all of the following roles being played.

An *encourager* praises, agrees with, and accepts the contributions of others. He offers commendation and shows warmth toward other members. His code may be verbal or nonverbal. He may say, "That's a good thought," or he may only smile and nod in agreement.

In a slightly different role, the *harmonizer* mediates differences among members. He is the go-between who points out the merits of both sides of an argument, who relieves tension with a jest or a joke, who shifts the discussion direction if there is too much trouble ahead.

Then there is the *compromiser,* who does his own harmonizing when there is a conflict with his ideas or opinions. He may compromise by yielding status, admitting his error, or disciplining himself to maintain group harmony.

The *expediter* attempts to keep all communication channels open by encouraging the participation of all members. He attempts to change consistent receivers into senders, and listeners into talkers. He may say, "I would be interested to hear what Joe has to say about this." Or he may try to regulate the channels of communication by setting time limits or suggesting procedures that ensure all members a chance to speak.

Negative Roles

Unfortunately we cannot complete the discussion of roles played by group members without mentioning those played by the "noisemakers." When a member wants to satisfy an individual want or need he may play one of a variety of roles that interfere with intended communication. He produces noise in the communication channel that blocks the reception of messages. Be on the lookout for these roles.

The *aggressor* always has something to say but his intent is negative rather than positive. He produces noise by deflating the status of others; by expressing disapproval of the values, opinions, or acts of fellow members; by questioning the group's purpose for being; by joking aggressively; or by trying to take credit for another's contributions.

At the next table sits the *blocker,* who maintains a stubbornly negative attitude toward everyone and every idea. He disagrees or opposes without sound reason and will attempt to revive issues that have been rejected or bypassed.

Behind him is the *recognition-seeker,* who works in various ways to call attention to himself. He boasts, reports personal achievements, and is constantly worried about being placed in an inferior position.

The *playboy* may be one kind of recognition-seeker. He shows his lack of interest in the group by being cynical or nonchalant. He ignores the discussion mainstream and carries on his private conversations with the fellow beside him.

On the other hand, the *dominator* also calls attention to himself, but in a different way and for a different reason. He attempts to assert authority or to demonstrate superiority by manipulating the group or certain members of the group. He may do this by encouraging members to "take sides," placing himself in the leadership role for one faction. He succeeds in splitting one group into two and replacing group communication with two-way communication between opposing sides.

Finally there is the noise produced by the *special-interest pleader,* who tries to conceal his own prejudices or biases in the "cause" of some other group or interest. Be alert for the start of a communication failure when a group member says, "I could agree with this proposal, but I think we should consider the needs of the small businessman."

IMPROVING GROUP COMMUNICATION

By appreciating the dynamics of a group environment we can consider measures to improve communication among the members of the group.

1. Communication will be most effective when each member

of the group has a reason for belonging and when that personal reason is related to the broad objectives of the group. Conversely, communication breaks down when people are arbitrarily assigned to a group and have no personal reason for belonging. When structuring a group for a specific purpose, therefore, select members whose personal interests, ambitions, and goals are compatible with those of most or all other members of the group.

2. Within the broad framework of policies and purposes, specific group goals should be internally established rather than externally imposed. Communication will be most meaningful when the goals of the group are the same or similar to the individual goals of the members.

3. As a member of a group, appreciate the possible reasons why some members participate and communicate while others do not. Start first by analyzing your own communication behavior. Can you identify and isolate possible blocks that keep you from communicating within the group? Do you recognize how you adjust to those blocks in a negative or a positive way? Once we understand our own communication behavior, we can play a more effective role in helping others overcome communication blocks.

4. Encourage members to play those roles that contribute harmony and direction to internal communication. Recognize and praise the contributions of those who serve as initiators, information-seekers, information-givers, and others who make similar positive contributions to the environment of discussion. By so doing, you will encourage others to play similar roles.

5. Identify and reduce the causes of noise in the communication system. Seek out the reasons why some members play negative roles and, if possible, eliminate those reasons. Try to compromise the differences between a member's personal goals and ambitions and the objectives of the group. At times it may be desirable to adjust the group goals to more nearly match the personal goals of the members.

6. Provide a permissive, congenial group atmosphere for communication. Make each member feel welcome, wanted, and

needed. Provide for the physical comfort of members, and make sure all members can hear one another and can see the visuals if visuals are used.

7. Break large groups into small ones so that all members have an opportunity to participate.

8. Practice skills of listening.

CHAPTER 6

Communication and Social Action

We initially considered the communication process within the two-dimensional environment of sender and receiver and then placed a number of sender-receiver combinations within the more complex group environment.

Now we should examine communication as it functions within a given social system made up of individuals, groups of individuals, and a variety of social institutions such as schools, churches, political parties, and government units.

Within the environment of a social system the purpose of communication is to accomplish social action. At some time nearly all of us are involved in efforts to improve our social system through social action. We, along with others, seek action to correct faults in the system or to help a good system become better. We can accomplish such action only with effective communication.

A social system may be described as any identifiable combination of individuals, groups, and institutions with a reason for

53

being. A nation is a social system, and so is the United Nations, representing many nations. A state comprises a social system, and so do each of the counties within the state and each of the townships, cities, and towns within the county.

Using the above concept we can identify both large and small social systems. The list may include farmer cooperatives, school districts, universities, public-health districts, city ghettos or sections of ghettos, labor unions, and trade associations.

All social action takes place within *some* system, and the environment of the system affects the role of communication.

THE PROCESS OF SOCIAL ACTION

When we talk about social action, we must again use the familiar and perhaps overworked term *process.* Social action is the process of carrying out an action program within a social system. Social action, then, is the *process* by which problems are identified, solutions proposed, goals established, plans made, and steps taken to carry out plans to accomplish goals.

Unless we completely remove ourselves from society, it is difficult to avoid involvement with some social-action program. At any given moment some community or some social system within the community is involved in programs to improve recreation facilities for children, build a new hospital, reduce racial tensions, control stray dogs, eliminate air and water pollution, raise taxes, lower taxes, bring new industry to the city, keep industry out, ban the bomb, eliminate crime.

We may be involved as one of those who identified the problem, as an originator of the solution, as a consultant or a member of a committee, or as one of the hundreds who must vote either yes or no on a proposition.

Regardless of how we are identified, or the role we play, we are involved in the communication process as a sender or as a receiver. In this discussion, though, we will assume that we, as educational leaders, have been placed at the leading edge of the action. We have a prime responsibility for the action program—

for seeing that something is accomplished. We communicate with individuals, alone and as members of groups. By examining the process of social action we can see where, why, and how communication must take place.

For convenience in this discussion we will select an example and design a model of the social-action process. A word of caution: If we asked ten people to design a model of an automobile we would end up with ten different models. Each would be different, but all would have essentially the same component parts —engine, chassis, wheels, body, and a means of transmitting power from engine to wheels. Similarly, there are different models of the social-action process, but all feature similar component parts and have comparable mechanisms for *power.*

Our model features a familiar example—*the need to improve medical facilities for the community.* The need exists, the time is now, and we are involved. What are the considerations? How does action take place? Where does communication fit in?

The Social Situation

Before a mountain climber heads for the highest peak in the range he surveys the scene and studies the situation. He knows he is not the first to attempt the climb. Who has gone before? What routes did they take? Where did they run into trouble, have to fall back and start over? In what season did they make their attempt? Will conditions be different now?

To achieve social action we must also survey the scene and study present and previous situations. We want to improve medical facilities in our community. Have previous attempts been made to get such facilities? Who tried? Why did they fail? What other needs does the community have? How competitive are those needs? Where is the community in its life-cycle? Young? Middle-aged? Old? Financially, is the community rich, poor, or in between? What medical facilities are available outside the community?

These questions and hundreds of others must be asked and answered to describe previous and present social situations. The knowledge will guide our communication effort. It will help us identify and analyze target audiences, select appropriate messages, use message codes and appeals most effectively, and zero in on specific purposes. Past failures, in fact, may have been directly associated with faulty communication.

The Start of Action

Social action begins when two or more people agree that there is a problem *and* that something should be done about it. Agreement on a problem is not enough. There must also be agreement on the need for action—something should be done. There is need for improved medical facilities in this community, *and* we should take action to get those facilities. There are numerous examples, of course, where a successful social-action program started with a single, inspired individual. Most of us, however, need the support of a few others before we are willing to translate problems into action programs.

As someone who joins others in saying that "something should be done," we may be *within* the social system, or we may be related to the social system and represent *outside* interests. As a parent we are an *insider,* concerned about better medical facilities for our children and our neighbor's children. As a teacher, social worker, or extension agent we are related to the system but in a position to gain the support for action from outside people and other social systems.

Those who join us in our cause may have common interests or complementary interests. Other parents share common interests with us in wanting adequate medical treatment for children. The local contractor sees in the action an opportunity to build the facilities. His interest is complementary. Common and complementary interests need not conflict, but they should be recognized.

Regardless of the interest base, some small group of people must eventually say, "Let's go! We have a problem and we are ready to see if something can be done about it." Some sociologists refer to this group as the *initiating set,* the first few who initiate the action.

There may be only one initiating set or there may eventually be three or four as the direction for action is formulated. As a parent we may be a member of the first set, composed of the director of the social-welfare program, a local doctor, and a member of the city council. We may have discussed the need for medical facilities during a chance meeting at a local restaurant or after the regular meeting of our club. But at some point our group agrees to initiate action.

We may then go home, find keen interest among a few of our neighbors, and form a supporting group—a second initiating set. The welfare director does the same thing with a few of his associates, and so does the doctor. The council member knows that a few of his associates believe the same way he does, so a fifth set is formed.

Communication must now take place within each set and among the various sets. Communication liaisons are established. We may agree to meet a couple of times a week to talk over needs, procedures, and courses of action. Each of us communicates the concerns, attitudes, experiences, and suggestions of those in our particular group. Gradually there is assurance that we are on the right track, and we are ready for the second stage of the process.

The Legitimization Stage

In almost every social system the action program seems to depend upon the *approval* of certain people, groups, or organizations. They seem to have the right—the real or implied authority, the community position—to indicate whether or not ideas, plans, or action programs are legitimate. Again some sociologists have coined a word for these people or groups. They call them *legitimizers.* You probably have heard this term many times during recent years.

Our task as a social-action leader is to identify the legitimizers, communicate with them, and win approval for our proposed action program. With respect to our medical-facilities program, the number and type of legitimizers may vary. We may need only a favorable nod from one or two people. The chairman of the county medical society may be one. Another may be the town's oldest and wisest doctor. Such individuals are logical choices, but some legitimizers do not seem to fit logically into the social system.

The League of Women Voters may be strong enough to block social action despite support from the county medical society and the doctors in town. We may find we need the supporting voice of the distinguished gentleman who was mayor of the community fifteen years ago and has not held public office since. The community citizens, though, still accept his judgment on what is good or bad for the community.

Some people are legitimizers because they hold key positions with labor unions, professional organizations, political parties, or social groups. Some play the role because of family prestige, money, unique knowledge, or soundness of past judgments.

Successful identification and communication with legitimizers may pave the way for acceptance by others and provide an additional input of ideas into our program. Because of his position, the legitimizer may see weaknesses in our plan, suggest alternative routes to follow, recall comparable programs that succeeded or failed.

Most of our communication with legitimizers, of course, will be on a face-to-face, person-to-person basis. But there will be no other time in our action program when the lessons of effective communication need more careful application.

What do we expect to accomplish from our communication with a particular legitimizer? What is our purpose? Do we seek or need only approval—an agreement with our plans, a promise not to block or interfere? Do we need something more—active support, the use of his name, position, and prestige?

What are his wants or needs that we must appeal to? He is our first audience and he may be a legitimizer *because* he has special wants and needs. He may want reassurance of his position and prestige, recognition for his wealth or his role in the community. He will support our program only if it satisfies him to do so. Our communication must assure him of such satisfaction.

Message content and code are equally important. Our *language* must assure him that we know enough about the problem to warrant his attention. Our *code* and *treatment* must show evidence of respect and appreciation for *his* knowledge and *his* role. And we must be ready to play the attentive role of the receiver in the communication process. He wants us to listen to his ideas, his opinions, and his experiences.

FROM LEGITIMIZATION TO DIFFUSION

Three social-action steps have been taken: a social-action need has been identified; an agreement for action has been made; the concept has been approved by the legitimizers.

We are now ready for the next stage in the process of social action—the spreading of the idea among the citizens of the community, or at least among those citizens who must approve the action. This phase of the process has become known as the *diffusion stage*.

At this stage we are more concerned with the what than the how. We and the legitimizers agree that there is a need for improved medical facilities and that something should be done about it. Do others in the community agree with this need—see it the same way we do? Are their concerns active or passive? Can they be moved to get behind specific action plans, or will they only listen and talk about the problem? The need now is to expand our audience, to diffuse the idea, and to measure the reactions.

If everyone shares the same sense of need for improved community medical facilities and the same desire for action, the social-action process will function almost automatically. But they don't. The task during the diffusion stage is to make people aware of a problem and to identify the need for solution as *their* need. There are various ways to accomplish this.

One way is through basic education—to communicate the facts of a situation to an audience previously unaware of the facts or of the meaning of the facts. What is the level of present medical services? How do they compare with other communities and with established standards? Where are the major deficiencies? How many people must leave the community each year to seek specialized assistance? What kinds of specialized assistance might be brought to the community?

Surveys can be used to help people identify their problems and to translate them into needs for improved medical facilities. Most of us avoid thinking about doctors and hospitals unless we or close friends have been ill recently. A well-designed questionnaire helps us focus and project our thinking.

During the diffusion stage we may also establish a number of study committees to examine specific aspects of the action program. We may ask one group to consider the special medical needs of the older people. Another may study the physical requirements—land, buildings, construction needs. Such study groups actually become diffusion groups as they seek and exchange information and communicate with one another.

During this stage we make use of a variety of communication channels to reach our many audiences with related messages. Through face-to-face channels we talk to a wider circle of friends and neighbors, speak before service clubs and professional groups, and hold discussions before and after meetings called for other purposes.

We encounter many of the roles previously discussed. Fred is consistently against the whole idea because the community didn't support his plan for a baseball park. "If people played more, they wouldn't be sick all the time." Max is for it if a way can be found to raise the money without increasing property taxes. Jane wonders if people shouldn't get into the habit of going to a larger city where there are more medical specialists.

Since the action plan is community-wide, we use public media channels. News stories explain the idea. The needs are outlined by a panel on the local radio or television station.

Audience attitudes and concerns need careful attention. Rumor and misinformation can be diffused as quickly as facts. The appeal of "danger to health" may create more opposition than support.

The diffusion stage may last a few weeks, months, or even a year or two. If action is called for too soon there will be resentment and charges that "someone is trying to ram a plan down our throats." If action is postponed too long we lose momentum and supporters will drift away to other programs and other causes. The time span will depend partly upon the adequacy of the communication effort and the leaders' sensitivity to the feedback from the public. There is a "right moment," though, for the process to move from the diffusion stage to the action stage.

Movement to Action

In the action stage our efforts shift from winning support to winning commitment for action. The need for improved community medical facilities has been expressed, the idea has been approved by the legitimizers, and the appropriate segments of the public understand the need and seem willing to support a reasonable program of action. *How* can the community achieve better medical facilities?

Obviously some thought has been given to *how* during all of the previous stages, but past thinking must now be structured in terms of specific goals and objectives. Is our objective to meet minimum standards, average standards, or ideal standards? Do we want to achieve those standards immediately or during the next five years?

Alternative goals must be spelled out, communicated, and evaluated on the basis of responses from the audience. In time this process will bring agreement on a specific goal, and attention can be directed toward alternative methods for reaching that goal.

The community has now agreed that the immediate goal for action is to meet average standards for medical facilities and services, and these standards have been translated into size of buildings, number of hospital beds, kind of specialized equipment, and units of related auxiliary services. What reasonable alternatives for reaching this goal should our community consider? Should the present hospital be remodeled and enlarged? Should a completely new hospital be built? Through increased taxes? Medical fees? Contributions? Should the facilities be located downtown, at the edge of town, or in the country?

In most cases, relatively few people are involved in selecting the final goal and the action plan but communication is needed to keep the public informed and their support active.

More people become involved when action moves into the specific plan-of-work stage. Time schedules are agreed upon, working committees are appointed and assigned specific responsibilities, outside consultants are hired if needed, building specifications are spelled out, and additional land is acquired. It is now that the community mobilizes and organizes its talents and its resources. Agreement on need and passive support must be turned into active support demonstrated by contributions of time, money, and talent.

If the social-action process has been well managed up to now, the action stage should be free of major opposition and blocks. The purpose of communication changes from gaining acceptance of need to informing people where and how their contributions can be made. Letters are mailed inviting people to serve on various working committees. News stories report the progress of the land-acquisition group. The downtown bank has a model constructed to show what the improved facilities will look like. The public is informed as each objective is accomplished.

NEED FOR EVALUATION

This simplified model of the social-action process may suggest that the process, if correctly handled, flows in a straight line from the time the idea is initiated until the program is completed. This is not so, of course, because some form of evaluation must be built into each stage of the process.

The original idea should be evaluated in terms of its appropriateness, timeliness, practicability. Modifications may be called for, new ideas incorporated, old versions discarded. New directions may result from further evaluation at the legitimization stage.

Evaluation should be continuous during the diffusion stage as public attitudes are sampled, new people are involved, and both positive and negative feedback are measured.

There will be a similar need for testing during all phases of the action stage as working committees go about their assigned tasks, consultants report, and plans of work encounter unforeseen snags.

While much of the evaluation may be informal, it should not be left to chance. How well have we done so far? Are we on schedule? Did we pick the right route? Does our plan for the next stage still seem correct? Can we now see easier routes?

It would be foolish to follow a plan for social action without evaluating the success and failure of each step in the process that leads to program accomplishment.

THE FUNCTION OF COMMUNICATION

It should be obvious that the process of communication is intimately associated with the process of social action within the social system. More positively, the success of social-action programs is, in fact, dependent upon effective communication.

At each stage of the action process audiences must be carefully identified and analyzed in terms of knowledge, attitudes, and communication behavior. At the legitimization stage there may be an audience of only a few, while at the diffusion stage the general public, or a large share of it, may constitute the audience.

Audience analysis provides the basis for identifying communication purpose, and purpose must be related to the interests, wants, and needs of the audience in terms of the objectives of the action program.

Audience analysis also provides the basis for selecting specific messages, for determining message treatment, and for using particular channels of transmission.

In short, the leaders of social-action programs must continually ask, "What messages do we want to communicate, to whom, in what way, for what purpose?" Meaningful social action can only be accomplished by informed and motivated people, and communication is the key to information and motivation.

CHAPTER 7

Communication and the Adoption of Ideas

For years social scientists have probed the intriguing mystery of why and how people accept and adopt new ideas and practices. In their studies they have examined the role of communication in this mystery.

It would be helpful if we could report here that the mystery has been solved; that we know for certain why and how people accept and adopt new ideas; and that we can explain the unique role of communication. Unfortunately, we cannot. Social-science research lacks the precision of physical-science research. People are complex, and their behavior is difficult to predict with complete assurance.

We can, though, review some of the clues to the mystery— clues that later may be confirmed as true or false or partly true and partly false. You can test them against your observations of the way you and your friends accept and adopt new ideas.

THE ADOPTION PROCESS

Rural sociologists have been deeply involved in studying how farm people adopt new practices. This is not surprising. For more than fifty years, the Cooperative Extension Service in each state has provided farm families with technical information to encourage changes in farming practices. The sociologists, therefore, have had a clearcut communication *purpose* upon which to base their research. With audiences identified, it has been easy to relate purpose to audience.

While the environment of an agricultural community differs from a city environment, the difference is less than in former years and the people in both environments probably follow similar adoption patterns.

Steps to Adoption

Studies indicate that in many cases a person takes five steps before he adopts a specific practice. Check these steps against your experience in adopting a new practice.

Step 1—Awareness.   Before we can try something new and different, we must first know about it. We become *aware* that the *new thing* does exist. We understand that there is a new way to grow corn, a new product that will increase gas mileage, or a new theory on raising children. But we have few details.

Step 2—Interest.   Now we start relating the awareness to our particular situation. We become interested in the application of the new thing to our wants and needs. We ask: How does it work? What will it accomplish? How will it help me? Can I get it? What will it cost? Because of interest, we seek more information.

Step 3—Evaluation.   The information we sought in the interest step gives us a basis for completing a mental evaluation. We relate cost and effort of this new thing to the cost and effort of other new things we are interested in. We use past experiences with similar ideas and practices to anticipate returns. We pose "yes," "no," or "maybe" questions and seek answers for our own satisfaction. Does the new thing "fit" us?

Step 4—Trial. At the dinner table we are asked if we want a serving of a new food combination. We have heard about it, know how it is made, and suspect that we might like it—awareness, interest, and evaluation. So we say, "Well, I'll try just a bit." The farmer believes a new seed variety may be better than the one he has been using, so he tries it on a few acres. The new gas-mileage stretcher seems to have possibilities, so we try it on one tank of gas. We are testing our mental evaluation against actual experience.

Step 5—Adoption. The farmer is convinced that the new seed variety does yield more than the old, so next year he switches varieties. Gas mileage is improved by the additive, and we become a regular customer. We like the new food and ask our wives to borrow the recipe so we can have it at home.

Effects of Complexity

In adopting some practices we may go through the five steps within a few hours—from the time we sit down to dinner until we finish eating. With others it may take years to complete the five steps. In general, the more complex or expensive the practice, the longer it takes to move from awareness to adoption.

We can categorize the degrees of complexity and attach labels to them. This helps structure our thinking, but we should remember that often some of the least complex concepts are the most difficult to sell.

Change in materials. Changing materials is the least complex practice. People switch brands and materials frequently—and easily. Advertisers count on this. There seems to be a new brand of soap or detergent on the market each week, and many women move from awareness to trial to adoption without much stress. The same observation may be made about hair styles and hem lengths, although the stress may be greater. Farmers who have had favorable experiences with a new variety of wheat accept subsequent new varieties quickly.

Change in practice. Changing a practice is more complex. Take shaving with an electric razor, for example. We now ask men to do more than shift from one brand of shaving cream to another. We ask them to change their method of shaving—to go from the safety razor to the electric razor. They must change habits as well as materials. As discussed earlier, habits are learned over a long period of time. We are reluctant to give them up. Most men will take longer to evaluate this new way. They may borrow a friend's electric razor and give it a try before deciding to switch to the new method.

Innovations. Men shave every day, but they may never have played golf. Our friends play golf. We watch golf matches on television. Manufacturers keep trying to sell us clubs, balls, and bags. We have been aware of the game for years and have grown more interested lately, since the doctor advised us to get more exercise. But would we like the game? Should we take lessons? Would we look foolish out on the course? Better think about it some more—evaluate. It might not hurt anything to see if we could hit the ball. We could borrow some clubs and sneak out to a deserted playing field first. Give it a try.

Finally we adopt the innovation of a new game and start bragging about breaking 100. Innovations are placed in the third category of complexity because they generally involve "first time" experiences—driving a car, growing orchids, going back to school after being out twenty years, using chemical weed-control methods for the first time.

Life patterns. Changes that involve adjustments in basic life patterns are the most complex of all. The farmer who is considering a switch from dairying to beef production must adopt concepts that change his entire farming pattern. His decision to change enterprises combines a whole series of other adoptions involving materials, practices, and innovations. Life patterns must be changed when we move from one occupation to another. Those who voluntarily decide to retire early do not make the decision easily. Often there is little or no opportunity for us to go through the trial stage when changing life patterns. We go all the way or not at all.

Who Adopts When?

Social scientists also have characterized the people who do the adopting and have assigned labels to the various categories. You probably have heard and used these labels but we will review them briefly.

Innovators. In every social system there are a few people who always try the new thing first. Certain farmers try new chemicals for weed control several years before anyone else. Fashion trends are adopted first by a relatively few women in the community.

For any idea, concept, or practice there are always a few who are first. They are the innovators. Usually, but not always, they are successful in their fields, and usually they are in a relatively high income bracket. Their status in the community is secure. From the standpoint of prestige and money they can afford to take risks and make mistakes. Often, but again not always, they take the lead in social action programs. And they may not be legitimizers.

Early adopters. This group of people is just a step behind the innovators in the adoption time sequence. They are willing to let the innovators prove the practice or make the mistakes, but they watch closely. With a little more experience and prestige they move easily into the innovator category.

Informal leaders. Innovators and early adopters often are just a little too far ahead of the crowd. The informal leader finds his place between them and the group that makes up the majority. The informal leader is not always best, right, or successful, but he is known for good judgment and he has good relationships with nearly everyone around him. He adopts an idea or a concept only after it has been proved in practice by the innovators and the early adopters. Then he says, "This is a good way; follow me."

The majority. This is the big group that follows the leaders. They are confident that the risks have been reduced or eliminated. Few questions remain. The case has been proved. But even now, people in this group usually go through the trial step before going all the way.

Non-adopters. For every idea, concept, or practice there are a few final holdouts: some by choice and some by circumstances; some because they do not believe and some because they cannot afford the changes; some who may have different sets of values. They are the non-adopters.

THE ROLE OF COMMUNICATION

At this point the mystery deepens. There are plenty of clues with all sorts of interpretations when we relate communication to the various steps of adoption or to the categories of people who do the adopting. This is not surprising when we remember that type and complexity of messages influence channel selection; that communication behavior determines both message code and treatment; and that social systems affect the way the receiver responds to a message. Even so it will pay to review what we think we know about the role of communication in the adoption process.

Communication Behavior of Adopters

People who are innovators or early adopters of an idea have a higher degree of communication *sensitivity* than the informal leaders or the majority. They receive and interpret more messages from more sources. They have more face-to-face contacts with people, belong to more groups, participate in more social action programs. They subscribe to more newspapers and magazines, and they read more thoroughly and more critically. They may not spend more time than others listening to radio or watching television, but they listen and watch more selectively.

Innovators and early adopters either have stronger wants and needs or they are more impatient to satisfy them. They are more interested in recognition and new experiences than in response and security. They often are so far in front of the crowd that they are recognized but neither admired nor followed. But they don't care. They are intrigued by the unknown and the untried, and they respond to messages designed to appeal to the new and different.

The communication behavior of the informal leader is not much different from the behavior of the majority. In fact, he moves within the same groups and the same systems as the majority, and this mutual familiarity provides one basis for his leadership role. The majority says, "He is one of us. He goes where we go, reads what we read, hears what we hear, and believes as we do." But there is a difference. The informal leader receives the same channels as the majority but he interprets messages somewhat more critically. He reads more closely, listens more attentively, and thinks a shade more clearly.

People in the majority category do not subscribe to as many channels of written communication. They watch and listen less critically but they still depend most on the mass-media channels to take them through the awareness and interest steps of the adoption process. They look more to others—friends and neighbors—for guidance through the steps of evaluation, trial, and adoption. And they look most to the informal leaders.

When you think about it you can find all kinds of exceptions to the general rule. There may be innovators who subscribe only to *The Wall Street Journal,* seldom listen to radio, and wouldn't have a television set in the house. In fact, they may be the originators of a given idea or practice.

At the same time there are persons who fit into the category of the majority whose outward communication behavior is identical with that of the innovator or the early adopter. For a variety of reasons, however, they do not want to be out in front. They prefer to move with the majority.

Channels by Adoption Stages

For the most part, studies of how adoption takes place have been restricted to measurements of past happenings. Measurements are taken after things happen, to find out what combination of forces caused them to happen. There is little opportunity to consider what might have happened if a different combination of forces had been employed.

With respect to agriculture, for example, social scientists have selected certain adopted practices and then traced the history of adoption to determine the role of communication. From this approach they conclude that personal communication played a certain role at this or that stage. The use of mass-media channels had certain other roles at certain other stages. This is fine so long as we confine our conclusions to historical happenings. There are dangers, though, when we attempt to project what happened in the past to what is likely to happen in the future.

Many studies, for instance, show that farmers get more of their information from farm magazines than they do from daily newspapers, radio, or television. But this is a little like proving that women get more housekeeping information from housekeeping magazines than from physical culture magazines. What else? The housekeeping magazines carry housekeeping information and the physical culture magazines don't. Farm magazines are in business to communicate farm information, whereas other public media may carry little, if any, farm information.

With this viewpoint registered, we can go ahead and review some of the clues regarding channels used at various stages of the adoption process.

As might be expected, studies of the adoption of agricultural practices in this country seem to agree that most farmers become *aware* of a new idea or practice through one or more of the mass-media channels of communication—magazines, newspapers, radio, or television. At least farmers usually mention one of these channels when asked where they first heard about an idea. If newspapers, radio stations, and television stations carry farm news and information, we may assume that the more newsy, simple ideas and concepts are reported first on those channels, and that is where the farmers hear about them. The more complex ideas and practices are usually reported in the farm magazines.

At the awareness stage, farmers depend less on person-to-person communication channels than on mass-media channels. Some studies have ranked sources from which the farmer receives information in the awareness stage. They show government agencies coming in first, friends and neighbors second, and salesmen and dealers third.

The same ranking of channels and sources seems to apply at the *interest* stage of the adoption process. Once aware, the farmer still looks first to the mass-media channels for more information about the practice, and the person-to-person channels are in second place. Sources hold the same rank as in the awareness stage.

At the *evaluation* and *trial* stages the situation changes. Channels and sources are mixed up. Person-to-person channels having neighbors, friends, and government agencies as sources move into first place; the mass media channels hold on to second; but person-to-person channels having dealers and salesmen as sources end up third.

At the *adoption* stage the farmer depends upon self-communication. His actions are based upon his own experiences during the trial period. He decides for himself whether the yields are higher, the cattle are faster-gaining, and the paycheck is bigger.

Surprisingly enough, however, it may be at or immediately after the adoption stage that a person is most receptive to messages about the practice from a variety of sources via a number of channels. He seeks confirmation and approval of a decision already made. He talks to friends and neighbors who have tried or who are trying the practice. He reads magazine stories about the practice with almost the same thoroughness that he did when still trying to decide his course of action. For this reason salesmen and advertisers would do well to remember that customers who have already bought are one of their most important audiences. It is poor policy to win one customer with communication attention while losing another from lack of attention.

COMMUNICATION AND COMMON SENSE

Past research provides clues to the mystery of why and how people adopt new ideas and practices, and it suggests how communication fits into the adoption process. Our task, then, is to match these clues with our knowledge of (1) the simplicity or complexity of the idea or practice we are trying to get adopted, (2) the characteristics of the target audience, and (3) the nature of the social system in which the audience is located.

If we were the "expert" and someone came to us for help in getting an idea across or a new practice adopted, we would first get answers to some rather specific questions. How much change in behavior is required to adopt the practice? How many people do we want to change? Where are they? Who are they in terms of attitudes toward "new" ideas? What do they read, watch, and listen to? What channels are available? How do the messages "fit" with the channels that we can use?

We would then check our answers against the following commonsense observations:

1. It is logical for the mass-media channels to play a leading role in making large audiences aware of and interested in a new idea or practice. Common sense tells us this when we consider the saturation of mass media, the millions of dollars spent for advertising and sales promotion via the media, and the outpouring of educational information to and through the media. Skill in using the mass-media channels, therefore, is extremely important for anyone who has the job of communicating effectively with large numbers of people.

2. We also may assume that, for certain ideas or practices, the mass-media channels can take audiences through all five stages of the adoption process—with or without assistance from other channels. We get many of our ideas and formulate many of our opinions by reading, watching, or listening to messages that come to us via such channels. We are also influenced to try new products or to switch brands of the same general product line.

3. The mass-media channels are not well suited for messages

that demand major changes in our behavior, or for teaching us new and complicated skills. We need personal channels to teach us how to drive a car, although we can learn improved driving procedures by watching television.

4. The more complicated the practice, the greater the need for channels that provide continuous feedback so that questions can be asked and answered, language clarified, and instructions repeated.

5. In the final analysis, most people adopt new ideas or change practices because of exposure to a number of messages, from several sources, received through a variety of channels. Some channels, especially the mass media, make us aware and interested and may lead us to a tentative decision. We may turn to other channels and other sources, especially personal ones, for additional information, for other judgment, or for support of our tentative decision. It may be somewhat academic to attempt to assign major credit to a particular source or channel for our final decision.

Part II

THE SKILLS OF
COMMUNICATION

Man's progress depends in large measure upon his mastery of the skills of communication. Without such skills he cannot expect to be either heard or understood.

CHAPTER 8

The Importance
of Listening

Have you ever sat in a restaurant and said to the "attentive" waitress, poised with her pad and pencil, "I would like a cup of coffee, please, with cream and sugar," only to have her ask, "Black, or with cream?"

Or have you approached a ticket counter and asked for a round-trip coach ticket to Chicago, Syracuse, or someplace else and experienced a response of two questions? The first: "One-way or round-trip?" The second: "Coach or first-class?"

You mention to the boss that you are taking next Monday afternoon off to go to the ball game. But when a special job comes up Monday morning the boss insists he never "heard" you say anything about the ball game that afternoon.

After experiencing a succession of such simple but frustrating breakdowns in social communication, you start to believe that "everybody talks, but nobody listens." Unfortunately that may be close to the truth. Many communication failures, both important and unimportant, cannot be traced to wrong messages, poor language codes, or faulty channels. The failures result from faulty listening on the part of the receiver, and much of the communication effort is wasted.

Many of us believe that we could communicate better if we only had more skill in writing, speaking, or illustrating. Our jobs call for writing news releases, performing on radio, and appearing on television. We are eager to become better writers, speakers, and broadcasters. We give little thought to our skill, or lack of it, as listeners, yet, it is doubtful if any of us will ever communicate well unless we learn to listen well. So in discussing ways to improve communication skills, let's start with the importance of listening.

WE LISTEN TO MANY

Technically, of course, it is incorrect to say that "everybody talks but nobody listens." Whenever someone talks, someone listens—or tries or pretends to listen. If you doubt the importance of improving listening skill, keep track of how you spend your communication time for a couple of days. How much time do you spend reading? Talking? Watching? And how much time do you spend listening? The totals may surprise you.

In one study a number of years ago, Paul T. Rankin, who was supervising director of research and adjustment for the Detroit Public Schools, asked sixty-eight persons to keep accurate records of their communication time for two months. On the average, this group, representing a number of occupations, spent 9 percent of their communication time writing, 16 percent reading, 30 percent talking, and 45 percent *listening*. The group members spent 61 percent of their time receiving messages (reading and listening) and 39 percent of their time sending messages (writing and talking). But on the receiving end, they spent three times as much time listening as reading.

We need to improve our listening skill simply because we spend so much time at it. Without listening skill, much time is wasted.

Other studies support this claim by showing how little of what we hear is remembered. In general these studies show that, immediately after listening to someone talk, we remember only about half of what we heard. Two months after listening we remember only about 25 percent of what we heard. By improving our listening skill we hear more, remember more, and use our time more efficiently.

KEY ROLE IN COMMUNICATION

If you wish to speak with a man, listen first to his talk. Skill in listening is a prerequisite for learning, for using all other communication skills, and for managing the process of communication.

Listening helps us know and understand our audience. Through listening we appraise the audience's general level of knowledge, as well as its specific knowledge concerning our message. We take readings on attitudes, prejudices, and mental blocks. Listening also tells us much about the potential receiver's motivational wants and needs. By listening we learn better how to select messages, language codes, and appeals.

Spend an evening listening to a group of people who represent an audience you want to reach. In normal conversations people generally reveal where and how they "learned something." Listen for the clues. Do they quote other people with whom they have talked? Do they mention the things they read in their local papers? Or heard on radio? Are the latest books discussed? Are they using the language of the mass media?

We also listen to evaluate the success or failure of our communication effort. Listening will tell us whether our message is being received, whether there is true reception or only polite attention. By careful listening we know whether the stirring in the audience is resulting from the impact of our message, or from the boredom of sitting until we finish saying what they are *not* listening to.

OUR HABITS OF POOR LISTENING

By the time we are adults most of us have acquired our listening habits and skills. We acquired them, as we did other habits, during a long period of time and for a variety of reasons. And we do not change habits easily. We cannot switch from being a poor listener to being a good listener by simply deciding to change—or by reading the few pages that make up the chapter of this book. We can start, though, by taking a look at the kind of listening habits we now have and by deciding whether our habits are good or bad. Here again we can benefit by listening to Ralph Nichols and other specialists who have identified a number of bad listening habits. For each one we will suggest ways to break the habit.

Partial Listening

All of us can think faster than the average person can talk. Most speakers move along at about 125 words per minute— some faster and some slower. If we could measure our speed of thought it might come out something like 400 or 600 words a minute. Listening doesn't demand all of our thinking time, so we tend to make use of the "extra."

We listen along at 125 or 150 words a minute and "think along" with the remaining time not needed for listening. There is nothing wrong with that if we direct our thinking toward what is being said. But often we don't. We let our minds wander, picking up thoughts here and there, playing with them for a while, and then we give our attention back to the speaker as we listen for another "bit." Every so often, though, our minds pick up a wandering thought and we stay with it longer than we intended. By the time we get back to the speaker we have lost a good part of what he was saying. At that point we have two choices. We can listen intently and try to pick up the continuity of the message, or we can decide that the effort is too difficult and turn the speaker off.

We are usually most guilty of partial listening when we think

we are unobserved and when we are not expected to respond—
in a big group meeting, while listening to radio, or any time that
we think we are hidden by a crowd. But the habit of partial listening often carries over to person-to-person communication.
Even when talking with a friend or a business associate, we give
in to our wandering thoughts and miss half or all of the intended
message.

Solution. You can start controlling this bad habit by concentrating the extra thinking time on the message itself and on
the intent of the speaker. Make sure you truly understand what
the speaker intends to say, and listen for his main points. Think
about the way he is structuring his message, the evidence that is
being used, the logic of his position.

As you go along, think back over what has been said and see
if you can anticipate the next parts. Summarize mentally. Can
you learn anything from the way the speaker sends his message
—his gestures, the way he stands or moves about, his facial expressions?

Emotional Blackouts

We all bring to the listening side of the table our own set of
emotions, preconceived notions and beliefs, and our attitudes toward people, ideas, and concepts. We want our emotions appealed
to, our beliefs supported, and our attitudes confirmed. When this
doesn't happen we turn our listening mechanism down or completely off.

We have decided that we cannot put much stock in the opinions of men with long hair, beards, and mustaches. The speaker
has long hair, a beard, and a mustache. So we spend our time
listening for confirmation of our opinion rather than listening to
what the fellow has to say. Our prejudice blocks our ability to
listen. We spend time analyzing the sender rather than receiving
the message.

We may also have some pretty firm ideas about parent-child relationships. And the first time the speaker, be he friend or foe,
suggests that adults are responsible for misunderstandings be-

tween adults and youth, we start building an argument and stop listening to the basis for his point of view.

Solution.   Listen now; argue later. You lose nothing by at least hearing what the other fellow has to say. You may find that he is more on "your side" than you thought. If not, there will be plenty of time to raise questions and present another viewpoint.

Message Blackouts

We often use the message as the excuse for not listening. We decide early in the game that the speaker's subject is uninteresting, too difficult to grasp, too simple to waste our time on. We mentally excuse ourselves and let our minds wander around the countryside of our fancies. We may even look to others to support our judgment. A nod there, a smile here, or a shake of the head is enough to reassure us, and we stop listening completely.

Solution.   Few messages will be exactly tuned to the wavelength of your interest. Some will seem complex and others simple. But by listening you add some small bits to knowledge and understanding. The difficult message gives you a chance to sharpen your ability to think and reason. Listen for new words, or old words used a different way. Jot down phrases or statements to clarify later. By listening and thinking, you can elaborate on the simple message by directing attention to the missing segments and by making more subtle interpretations.

Speaker Dismissal

Some speakers seem to turn us on, while others turn us off, whether the environment is a big meeting or a casual conversation. We dismiss some speakers and stop listening for many reasons—style of clothes, tone of voice, use of gestures, physical appearance, platform mannerisms. We either mentally turn away or concentrate our attention completely on the man himself, but the result is the same—faulty listening and missed messages.

Solution.   Keep in mind that Albert Einstein did not make a commanding impression, but he had something pretty important to say. Concentrate on the message and not the man. You are not selecting him as a business partner or a fishing companion. If he has something to say it doesn't matter if he is tall or short, fat or thin, colorful or drab. But you will never know unless you listen.

Faking Attention

There are times when we pretend to listen and substitute a listening posture for the real thing. We give the speaker or our friend across the table our "undivided attention." We seemingly ignore all distractions, look him straight in the eye, smile, nod at appropriate times, lean forward as though to hear better, and yet miss everything that is being said because we are not listening. Unfortunately the mere act of pretending may require more mental effort than listening. And it is doubtful if anyone is being fooled, least of all the speaker.

Solution. Mentally trade places with the speaker and analyze your reactions when you realize that your listeners are only pretenders.

Pencil Listening

We may listen poorly because we are one of several kinds of pencil listeners. We are convinced that we can doodle and listen at the same time, and at first we may be able to. Soon, though, we become so intrigued with our artistic doodles that the speaker's message is lost forever.

On the other hand we may believe that the secret of listening is to take a lot of notes. Soon we are so involved with the physical task of note-taking—in proper outline form, of course—that we can't keep up with the speaker's rate of even 125 words per minute.

If we are fact-seekers we listen with pencil poised for the facts of the message. But as we search and record we miss the interpretation the speaker is giving his facts. We have the facts but failed to get the message.

Solution. Keep in mind that the intent of most messages is to communicate ideas. Facts and their interpretations are used to present or support the idea. If you listen attentively you can usually remember the three or four main ideas the speaker hoped to communicate. Use the pencil to note ideas and a few facts, if you must, but forget the detailed notes unless you plan to give the same speech yourself. In that case, ask the speaker for a copy of his talk.

FROM POOR HABITS TO GOOD

While we should direct part of our attention toward correcting poor listening habits, we can also set about acquiring some new or improved habits. Such newly acquired habits may, in fact, help drive out the old ones.

Many of our listening faults result from social or professional environments in which we are *required* to listen whether we want to or not. We are *expected* to listen to our wives or husbands, to our children, to those attending the same dinner parties. At work we must listen to our associates, attend staff meetings, take part in conferences, and participate on committees because the job demands it. So we think we can beat the system by being physically there and mentally off somewhere else.

There is another way to beat the system, though. We can set a goal of being one of the world's ten best listeners—or at least one of the ten best in our office or on our block. In addition to being one of the most popular persons, we also will acquire a basic skill of communication.

Check Attitude and Atmosphere

Assume for the moment that you are in control of the situation. Your objective is to listen and learn. You are the receiver in the communication process. The other fellow is the sender. Are the conditions right for the process to begin?

Check your attitude first. Can you put aside the project you have been working on or problems you have been thinking about? Can you postpone the telephone call that should be made and put off the instructions you intended to give someone? Have you used the mental eraser to remove the lingering thoughts and distracting notions that may interfere with your reception of the message?

What about the sender? Are you convinced that he is worth listening to? Can you ignore for now his funny habit of looking at the floor when he talks, or the way he blinks his left eye? Can you accept his color, his race, his religion?

Do you have built-in opinions about the anticipated subject? Are you ready to reserve judgment or is your mind already made up?

Now about the atmosphere. You may like a fresh gale blowing through the north window, but the effect may be to freeze out the person who is talking. Are you *available,* or have you blocked out communication with a fourteen-foot-wide desk between you and the sender? Or do you frighten him off by sitting or standing too close? The physical environment may be more important than you think. It is almost impossible to speak or listen if the telephone rings every three minutes, whether you answer it or not. Can you defer phone calls until later?

If attitudes and atmosphere are right you are ready to turn on the receiving mechanism with a smile, a greeting, and an invitation to be comfortable. In effect you will have said, "Welcome, my friend, I am glad to see you and I am interested in what you have to say. I may not agree with everything, but be assured that I will listen."

Keep Channels Open

You have made a long-distance telephone call to an associate, but at the most critical point of your conversation the line goes dead. There is a break in the circuit. The channel is closed. When you complain to the operator she informs you that all of the circuits are busy now and she will call back. Or she replaces the call but you find it difficult to get back to the critical point.

The art of good listening includes the skill of keeping the channel open and avoiding the short circuits. Perhaps the best way is to avoid the sins others commit when they listen to you.

Chances are that you have been around so-called listeners who are expert circuit-breakers.

There is the fellow who lets you say five sentences and then says he knows exactly what your problem is and what to do about it. You know that your first five sentences weren't about the problem at all but were intended only to open the door. He closes the door before you can walk through.

Then there is the "I've got problems, too" circuit-breaker. You wanted his advice on your problem, but he listened only long enough to be reminded of all the problems he has.

You probably have had experience with listeners who can do five things at once. They can listen to you, talk on the telephone, read a piece of mail, clean their fingernails, and smoke a pipe. They reassure you by saying, "Go ahead, I'm listening." But you know they are not, and they know they are not. The channel was closed a long time ago.

Some people seem to listen while doing their physical exercises. They stretch, yawn, crack their knuckles, walk around the room, pace behind your chair while offering little grunts of encouragement. Since you can't tell whether the grunts signal attention or boredom, you figure you may as well give up.

With a little thought, you should be able to identify a number of other techniques people have used to close the channel that you hoped would stay open. Your task is to avoid those techniques, and apply the golden rule of listening: *Listen to others as you would have them listen to you.*

Respond to Reassure

We hope we haven't suggested that the good listener is one who sits at perfect attention without saying a word or changing his expression. Such lack of action may provide the best circuit-breaker of all. Your visitor will be so unnerved and unsure of himself that he will completely forget what he wanted to say.

Skill in listening demands response on the part of the listener —the kind of response that reassures the speaker that he is being received and interpreted.

Your nonverbal response will register first. This doesn't mean that you have to smile benevolently the whole time or nod continuously like a bird drinking water. The speaker knows that his message isn't intended to provide constant smiles or chuckles of appreciation. It is more serious than that.

At the same time, if you react too strongly to a negative message you may encourage a withholding of facts to soften the blow. The speaker thinks, "This fellow doesn't like what I am saying, so I had better not say it."

Keep your nonverbal responses moderate. Avoid too much of any response—humor, sympathy, surprise, horror, shock, amazement, shame. But you contribute little by being the strong, silent, unemotional type because a part of the speaker's purpose is to tap your emotional responses.

Your most reassuring verbal responses will be in the form of appropriate questions that encourage the speaker to continue with his message. You can use questions to seek additional facts, to clarify an interpretation, to understand better the speaker's point of view. In one way or another they should all say, "Tell me more. I find this interesting, and I think I understand." Avoid questions that challenge the speaker's authority, his grasp of the facts, or his motivation. One of the most effective ways to close the communication channel is to *dare* the speaker with a skeptical question that starts out with the phrase, "Are you really sure?" or, "Do you expect me to believe?"

You can also reassure by making affirmative responses. You may repeat a key point that he has made, offer a comparable example, or suggest a supporting piece of information. By so doing you are letting him know that you understand what he is saying even though you may be reserving judgment until he has completed his message.

Keep the Door Open

Most of our person-to-person communication experiences are not single, isolated episodes. Our role as listener may cover a long period of time and include a number of listening sessions.

The first session, in fact, may be only a preliminary survey on the part of the fellow across the table. He may be testing the water by introducing only a fringe aspect of the real problem that he eventually wants to discuss. He is interested in finding out if the door is open for his return.

The best way to close the door on future discussions is to fail to listen the first time. The next-best way is to let the other person know that you don't anticipate future discussions. Say something such as, "Well, I'm glad we got this all talked out now, and I'm sure you won't have any more concerns with the problem." You can be fairly sure that you will not hear about the problems any more.

You keep the door open by letting him know you are prepared to listen again. He will know that he is welcome back if you say, "Maybe we have carried this problem about as far as we can today. Let's think about it some more, see if there are some points we have missed, and have another session on it next week if you would like." This leaves the option up to him, but the door is open.

Listening is the path to knowledge, and knowledge is the key to effective communication.

CHAPTER 9

Good Writing from Good Writers

We listen to learn. We write to persuade.

When writing, we reverse our position in the communication process. We change from receiver to sender.

Writing is not only a means of communicating thoughts, ideas, and information of the moment, but also a method of recording and preserving for the future. The written word lasts longer than the spoken word, but, unfortunately, poor writing may last just as long as good writing.

The contributions of good writers and their writings are universally recognized. The lost contributions of men and women who know but cannot write are deplored. Someone once said, "Men who know something but can't write so that others will understand must be considered the inarticulate components of our society." Education and business leaders champion the cause of effective communication and the value of writing skills. Note the following quotations:

One's accomplishment is, in a very real sense, dependent upon the quality of his communication with others.—J. C. Warner, President, Carnegie Institute of Technology.

There is no greater problem than that of effectively presenting thoughts and ideas. I believe that the student who learns to communicate through speech and writing will make himself more valuable in whatever work he selects.—Frederic N. Schwarz, President, Bristol-Myers Company.

The accurate transmission of ideas and facts from one mind to another is a complex process with many pitfalls, especially when the communication must be in writing. The man who wishes to advance must exert himself to improve his communication skill. His goal should be not merely to be understood, but to write so that he cannot be misunderstood.—Harry O. Bercher, President, International Harvester Company.

Today's leaders are frequently men and women who have mastered the art of communication. They know how to get their ideas across. —Robert Sarnoff, President, National Broadcasting Company.

CHARACTERISTICS OF GOOD WRITERS

If we accept the proposition that good writing can come only from the pens and typewriters of good writers, we must turn first to the writer and consider his attitudes, purposes, knowledge, and writing skills.

Attitude

Few people do anything well that they truly dislike doing. The homemaker who dislikes sewing will seldom make a perfect dress. The farmer who dislikes livestock will probably have an inefficient cattle-feeding operation.

Writing is no different. Writing can be a stimulating experience or drudgery. If we consider writing to be drudgery we will never —repeat, never—be good writers. The man who continually insists that he is a poor writer probably is, and he will have trouble becoming a better writer unless he can alter his attitude.

This does not mean that writing must seem easy before we can have a positive attitude. The man who says writing is easy may be speaking about *his* kind of writing. His writing may not be good writing. Writing, like any other creative task, is often difficult, but it can still be stimulating and pleasurable. The good writer regards his writing as an extension of himself, and only good writing will reflect his best qualities.

Obviously, attitude cannot be bestowed. Nor can a positive attitude be taught in class or in books such as this. Each person must have his own reasons for wanting to be a good writer.

Purpose

Poor writing often comes from writers who lack purpose or who put words on paper for the wrong purpose. Then why do they write at all? Because it is expected of them. Writing is a requirement of their jobs, and they comply. Wrong purpose. Poor writing.

Our job requires that we submit a monthly narrative report covering the work accomplished. So we write the reports with the mistaken notion that the purpose is to satisfy the job requirement. Wrong purpose. Dull, dry reports that don't say anything.

We promise the local editor several news stories each week. After a couple of weeks the purpose of writing news stories becomes one of satisfying our agreement with the editor. Wrong purpose. Lifeless, meaningless news stories that waste newspaper space.

We are drafted by our group to prepare a summary of the plans for the proposed new community medical facilities. We want to prove that we are doing our share of the work in the group and write the report. Wrong purpose. Summary fails to stimulate anyone to further action.

Rhetoric instructors in high school and college attempt to teach good writing by having students write themes on assigned subjects. Students write to please the instructor and get a grade. Wrong purpose. Stacks of poorly written themes.

Writing should influence the reader in some identifiable way. If we don't know why or how we want to influence the reader, we should forget about writing.

Knowledge

Knowledge of both audience and subject is perhaps more important in writing than in most forms of speaking. The readers of our writing cannot tell us at the moment whether they understand our message. They cannot provide continuous feedback. As writers we must select content and language that permit easy reception and interpretation.

APPROACH TO GOOD WRITING

We have all had the experience of reading a truly good piece of writing—a report, special letter, news story, feature article, or book. We were impressed by the organization, coherence, and readability. The writer seemed to write effortlessly. He must have sat at his desk and let the words flow.

We were right about the ease of reading. We probably were wrong about the ease of writing. The writer had something to say to us and he knew how to approach his task. His writing, like that of all good writers, probably resulted from professional attention to these four equally indispensable steps to good writing: (1) researching, (2) drafting, (3) redrafting, and (4) polishing.

Researching

Good writing often has been compared with an iceberg. The part that "shows" is only a small fraction of the total. Once a good writer has identified his audience and his purpose, he collects, analyzes, evaluates, and organizes his information. He anticipates the kinds of questions his readers might have, gathers the bits of knowledge that will contribute answers, arranges the bits in logical order, and decides which bits can be used and which discarded. He sorts out facts from opinions, determines how much supporting evidence he needs, and tests the quality and validity of the opinions. Before he starts writing he may have two times, four times, or ten times as much information as he will eventually use. But the nature of his research determines whether his final written product is good or poor.

Drafting

To provide continuity and flow, most good writers try to get the first draft on paper quickly. At this stage they do not worry about such technicalities as sentence structure, grammar, punctuation, or style. They want the draft to reflect movement, spontaneity, and life. The good writer is more interested in substance than in style. He wants to get his main ideas recorded and related to each other, and he tries to do this quickly.

Redrafting

After the first draft "cools" for a bit, the writer can take a fresh look. He may change the structure, rearrange paragraphs, add a section here, and take out some material there. He decides whether he needs more evidence to support a point or whether he has overburdened a clear concept with too much evidence. He may conclude that the logical beginning of the piece is buried in the middle, and he changes that.

The complexity of the subject and the precision of the writer determine whether one or five redrafts are needed.

Polishing

Once the writer is satisfied with the substance, the structure, and the flow, he is ready for the final polishing job. At this stage he is looking for a slightly more appropriate word, a more forceful sentence, a minor shift in emphasis. Now he pays close attention to the consistencies of grammar and the appropriateness of punctuation. He takes out the meaningless words, the vague references, and the redundant paragraphs. It is here that he adds the final touches of "style."

BUT NOT FOR ME

About now, you start turning the reception knob to "off." You want to be a good writer, but you have no intention of writing the world's best article or winning the Pulitzer Prize for literature. The need to research a subject, draft, redraft, and polish seems a bit too much. But don't back away from our suggestions or let them scare you off.

Obviously your approach to the task of writing an article for *Life* magazine would differ from that of writing a news story for the local paper. You probably agree that the *Life* article is "worth" researching, drafting, redrafting, and polishing. But you are certain there is an easier way to write the local news story. There is, but only with respect to the time required to take the steps and not in the steps themselves.

You probably are an authority for the story you plan to write for the local newspaper. You have the necessary facts in your head or readily available from other sources. Your research, therefore, may require only a few minutes, but you still must take the step. Relate audience to purpose to message. If you fail to take the step, you may omit information that your readers need most.

With any skill at all, you say, you should be able to combine the drafting, redrafting, and polishing steps into one step. Just put the story down on paper and send it off to the editor. Many people do this, and many people are poor writers.

A complete redraft of the story may not be needed, but you are an unusually gifted writer if you can achieve perfection on the first try, even with a simple news story.

With some writing you may be able to combine redrafting and polishing in the same step. There is nothing wrong with that, and we don't want to be so stuck on steps that we forget purpose. The final polishing, however, often separates adequate writing from excellent writing. You can decide whether your goal is adequacy or excellence.

CHAPTER 10

Writing for Easy Reading

The most beautiful writing in the world is wasted if the writer alone knows what he is saying. With good writing, the reader knows what the writer is saying.

The reader has a choice of things to read. He bases his choice on two factors: interest in the subject and readability of the writing. He may even turn away from an interesting subject if the writing is difficult to read.

Not all easily read messages, however, are worth reading. Some writers are expert at making writing readable, but have little that is worth saying. We must combine good writing with worthy subjects.

Writing for easy reading means following four writing habits:

1. Using *words* that readers understand and grasp quickly.

2. Putting *sentences* together logically and concisely.

3. Organizing sentences into short *paragraphs,* tying them together with transitional words and phrases.

4. Organizing paragraphs into the *form* that is suited to the purpose for which the writing is intended.

THE RIGHT WORD IN THE RIGHT PLACE

As writers our task is to spot difficult words and to substitute easier words without changing the meaning. We anticipate words our readers may find either difficult or easy, and we appreciate the variations in meaning that readers may give to certain words.

While there is no way to guarantee that we will always pick the easy word over the more difficult, the following guidelines should help:

1. *Long words with many syllables are often difficult words.* Many of our English words began as Latin or Anglo-Saxon root-words to which prefixes and suffixes have been added. The more we add to the root-word, the more difficult the final word becomes.

Take the word *unbearable.* The root of the word is *bear,* meaning "to carry." We add the prefix *un* and the suffix *able* to get the word *unbearable,* which is vague and abstract. This is the way in which many of our long words are built.

We don't have to look far in everyday writing to find long, complicated words of many syllables. Here are just a few: *consultation, consequently, revolutionary, coordination, assimilation, acquisition, pathological, incomprehensible, discretionary.*

2. *Words that are new and little used are often difficult words.* Some twenty or more years ago, chemists discovered a new type of washing compound that had certain advantages over soap. This compound was identified as a *detergent.* This was a new word, and when it was first used not one person out of a hundred had the faintest idea what it meant. And today, a lot of people still would have a hard time defining the word.

We are continually coming across new words. And we like to use them. The trouble is that we don't bother to explain the meanings of such words to our readers. We may get credit for being smart, but the audience doesn't understand what we are writing about.

3. *Words that have meaning in a particular profession or trade may often be difficult for the average reader to understand.*

Every profession develops a special language, which may consist of some newly coined words plus a lot of old words with different or highly specialized meanings. Such words are often called jargon. Jargon is fine when members of a profession are talking among themselves, but most people outside the profession simply don't understand the language. Economists, sociologists, and communication specialists are great users of jargon. Here are a few examples: *correlation analysis, marginal input, optimum output, protectionism, inversion, potential, standardization, cognitive dissonance.*

4. *Words that have many different meanings may be difficult and confusing to the reader.* Foreign students agree that the English language is one of the most difficult to master because so many of our words have different meanings. For example, the word *block* may have ten or twelve different meanings. It can mean a block of wood, a block on the football field, a railroad block, a part of a block and tackle. The same is true of the word *fast.*

5. *Words that are trite and overused contribute to poor writing because the reader is bored with them.* Probably one of the most overused words in the English language is *very.* In writing or speaking, we say that something is very long, very high, very hot, very cold, very nice, very bad, very good. The question one must always ask is, "How very is very?"

To illustrate, we have listed below some words writers use every day. There is nothing wrong with these words but they tend to be difficult for the reader to grasp quickly and easily. Opposite each, we have suggested a substitute that is more common and generally easier to grasp and understand. You may think of substitutes that are even better.

abbreviate—shorten	indicate—show
accelerate—hasten	ineffectual—useless
accomplish—carry out	innocuous—harmless
accordingly—therefore	interrupt—hinder, stop
actuate—put in action, move	inundate—flood
additional—added	isolate—set apart

aggregate—total
agitate—shake, stir, excite
alleviate—make easier
ameliorate—improve
antithesis—opposite
apparent—clear, plain
append—add
appropriate—proper (adj.),
  set aside (v.)
approximately—about
ascertain—find out
assimilate—absorb, digest
beneficial—helpful
bilateral—two-sided
circuitous—roundabout
coagulate—thicken
cognizant—aware
commence—begin
commodious—roomy
conception—thought, idea
conjecture—guess
considerable—much
contiguous—touching, near
criterion—rule, test
deficiency—lack
development—growth
deviate—turn aside
diminution—lessening

judicious—wise
liberate—free
lucid—clear
luminous—bright
manifest—clear, plain
manufacture—make
minimal—smallest
mitigate—make mild, soften
modification—change
nebulous—hazy, vague
neutralize—offset
objective—aim, goal
oblique—slanting
observation—remark
observe—note
obsolete—out-of-date
occupy—take up, fill
operate—work, run
orifice—opening, hole
paramount—top, chief
partially—partly
participate—take part
penetrate—pierce
periphery—outer edge
practicable—can be done
present—give
principal—main, chief
problematical—doubtful

What words could be substituted for those listed below without changing meanings?

discussion	external	procedure	stringent
disengage	fabricate	proximity	subsequently
disseminate	facilitate	quadrilateral	substantial
distribute	fluctuate	quiescent	sufficient
dominant	formulate	recognize	suitability
duplicate	fragment	reconstruct	supersede
effect	frequently	refrigerate	tabulation
elevation	generate	remainder	technicality
emerge	gravitate	reproduction	terminate
emphasize	identical	requisite	ultimate

encounter	immediately	saturate	unavailability
endeavor	impair	segment	undulations
entirety	inclement	segregate	uniformity
equivalent	inapplicable	selection	utilize
evident	incombustible	similar	variation
expedite	increase	situated	visualize
expunge	indeterminate	solitary	voluminous

When we substitute easy words for difficult ones we usually end up with words of fewer syllables. One way to check your writing for probable ease of reading is to count the number of syllables in a 100-word sample. In general, the more syllables in the sample, the more difficult the reading. Easy reading contains from 100 to 130 syllables per 100 words. Standard reading permits from 130 to 160 syllables for the same number of words. If your writing contains more than 160 syllables per 100 words it may be difficult reading for the average person.

In the following example the writing of the original message averaged 165 syllables per 100 words—difficult reading. The rewrite averages 117 syllables per 100 words. You can decide whether the rewrite says the same thing as the original and whether it is easier to read.

Original: Retention of a position is not a vested right to which the incumbent is entitled by virtue of possession, but is conditioned upon his maintenance of high standards of performance and the continued need for his services.

Rewrite: No one has a right to his job just because he is holding it. An employee may expect to keep his job only if he is doing his work well and if there is still a job to be done.

Try your hand at rewriting the following messages to change them from difficult to easy reading. Aim for fewer than 130 syllables per 100 words. We have indicated the syllables per 100 words for each example, and each is in the difficult range.

Original (200 syllables per 100 words): Your use of land during the years ahead will depend on allotment levels, characteristics of your soil, present soil quality, soil improvements made, equipment available, and the relative prices of various crops. Alternative crops must be considered individually. Explore the situation with your local farm adviser, who can give personal counsel and furnish helpful printed material on various crops.

An important consideration in today's complex economy is the marketability of alternative crops. Safflower in particular deserves advance arrangements, for it is produced entirely on contract.

Original (181 syllables per 100 words): Under an ideal capital structure, it usually is desirable to borrow seasonal capital requirements even though the members are in a position also to provide this capital. There are a few cooperatives in Oregon in such excellent financial condition that they hardly ever borrow any funds. During several months of the year, however, they carry excessive cash balances. In most cases it would be better to distribute some of these funds to the patrons and borrow during the peak season. The patrons probably would be able to employ this additional capital productively on the farm. Associations that are able to obtain all of their facilities, equipment, and normal operating capital from the members will not encounter any difficulty in borrowing for seasonal needs at a reasonable rate of interest.

TURN LONG SENTENCES INTO SHORT ONES

As we learned a long time ago, a sentence is simply a group of words that express a complete thought. A basic sentence contains a subject, a verb, and sometimes an object.

As children we learned to write simple sentences: "I see a dog." "He hit me." "I won't (play) (go) (come) (stop) (sit) (stand)." A child's writing may be tiresome, but it communicates.

By adding words and phrases we make the thought of a simple sentence more refined and more exact. We also make the sentence more complex. We become still more complex when we attempt to express two or even three thoughts in the same sentence. And we make a final, horrible mess of writing when we attach two or three qualifying phrases or clauses to each of the two or three thoughts.

Example: If not more than two-thirds of the county Extension workers ask for pay raises, and not more than one-third ask to have their salaries doubled before the next biennium, some consideration will be given to merit increases for those whose salaries are below the minimum, assuming money is appropriated by the legislature and if it isn't needed for something else.

There are a number of ways to measure the complexity of a sentence. The easiest way is to determine the length of the sentence by counting the number of words. *In general, the shorter the sentence, the easier the reading.* The average sentence length of most *Reader's Digest* articles is around seventeen words— fairly easy reading.

It's easy to find the average sentence length of any passage. Just count the total number of words and divide by the number of sentences. In counting sentences, figure a colon or a semicolon the same as a period, provided there is a complete sentence on each side of it.

It would be an obvious mistake, of course, to make all sentences the same length. Such writing is choppy, dull, and uninteresting. The good writer strives for variety. There is nothing wrong with an occasional long sentence if it is properly constructed. The reading difficulty comes when all sentences are long and when many of them are improperly constructed.

Here are some examples of how long sentences, even though properly constructed, can be turned into more easily read short sentences:

Original: A few seedlings in progenies from the best selections fruited this past summer and while these represent only a tiny fraction of the more than 5,000 seedlings in this group, the prospects are quite encouraging, at least in regard to size and color. (One sentence —43 words.)

Rewrite: A few seedlings from the best selections fruited this past summer. These represent only a tiny fraction of the more than 5,000 seedlings in this group. But the prospects are encouraging, at least in size and color. (Three sentences—average 13 words.)

Original: The major market for Concord grapes on an industry-wide basis is for unfermented juice in the processing industry and there is little argument that Concord is tops at the present time because of the highly desirable flavor characteristics of its pasteurized juice and juice products. (One sentence—46 words.)

Rewrite: Concord grapes find their greatest market as unfermented juice for processing industries. The highly desirable flavor of Concord's pasteurized juice and juice products makes it the most popular grape at the present time. (Two sentences—average 17 words.)

Original: Work on improved techniques for growing and handling tomatoes under the direction of J. P. McCollum and R. W. Hepler, University of Illinois, revealed that significant greater gross returns can be realized from tomatoes grown on paper mulching on the ground than from tomatoes grown either on the ground or staked (but not pruned). (One sentence—54 words.)

Rewrite: J. P. McCollum and R. W. Hepler, University of Illinois, worked on improved techniques for growing and handling tomatoes. Paper-mulched tomatoes brought greater gross returns than unmulched tomatoes or staked tomatoes that were not pruned. (Two sentences—average 18 words.)

Now let's take a look at some rewrite jobs on long sentences that are improperly constructed:

Original: A federal court of appeals has ruled that if a (chemical) substance can be used safely by observing certain precautions and they are known to persons using it, the substance is not inherently dangerous and the manufacturer cannot be held to strict liability for damage resulting from negligent use. (One sentence—49 words.)

Rewrite: Manufacturers should indicate on the labels of chemical containers whether the substance is dangerous. They should also specify certain precautions for safe use of the chemical. If a manufacturer takes these steps, he cannot be held liable for damages resulting from careless use. A federal court of appeals has made this ruling. (Four sentences—average 13 words.)

Original: This same court has also ruled that the test as to whether or not a label on a (chemical) container is adequate to inform those using it of danger of improper use is whether the "ordinary prudent man" can understand it. (One sentence—41 words.)

Rewrite: This same court has also ruled that labels on chemical containers must be written so the average person can understand them. (One sentence—21 words.)

Original: Working to outline detailed recommendations for self-feeding programs, R. N. Van Arsdall, Agricultural Research Service economist at the University of Illinois, recently interviewed forty-nine Illinois cattle feeders who are currently using horizontal self-feeding silos. (One sentence—33 words.)

Rewrite: R. N. Van Arsdall recently interviewed forty-nine Illinois cattle feeders who are using horizontal self-feeding silos. On the basis of these farmers' experiences, he has outlined detailed recommendations for self-feeding programs. Van Arsdall is an agricultural research economist at the University of Illinois. (Three sentences—average 14 words.)

Improper or awkward construction is not always confined to the long sentence. Here are some examples of how a rewrite job can improve the communication ability of average-length sentences:

Original: We are half of the opinion that an orchard sod may as well shift for itself, weeds and all. (One sentence—19 words.)

Rewrite: We believe that an orchard sod may as well shift for itself, weeds and all. (One sentence—15 words.)

Original: Passing the material through a screen to obtain a homogeneous condition will aggravate rather than alleviate this condition. (One sentence—18 words.)

Rewrite: Passing the material through a screen will only make matters worse. (One sentence—11 words.)

Original: The price per pound of meat varies inversely with the weight of the cut. (One sentence—14 words.)

Rewrite: The heavier the cut, the less it costs per pound. (One sentence—10 words.)

Original: In St. Louis alone there are seven storage plants having a total capacity available for apples sufficient to accommodate 460,000 barrels of apples. (One sentence—23 words.)

Rewrite: In St. Louis alone there are seven storage plants that will hold a total of 460,000 barrels of apples. (One sentence—20 words.)

Original: An interpretation of the symptoms shown by a poisoned animal, leading to diagnosis, and the treatment prescribed following the diagnosis, require the skill of the trained veterinarian. (One sentence—27 words.)

Rewrite: Animals suffering from poisoning require treatment from a trained veterinarian. (One sentence— 10 words.)

You can often shorten sentences and make writing more readable by simply cutting out or chopping down pompous and often useless phrases. What would you substitute for the following phrases?

of the order of magnitude of	in the case of
for the purpose of	in view of the fact that
in the nature of	with a view to
along the lines of	despite the fact that
prior to	give consideration to
subsequent to	have need for
in connection with	give encouragement to
with respect to	make inquiry regarding
with reference to	comes into conflict
with regard to	give instructions to
in the amount of	(he) is of the opinion
on the basis of	make an adjustment in
in accordance with	it is our understanding that
on the occasion of	there are two questions which
in the event that	

The sentence length in the examples below ranges from 49 to 68 words. See if you can make the message more readable by saying the same thing with shorter sentences—and, let us hope, easier words. Aim for an average of 12 to 18 words per sentence with enough variety to keep the reading active and alive.

Original: This study was designed to determine which of thirty drapery fabrics would be the best buy for use in women's dormitory rooms in Resident Hall "X" on the Purdue University campus and to select the most sun- and weather-resistant fabrics for use at those windows which would receive the maximum amount of sunlight. (54 words.)

Original: During an average year, the *Chicago Daily News* carries about 1,500 recipe suggestions for homemakers, and, according to surveys that have been made to determine just how effective this material is, most of these ideas are used by a large percentage of the readers, and you can find *News* recipes in almost all the homemaker recipe files in Chicago. (59 words.)

Original: In response to requests from home economics specialists working in countries abroad where the family laundry is a backbreaking affair of beating clothes on rocks at the edge of a river, a simple hand-operated washing machine has been developed by the International Cooperation Administration and the U.S. Department of Agriculture. (52 words.)

Original: The kind of skills a teacher might develop in her home economics students can be seen in the way our General Foods Kitchens handle a typical request, say from the marketing group of a product division, seeking advice on the package size and package directions of a new pudding. (49 words.)

Original: Canning has made possible the wonders of scientific explorations, of colonization, it has proven a priceless boon to the housewife, it has furnished profitable outlets for the products of the farm, the orchard, and the sea, it has reduced food costs for the average family, and has placed choice, nutritious, and wholesome foods within the reach of all, producing for America, in particular, the highest of living standards. (68 words.)

SHORT PARAGRAPHS MAKE READING EASIER

The long-winded speaker seems to talk for five minutes without taking a breath. The long-winded writer writes for five minutes without indicating a paragraph.

The paragraph serves a number of valuable purposes. It is the means of organizing the parts of the message into a logical sequence of movement. It can indicate a change in pace or direction. Paragraphs enumerate points in the message, without using numerals or letters. Most important, perhaps, paragraphs give the message "breathing room." The task of the writer is to make reading easy for the reader. Paragraphs help him do that.

Unfortunately there are no definite rules to follow in using paragraphs. But you may find these general guides helpful:

1. For almost any message, keep the first paragraph short— not more than a few sentences.

2. Use a paragraph each time you introduce a new thought or a new piece of information.

3. Use paragraphs when presenting a series of information items, even though the items are related.

4. Use paragraphs to present information supporting the major message.

5. Use paragraphs when enumerating, regardless of whether you use enumerating symbols.

Most writers have little difficulty in breaking a message into paragraphs. The trouble comes when they fail to tie the paragraphs together so that the message "flows." Good writing should lead the reader smoothly through the message from the opening sentence to the final one.

Transitional words and phrases are needed (1) to tie paragraphs together and (2) to give the entire message continuity and cohesion.

Transitional words and phrases are similar to road signs along the highway. Such signs let the driver know that he is on the right road and going in the right direction. They warn him when the highway curves or turns. Other signs tell him when he must change highways to get to his destination. If you have driven on a highway without road signs, you will realize how important they are. Transitional words and phrases are equally important.

Here are some examples of transitions that let the reader know that the writer is continuing down the same line of thought:

On this same subject, Brown emphasized. . . .
Along this same line, farmers will find. . . .
Another consideration. . . .
In addition. . . .

When there is to be a shift in direction of the message, transitions can warn the reader in this way:

Brown concluded. . . . (End of paragraph, letting reader know this part of message is over.)
On the other hand. . . .
Even though hog prices have gone up. . . .
From the standpoint of the consumer. . . .
On the opposite side. . . .
On the subject of supports. . . .

A well-known newspaper writer and columnist has a trademark of using one-sentence paragraphs. He is a good writer and he can get by with it. Most people can't. If every sentence is the same length and every paragraph is the same length, reading is like tasting one spoonful of oatmeal after another. It all tastes alike.

Practice your paragraphing skill on the two writing samples below. The first appeared in one of the leading newspapers in the Midwest. The second was borrowed from a "popular" college bulletin for homemakers. Where would transitional words and phrases help the reader?

Original: Houseflies have built up to high numbers over most of the state, says Extension Entomologist Gordon Barnes. Flies multiply rapidly. If nothing happened to their offspring, one pair of houseflies could produce 191,000,000,000,000,000,000 offspring from April to August. Flies are a nuisance around the house, and they are also important carriers of many diseases, because they carry filth wherever they crawl. Food is contaminated as flies come from filth and light on dishes or the food itself. Fly control should be threefold—through sanitation, screening and use of insecticides, says Barnes. Sanitation is very important to reduce breeding places for flies. Wherever possible, manure should be scattered at least once each week so that it will dry out. Garbage cans should be covered and garbage dumps and refuse disposals kept treated with insecticide. If a good job of sanitation is done, fly numbers can be kept low enough to control with insecticide applications. For a fast knock-down in barns or other buildings where fly numbers are extremely high, a dry bait is very effective, says Barnes. A residual spray in the same building may help to hold numbers down. Aerosol bombs containing pyrethrins may be used for fast knock-down of flies inside the home. Fly cord (cotton cord impregnated with parathion and diazinon) has been used successfully in buildings thickly populated with flies.

Original: A sufficient hot water supply is important in the performance of the automatic washer. The number of gallons of hot water used by the various washers ranged from sixteen to thirty-five gallons. (Since the rinse waters are tempered to $100°$ F. the amount might be slightly higher in winter when the supply was extra cold.) A thirty-gallon hot water heater could supply sufficient hot water for only two loads in the lower capacity and one load in the higher capacity machine without waiting for water to reheat. If the user is willing to change practices and wash one or two loads on different days during the week, a thirty-gallon water heater might suffice. If, however, she insists upon washing all loads in sequence on the same day at least a fifty- to seventy-five-gallon hot water tank will be needed to provide enough hot water to insure good performance.

CHAPTER II

Writing for Impact
and Interest

There is more to good writing than readability. Good writers have a second goal: they strive for impact and interest. They want readers both to understand their writing and to be moved by it. They seek emotional involvement and encourage readers to be active partners in the communication process. Easy reading aids understanding. Impact and human interest encourage action.

In addition to ease of reading, then, good writing has four other important characteristics: (1) appropriateness, (2) movement, (3) force and clarity, and (4) human interest.

APPROPRIATENESS

As important as it is, we need not dwell long on appropriateness as a characteristic of good writing. We stressed this need earlier when we discussed the *purpose* of communication.

We have said that writing should *fit* the audience and the

message. We obviously would write a children's book differently from a scientific journal article. We would strive for ease of reading and impact with each, but our writing would not be the same. Words that would be vague and meaningless for one audience would be completely understandable and meaningful for another.

Do not assume, however, that complex ideas and concepts must be expressed with big words and intricate sentence structure. You may be familiar with these famous words:

> In this case I have undertaken the journey here for the purpose of interring of the deceased, and from this point of view, I do not, however, propose putting anything on record in so far as praise of the deceased is concerned.

If not, you surely remember the edited version:

> I came to bury Caesar, not to praise him.

MOVEMENT

We studied English or rhetoric in school because we were required to. At the time, we did not study because we wanted to be better writers. Rhetoric was there, required, and we took it.

We did learn, though, that every complete sentence has a subject and a verb, and many sentences also have an object. The sentence "he hit me" gives us the subject (he), the verb (hit), and the object (me). We also learned about adjectives, adverbs, prepositions, participles, nouns, pronouns, clauses, prepositional phrases, and the whole bit.

Unless you are in school now or teaching writing, you spend little time diagramming sentences or thinking about the parts of speech. But writing skill is based upon effective use of the English language, and we need to review some of the things we learned in those English and rhetoric classes about writing that has movement.

Working Verbs

You have read some writing that seems dull and listless. The writing just lies there on the page without doing anything. It lacks movement because the writer has used mostly *being* verbs —verbs that tie together but do no other work. A being verb is always some form of the verb *to be,* such as *am, is, are, was, were.* It connects but suggests no action, and the sentence lacks movement.

On the other hand, the *working* verb does something. It never quite stands still. Sentences with working verbs have movement, and movement adds impact to writing. Take this example:

Bad weather *is* a frequent cause of crop loss.

There is nothing grammatically wrong with that sentence. Note, though, that the main verb is the being verb *is.* Why not use a working verb? What is the sentence about? Bad weather. What does bad weather do: It causes loss. So why not write:

Bad weather frequently *causes* crop loss.

By replacing the being verb with a working verb, we have injected action into the sentence. We have also made the sentence more direct by eliminating three words. Take another example:

Limestone *is* effective in promoting beef gains.

Action is wrapped up in the word *promoting,* so we can turn that word into a working verb by writing:

Limestone effectively *promotes* beef gains.

You can't, of course, eliminate all being verbs from your writing. Nor would you want to. Often they *are* indispensable. (How else, for example, could you construct this last sentence?)

For practice, decide how you would substitute working verbs for being verbs in the following sentences:

1. The shipment of tree seedlings *is* already under way in the state.
2. The cost of pelleting a ration *would be* prohibitive in many operations.
3. Feed consumption by the four groups *was* essentially equal.
4. Working verbs *are* needed for good writing.

For more practice, take another look at your rewrite efforts on the examples in the previous chapter. Note how many being verbs still linger on. Find working-verb substitutes.

Specific Verbs

Although all working verbs express action, some work harder at it than others. Such verbs as *to affect, to become, to appear, to accomplish, to act, to do, to make,* and *to have* are all working verbs. But they express abstract action. Give your writing more movement by using specific verbs.

When used alone, for example, the verb *to consume* does not pinpoint any specific action. It can mean *to eat, to wear out, to use up, to burn.* When possible, substitute the specific for the general or abstract. Achieve action and movement by having people eat things, smash things, burn things, and wear things out. Otherwise your readers will be consumed with boredom and indifference. Usually, the more specific the verb, the more economical the sentence, as the following example shows:

Cattle *have* a preference for corn ground in a burr mill.

Have is a weak, general verb. But the sentence contains the word *preference* which suggests more specific action. By replacing *have* with *prefer,* we come up with a leaner sentence:

Cattle *prefer* corn ground in a burr mill.

Even when specific verbs don't result in greater economy, they add flow and movement to sentences, as the following example illustrates:

Yearlings fed corn ground in a hammer mill, however, had the same weight gain, the same feed requirement per hundred pounds gained, and the same daily feed consumption as had yearlings fed corn ground in a burr mill.

By getting rid of the general and colorless verb *had* and changing the nouns *gain, requirement,* and *consumption* into verbs, we get a more forceful sentence:

Yearlings fed corn ground in a hammer mill, however, *gained* the same amount of weight, *required* the same amount of feed per hundred pounds gained, and *ate* the same amount of feed per day as did yearlings fed corn ground in a burr mill.

We are not suggesting that all abstract verbs should be tossed out, because sometimes the most specific verb is abstract. Be sure you have used the most specific verb available. Test your skill on the following examples:

1. Aerobic bacteria *can do* a satisfactory job of stabilizing liquid wastes without creating odors.
2. Lice *use* the animal's blood for food.
3. A little extra effort *means* more profit.
4. Control of flies *can be achieved* by spraying the house foundation every three weeks.
5. Powder-post beetles *make* tiny tunnels in the wood.

Active Verbs

You can add movement and directness to your writing by using active verbs (active voice) instead of passive ones (passive voice). Passive sentences move slower than active ones.

Active: The Mets beat the Cardinals.
Passive: The Cardinals were beaten by the Mets.

In the first sentence the subject is the *doer* of the action. In the second, the subject is the *receiver* of the action. The active sentence packs more punch by driving quickly to the point. Here is another example:

The best crime control is accomplished by well-trained police.

Who is the doer of the action? The police. What is the action? Not accomplishment, but control. When we put the words in natural order and use the more specific verb, we end up with an active sentence:

> Well-trained police control crime best.

You can easily identify passive verbs by looking for two characteristics: a form of the verb *to be* combined with the past participle of a working verb. You end up, then, with such passive verbs as *was beaten, is accomplished, are controlled,* and so on. Such passive verbs are used when the subject is the receiver of the action.

Before you change all of your passive verbs to active ones, note this exception: Use passive voice when the deed is more important than the doer. This happens when the doer is unknown. ("The tree was planted fifty years ago." "The treasure was never found again." "The true story was never brought to light." "The flowers were allowed to wither and die.")

Try rewriting the following sentences:

1. Covered runways *are built* on exposed surfaces by termites.
2. Your synthetic blankets *can be washed* by machine.
3. The fruit *is* then *packed* in sterilized jars.
4. High-germinating corn *must be used* when planting early.
5. Good writing *will be accomplished* by good writers.

If we think of sentences as shells in the communication gun, then verbs are the powder that determines the velocity and power of the shot. They determine the "bang" of our writing. With nonworking, nonspecific, passive verbs, our writing goes "pffft."

FORCE AND CLARITY

Good writers seek another dimension in their writing. They want writing to have *force* and *clarity,* to convey meaning with maximum impact and minimum loss. They test their writing for concreteness, conciseness, and sentence unity—the three ingredients of force.

Concreteness

Whereas verbs give motion to writing, nouns give body and weight. Writing that is filled with vague nouns and inflated terms lacks force. Choose nouns with the same care and precision with which you choose verbs. Follow these three bits of advice:

1. Always choose the simpler or plainer of two similar words. Down-to-earth words hit harder than pompous ones. Such words are usually shorter and easier to read in a sentence. (Check the word list in Chapter 10 again.)

2. Write in concrete rather than abstract terms. If you must deal in abstractions, give specific illustrations.

3. Use the most specific words you can find.

If you read the following example a couple of times, you can figure out what the writer is driving at. Maybe.

Technology determines the trend. It puts more constraints on the individual farms, because it allows little deviation from the trend. Progress has moved farming from a way of life to a full-fledged business. This change requires that the management decision be based on facts that can be measured from the study of good farm records. Unless a farmer's attitude toward the value of good farm records changes, he is apt to be left behind in the trends now being set by new technology.

You can translate the message into the following plain language:

Trends in technology have forced farmers to become businessmen. Like businessmen, they must believe in keeping records, keep them, and base their decisions on those records. Those who don't may go broke.

Here is a dandy example from a legal publication:

A landowner shall not willfully or intentionally interfere with any ditches or natural drains in any way that causes them to become so obstructed as to materially impede the flow of water.

After reading that sentence, most readers would have these questions: What does *intentionally interfere* mean? Is there always a difference between a *ditch* and a *natural drain?* Does *materially impede* mean to stop a third of the flow, half the flow, or two-thirds of the flow?

The following sentence carries the same message with more force:

A landowner should not stop up artificial ditches or natural drains.

Here is one for you to work on:

Today's challenge in agricultural education is to help the agricultural industry make adjustments consistent with national economic growth.

Conciseness

A good writer is known by the words he uses, but he is also known by the words he doesn't use. His writing is forceful because it is concise. He uses words as though each carried an expensive price tag. He is a word-miser.

Unnecessary words are like weeds in a garden. They compete with the needed words, sap sentences of vitality, and may choke out the message entirely.

To give writing conciseness, redraft and polish it. Practice word economy by cutting out useless words or rephrasing wordy constructions.

By Deletion:

~~The business of~~ stripmining often causes nearby wells to go dry. (− 3 words.)

All persons ~~who are~~ interested in soil conservation are welcome ~~to attend the meeting~~. (− 6 words.)

Much ~~of the~~ poor writing today could be avoided if ~~the~~ writers would ~~try to~~ think before they write ~~in the first place~~. (− 9 words.)

By Reconstruction:

Local taxes can furnish up to 40 percent of the ~~amount of money required~~ (required money). (2 words for 4.)

Make sure the house is ~~safe from a construction~~ ~~standpoint~~ (constructed safely). (2 words for 5.)

~~There may be times when~~ (Sometimes) extra words are justified. (1 word for 5.)

Once you get the hang of it, there is pure joy in cutting our useless words and phrases. Practice your hunting skill on the following examples:

1. Exhibitors will compete together in two separate live-weight classes.
2. Is there any legal restriction as to how a farmer may use surface water?
3. Researchers must find the power requirements needed to run the wheel.
4. Courts generally require proof of negligence on the part of the operator.
5. A will can designate who shall be the guardian of minor children.
6. If you find it necessary to press the binding, use a warm iron only.
7. Property tax is the only major tax levied by action of the county itself.
8. Volunteers must be single and at least eighteen years of age.
9. Good writing is usually the result of a writer's being willing to take the extra time that is needed for redrafting and polishing.

Unity

Sentence structure influences writing force. For maximum force, express only one main idea per sentence and place that idea in the dominant position. Don't let complicated sentence structure force your reader to detour from the main point.

Original: In Illinois alone, it is estimated that we need to provide 750,000 new jobs a year just to hold our own.

The main clause is *it is estimated that.* But the main idea is *we need to provide new jobs.* When we place the main idea in the main clause we get a better sentence.

Rewrite: In Illinois alone, we need to provide an estimated 750,-000 new jobs a year just to hold our own.

In checking your writing, look for phrases such as *it is felt that,* or *scientists find that,* or *it is generally believed that.* Those are danger signals. Chances are you have placed the main idea in a subordinate position, whereas the subordinate or supporting idea sits in the front row.

Original: Recent studies at the University of Illinois indicate that most people won't take time to read difficult writing.
Rewrite: Most people won't take time to read difficult writing, according to recent University of Illinois studies.

Original: Even if there were more jobs than people, many officials believe that some workers would be habitually unemployed.
Rewrite: Many officials believe some workers would be habitually unemployed even if there were more jobs than people.

Good writing, of course, accommodates variety in sentence structure. Every sentence, though, should tell the reader what is most important and what is less important. If it doesn't, he may not take time to figure it out.

We can help our readers identify main ideas and move smoothly from idea to idea, sentence to sentence, and paragraph to paragraph by using the transition words and phrases mentioned earlier. Consider these two sentences that contain related but separate ideas:

Ridding your house of termites can be a complicated job. You may need the services of a reputable exterminator.

What is the relationship between the two? The first idea leads to the second. If we consider them equally important we link them this way:

Ridding your house of termites can be a complicated job, *so* you may need the services of a reputable exterminator.

However, if we consider the first idea as subordinate to the second we link them this way:

Because ridding your house of termites can be a complicated job, you may need the services of a reputable exterminator.

The transition words help the reader put the emphasis on thoughts and ideas that you intend when you write. If you are fuzzy in your thinking and writing, you can be sure that he will be fuzzy in his reading.

If you remember your rhetoric classes you probably recall some discussion of *parallelism*. This is a form of sentence structure that helps relate two or more similar ideas of equal importance. The ideas are parallel, so you use a sentence form that shows the parallel relationship. Let's take a loosely constructed sentence and see how we can improve it through parallel construction:

Original: The inspection tag on poultry means that an inspector has examined it and it was processed in clean surroundings, not adulterated, and is truthfully labeled.

The sentence names four things that are on the inspection tag. But the sentence is somewhat hard to follow because each item is written in a different grammatical form. By making the items similar in form, we unify the sentence and make it easier to read. We can do this by repeating key words:

Rewrite: The inspection tag on poultry means that it has been inspected, that it was processed in clean surroundings, that it has not been adulterated, and that it is truthfully labeled.

Or we can avoid repeating the words and use similar grammatical forms:

Rewrite: The inspection tag on poultry means that it has been in-

spected, was processed in clean surroundings, has not been adulterated, and is truthfully labeled.

The misplaced modifier is another foggy-writing culprit. The
modifier, as you know, is the word, phrase, or clause that gives
additional information about the subject or the object of the sentence. When we put the modifier in the wrong place in the sentence we end up with it explaining the wrong thing. The sentence
becomes awkward and misleading:

Original: Lee Baker showed some slides of a project under way in
the district that offers feature-story potential.

The sentence seems to be saying that the district "offers feature-story potential." We know the writer intends to communicate that the project "offers feature-story potential." So the clause
starting with *that offers* should immediately follow *project*. But
if we merely transpose the words our example is still incorrect:

Rewrite: Lee Baker showed some slides of a project that offers
feature-story potential underway in the district.

Now we seem to be saying that the feature-story potential is
under way in the district. And that is not our intention at all.
But there is a way to get the job done:

Rewrite: Lee Baker showed some slides of a current district project that offers feature-story potential.

We have placed a modifier (*district*) immediately before the
noun (*project*) and another modifier (*that offers*) immediately
after the noun.

You might practice your modifier-placement talents on the
following two examples:

Original: The dog fund comes from fees collected from the licens-
ing of dogs, which are turned over to the county treasury. (You can
be sure the treasury doesn't want the dogs as the sentence seems to
suggest.)

Original: Trees are usually shipped by Railway Express or by United Parcel Service packed in wet moss. (The United Parcel Service would seriously object to being packed in wet moss.)

HUMAN INTEREST

We have been talking about how to make our writing easy to read and how to give it maximum impact. Even with these objectives accomplished, our writing may still lack a quality of *human interest.* The reader feels that the writing is about *things* and not about *him* or *people* in whom he is interested.

All of us like to read about people. We are interested in what people do and how they think. We want to know how today's "news" affects us and our friends. We read about scientific discoveries in terms of the significance of those discoveries on our lives —now and in the future.

We can add human interest to our writing by using personal rather than impersonal words and references. Personal words include all nouns that have masculine or feminine gender, such as *boy, girl, son, daughter, wife, husband, man, woman.* Personal words also include all pronouns that refer to people, such as *I, you, we, him, her, she, he.* Words such as *folks* and *people* also may be counted as personal words.

By using personal references in writing, we suggest a personal conversation with the reader. He gets the feeling that we are talking to him or about him, and he is motivated to learn more about what we have to say.

If we use from four to ten personal words per 100 words of copy, our writing will rate high on the scale of human interest. Some writing, of course, is easier to personalize than others. The use of too many personal words and sentences may irritate the reader. Writers of news stories for a newspaper tend to stay away from personalized writing. Feature stories, on the other hand, tend to be written in a personal style.

CHAPTER 12

Writing for Newspapers

What we have said so far about writing skill applies to writing for all kinds of channels—letters, memos, reports, proposals, themes, journal articles, direct mail, and news stories.

Regardless of channel, writing needs purpose, appropriateness, readability, impact, and interest. The channel, though, does determine the *form* or *style* of writing. Writing skill, then, means applying the characteristics of good writing to the *form* demanded by the channel.

Newspapers offer one of the most effective channels for communicating with people, so we need to fit basic writing skill to newspaper form and style.

KNOW YOUR CHANNEL

A newspaper plays a variety of communication roles within a social system—community, county, state, or nation. Before the days of radio and television the newspaper's primary editorial role was to report and interpret "news happenings"—those events and actions affecting the lives of people.

That role is still primary, although today much of the news is reported first on radio and television. A newspaper's secondary, but equally important, role is to confirm the news, add further details, and give additional interpretation. It is not uncommon for a person to read his evening newspaper while listening to the news on radio or watching it on television. Perhaps you have done this yourself. We seem to be saying, "Yes, we heard it, but we reserve judgment about believing it until we have seen it in the newspaper."

In the role of reporting, confirming, and interpreting "news happenings," newspapers appeal to the widest possible audience. They devote the most space to this role.

At the same time, newspapers provide a communication channel for special audience groups. Many women pay the most attention to the society pages, while many men find the sports page most interesting. The paper features other special sections for special interest groups—financial reports for investors, automotive features for the car enthusiast, garden pages, home-building sections, and so on. The stories may not report "news happenings," but they attempt to qualify as reports of something "new" —something the reader did not know before and wants to know now.

We can use the following characteristics to compare and contrast newspapers with other channels of communication:

Audience size. As one of the mass-media channels, newspapers can reach more people than any of the person-to-person or face-to-face channels, but they may or may not reach more people than radio or television. The circulation of the paper, the power of the radio or television station, and the reading, listening, and watching habits of the audience determine the advantages or disadvantages among the three.

Believability. As a rule, we tend to have a little more confidence in what we read than in what we hear. We know that our hearing may play tricks on us, so we tend to go along with the adage that "seeing is believing." Television provides "seeing" too, of course, but the exposure is more fleeting.

Timeliness. Newspapers reach more people more quickly than any of the personal channels, but not as quickly as radio or television does.

Completeness. Newspapers usually provide more details than radio or television, fewer than magazines and many other forms of written communication, and fewer than most personal channels.

Referability. If we miss news details on a radio or television newscast, we may or may not be able to catch them on a later broadcast. Newspapers provide a higher degree of referability. We can reread the story any number of times, and we can save the paper or clip sections for future reference. Normally, however, newspapers do not stay around the house as long as weekly or monthly magazines do.

Repetition. Newspapers may repeat news in successive editions and they often provide additional details or new interpretation of previously reported news. Radio often repeats news, with or without additional details, on successive hourly broadcasts. Because of the nature of its programming, television has less opportunity to repeat news than radio does, and may even do less follow-up interpretation than newspapers do.

KNOW YOUR EDITOR

A well-known Kansas magazine editor put his finger on the importance of local newspapers when he made the following observation:

The job of improving a community is too big for any one person or group, and it is getting bigger all the time. There is need for help. That help, powerful and effective, is available. It is the local newspaper. It is the one agency that can put all persons, groups, and interests to work as a team. A newspaper editor, sincerely interested in his community, probably can be of more help in reaching people with information than any other single person.

The key, of course, is the editor who is "sincerely interested," not only in his community but in us, our work, and our need to get information to people served by his paper. The best way to develop an editor's sincere interest is to know him and his paper and to appreciate the role he plays in the business of communicating with people.

Common Characteristics of Editors

While editors are all different, they have some characteristics in common.

Editors are in business to make money. The newspaper is the editor's bread and butter, and he has to run it with that fact in mind. Naturally, any editor wants to print all the news there is; but often there isn't room for everything. And a good editor will leave out a news story—even *your* story—before he will leave out a paid advertisement. It is well to remember this, and not be offended when it happens.

Editors are busy. Next to your job, they have about the most demanding job in the community. There is always a deadline; presses may break down and printers may get sick or quit; your story and other stories may be late—but still the public expects the paper to come out on time. It usually does, even if the editor and his staff lose sleep for three nights in a row. Because an editor is so busy, he may be unable to spend a couple of hours in friendly conversation if you happen to drop in during the day when the paper goes to press.

Editors are sincerely interested in the welfare of the people in the community. They want their neighbors to be healthy, happy, and prosperous. They are willing to devote a lot of space to information that benefits the people, if the information is legitimate, straightforward news. Most editors will even shut one eye to news that is actually publicity; but they can spot an attempt to get free advertising, and they don't like it. If you have sound information that the people of the community want and need, most editors will do everything they can to get it printed. But if you have something to advertise, put the material into a display ad and pay the regular newspaper advertising rates.

Editors are human like everybody else. They have good days and bad days. They have bills to pay and tax forms to fill out. They get the same kind of colds, headaches, and sore feet, and they suffer from the same sleepless nights that you do. Don't expect them to be calm, serene, and understanding for sixteen hours a day, seven days a week. They spend much of their time listening to the problems of other people, but once in a while they appreciate a chance to tell you something about their own problems.

Pay a Personal Visit

The most important first step in building sound, strong editorial relationships is to pay a personal visit to each of the editors in your area. Pick a time when the editor is least likely to be pressed with deadline work. On a weekly paper published on Thursday, the editor usually has the most free time on Friday afternoon or Saturday morning. Monday would be next best. Keep in mind that the closer the paper gets to its "press time," the busier the editor and the less time he has to talk with you.

Press time for an afternoon daily is usually between noon and three o'clock. Your visit with an afternoon-daily editor would be best timed for late afternoon after the paper is on the press. Morning dailies go to press at night, so there is more freedom for visits in the daytime. Around noon probably would be best.

With either a weekly or a daily editor, check with him by phone before stopping in. If you are making your first visit, don't take along a pack of stories you would like to get printed. But make your visit count. Talk about the baseball pennant race if you want to, but also get as much help as you can.

Get acquainted with the editor's problems. Find out just when he goes to press; when he would like to have most of his news copy in; whom it should be sent to.

If there is more than one paper in the community, there is

competition for news, for advertising, and for readership. Try not to play favorites. Pleasing everybody is a rough task but it is worth trying.

PLAY BY THE RULES

A newspaper has many sources of news—some good, some not; some dependable, others not. The number of pages in any issue depends upon the amount of advertising in the issue. There is a ratio between advertising space and editorial space (news, features, editorials). More advertising means more pages in the issue and more space for editorial matter. But there is never enough editorial space to handle all of the copy flowing into a newspaper. Some will always get left out.

You are one of the newspaper's sources of news. You are one of many who hope to use the newspaper channel for communicating with readers. You may have the skill to write news stories, but unless your stories are used your skill is wasted. If you know your editor and have visited with him about the newspaper business, you probably know most of the rules of the newspaper game, but it may help to review them briefly.

Meet Deadlines

All newspapers, whether weekly or daily, have a schedule of deadlines for different kinds of editorial matter. And each has a final deadline—the last minute that a piece of copy can be turned in for the day's edition.

A daily newspaper, for example, may have one deadline for business copy, another for society, a third for sports, and so on. It may feature a farm section only one day a week, a business section on another day. The sports section is usually the largest on weekends. Learn the deadline for the kind of news copy you send to the paper. Never fail to get your copy in well ahead of that deadline.

Respect the News

One of the basic characteristics of news is *newness*. The newspaper wants its readers to know about something as soon as possible after it happens. Readers want that too. This morning's fire is reported in this afternoon's paper. Last night's election is reported in the morning edition. If part of your job is to report the news of your work or the work of your organization, protect the newness of the news. Get the story to the paper as soon as possible after the happening.

If your group last night decided on a major fund drive to raise money for the new community hospital, get the story to the paper immediately after the meeting. That same night, if possible.

If you are a county extension agent and discover a new disease outbreak in the county, don't wait until it is convenient for you to write a story for the local papers. Do it immediately while the story still has newness.

Identify the Source

You may be sending news stories and features to a newspaper on a regular basis. If so, clearly identify yourself or your organization on the first page. You can do this with a printed masthead or by simply typing the source identification at the top of the page: "From Fred Jones, Medium County Medical Director."

In addition to the copy from his own staff, the editor receives stories from hundreds of sources each week. He throws much of this copy away after a quick glance—or no glance at all. You want him to identify your stuff easily so that it doesn't get thrown away.

Your group or organization may be identified as the source: "The University of Illinois News Service," or "The Macon County Soil Conservation Society," or "The Committee to Fight Air Pollution." (We are talking here about the source of the story itself and not necessarily about the source of information within the story.)

Keep the Copy Clean

Different editors have different suggestions on how they want news material prepared for their papers. In general, a good editor is interested in news even though it is written on the back of a paper sack and he has to stand on his head to read it. It is best not to take chances, though. Your news article will be better received and have more chance of getting in the paper if the copy is neat, attractive, and easy to read.

Have your copy typed, and use double-spaced lines. Triple spacing may even be better. Leave plenty of margin at the top and bottom and on both sides. You can turn in edited copy, but make sure your editing is neat and easy to read.

When sending more than one story to the paper, place each story on a separate page. The editor may want to use one and not the other. Identify each story with a simple one-line heading at the start of the story. Don't bother writing a headline because the editor probably won't use your version anyway. But the one-line heading lets him know what the story is about.

When sending a copy of the same story to a number of newspapers, make sure each copy is readable. Carbon copies are all right if the carbons are clear and free of smudges. Ditto and mimeograph copies are also suitable. It is often a good idea to indicate the distribution of the story at the top of the page. You can either list the outlets receiving the story, or use a phrase such as "Sent to Selected Newspapers."

Be Accurate, Brief, and Complete

Every editor has a right to assume that your news story or feature article is accurate. He expects names to be correctly spelled; dates, times, and places to be correct; facts to be facts; opinions to be identified as opinions. In other words, he wants your story to carry the truth insofar as you are able to determine and report the truth. Accurate reporting is the editor's business. He expects it to be the business also of every person using his channel of communication.

Because of the demands on his news columns from many sources, the editor expects your copy to be complete but brief. If all essential details of your message can be written in 100 words, do not use 120 words. Do not pad your message with unnecessary words or irrelevant details just to make it appear "more important" in print.

CHAPTER 13

The News-Story Form

Many people, including those who are good writers, have a mental block about writing new stories. They are convinced that newswriting is the unique domain of the favored few who were "born" with special talents or who acquired such talents through years of study at some journalism school.

Except for form, the requirements for news-story writing are the same as those for any other kind of writing. The writer must have a purpose, know the subject and the audience, and have basic writing skills. He completes his research, drafts his story, redrafts it if necessary, and polishes it. In short, good newswriting starts with good thinking, and is followed by logical organization and presentation of information in a language that is interesting, easy to read, and easy to understand. There is nothing particularly difficult about that.

We need to become familiar with the news-story form, to understand the reasons for the form, and to fit our writing to it.

ANALYSIS OF FORM

A newspaper always receives more information than it can use. Its objective, then, is to choose those stories of most interest to readers, and to present them effectively.

The newspaper also knows that readers spend a limited time reading the paper. Most readers pick and choose. They scan headlines, read parts of some stories, skip to other stories, and turn to other sections. Partly to make reading "easy" for readers, most newspapers use a form that is almost opposite that of a fiction story. The news-story form calls for reporting the gist of the information as briefly as possible at the start of the story—in the first paragraph or two.

With this approach, the reader grasps the main idea and gets the key facts by reading only the first few sentences. The rest of the story then elaborates on the main idea, gives more facts and details, and expands on the interpretation.

If you have been around journalists—or teachers of journalists—you may have heard this structure referred to as the inverted-pyramid news-story form. The "big" part of the story —the base of the pyramid—is at the top, and the additional details represent the tapering-down of the structure.

Newspapers have another reason for using this form of writing. When printers make up the pages of a paper they fit the columns of type within the frame of the newspaper page. If the column of type is too long for the available space, a part of the story must be left out. There isn't time to rewrite a shorter version and set it in type. The make-up man doesn't have time to read the entire story and select paragraphs to take out. It is easier and faster to start at the bottom of the column of type and take out paragraphs until the story fits the available space.

Actually, the news-story approach is similar to the way we report a bit of news when talking with our family or friends. If we witness an automobile accident on the way home from work, we don't tell the story by discussing the general hazards of automobile-driving these days. We blurt out the facts. "Saw a terrible accident at the corner of Green and Prospect on the way home. Two cars hit head-on. They think one person may not live. Three others were seriously hurt."

Chances are a member of our family or a neighbor will then ask, "How did it happen? Anyone we know? Who was driving?"

We then add as many details as we can. We give our version of the cause. We may recall that three other accidents have happened at that corner in the past year. We answer other questions.

If we were a reporter for the local newspaper, we would write the story in about the same way, and we would be following the accepted news-story form. We would tell the most important facts first, anticipate the kinds of questions the reader might ask, and provide information in the remainder of the story to answer those questions.

Some newspaper editors are critical of the traditional inverted-pyramid structure for news-story writing. They insist that some stories would be better told with a less rigid structure, letting the story flow in a chronological order with the main point in the middle of the story, or even at the end, rather than at the beginning. In their newspapers, you will frequently find stories that ignore the traditional form.

We mention this to assure you that there is no one best way— no perfect way—to write a news story. Not all experts agree. But you will always be on the safe side when using the traditional inverted-pyramid form. While you are at it, you may as well use the journalist's language to identify the form. The beginning of the story is called the "lead," and the rest of the story makes up the "body."

USING THE NEWS-STORY FORM

Once we understand the basic news-story form and the reasons for it, we can structure our writing to fit the form. Here is our formula for good news-story writing:

1. Start with clear thinking. Relate the message to the needs and interest of the readers.

2. Write in one sentence the main fact or facts, or the main idea, that you want the reader to know and understand. (At the moment, don't worry about whether it is a good sentence or not. Just get the point down on paper.)

3. Next, list the reasons why the main idea is important.

4. Finally, jot down all other bits and pieces of information that support the idea and complete the message.

Without knowing it, perhaps, you have outlined a news story.

Writing the Lead

When you write the main idea in one sentence you have written at least part, and perhaps all, of the news-story lead.

The lead is essentially a sharp summary of the story. Journalism teachers often tell students that the lead should answer the five W's and the H: Who? What? When? Where? Why? and How? That's good advice if not carried to the extreme. Better advice might be: the first few paragraphs should answer those questions. If you try to answer them all in the first sentence, or even the first paragraph, you may end up with a confusing, unreadable lead a mile long.

If you check a recent paper, you will find that most of the "news" stories have leads that feature some or all of the five W's and the H. Here are some examples from a local newspaper:

Federal Attorney Hans Walder (who) announced Friday (when) the arrest of a Swiss jet engine specialist (what) on charges of having sold secret plans of jet fighters (why) to Israel (where).

Some 2,000 employees (who) returned to their jobs (what) at the Firestone Rubber Co. plant in Ghana (where) Friday (when), ending a forty-day walkout for better working conditions (why).

The President (who) has proposed a $4.25 billion hike in Social Security reforms and benefits plus a new automatic locking of the system to the cost-of-living increases (what).
The President outlined his proposals Thursday (when) to a Congress apparently eager to go him one better on liberalization (where and why).

A twenty-six-year-old Urbana woman (who) was injured (what) Friday (when) in a two-car collision (how) at Lincoln and High (where).

Each of these leads gives the main facts of the story. For some readers the main facts are enough. Other readers will seek more details. They want to know how the authorities caught the spy, where he obtained the secret plans, how he smuggled them out of the country.

Businessmen may want to know how the Ghana Firestone strike will affect rubber prices, how the strike was settled, what the chances are for strikes at other plants.

Different readers will have different reasons for wanting more details on the President's Social Security proposals. What will the proposals mean to people now receiving Social Security benefits? Will the change mean increased taxes? Are the proposals likely to be approved?

The last example leaves out a critical item of information— the name of the injured woman. Her name and address were given in the second paragraph: "Sharon Glade, 210 Bristol Drive, was injured when a car slammed into the rear of her car as she was attempting to turn off Lincoln onto High." Now you know.

But you point out that you have no intention of being a foreign correspondent, will not be covering the Washington political scene, and have no plans for reporting accidents, fires, and other news happenings for the local daily. You represent the local cooperative extension service, the school district, the county medical society, or the county council for economic opportunity. What about leads for the stories that you might write? They're not much different, really. We can turn to any newspaper for examples:

Funds totaling $113,000 for the Campaign County Economic Opportunity Council (what) may be released in three to six weeks (more what), Rev. Errol Rohr, chairman of EOC, (who) reported Thursday night (when) at the EOC's regular meeting (where).

More than seventy-five amateur and professional artists (who) will exhibit their works (what) Saturday from 9 A.M. to 5 P.M. (when) in the Tenth Annual Sidewalk Art Fair (how) sponsored by the Urbana Association of Commerce (why). (The lead doesn't answer the question Where? and neither did the rest of the story, unfortunately.)

The Champaign County League of Women Voters (who) will review plans for the Constitutional Convention (what) at their first fall meeting at noon Friday (when) at the University Place Christian Church (where).

County Extension Agent Herb Gully (who) has advised local farmers to check their corn fields (what) immediately (when) for signs of corn borer infestations (why).

We don't suggest that these are perfect leads, but they give the reader the gist of the message. You can find better examples in any edition of your local paper. While you are looking, note the examples of leads that don't answer the five W's and the H. You should run across some or all of these types:

The "teaser" lead. The writer catches your attention with a question or a surprise statement. For example:

Did you ever get that sinking feeling when you took your driver's test?

That's what Mrs. X got Thursday. She drove the car into a river seven feet deep. She refused to give her name.

The summary lead. The writer has a number of actions to cover, and he summarizes those actions in his lead. For example:

Urbana's Board of Education placed nine high school students on probation, suspended another indefinitely, and expelled two others following a three-hour executive session at Thornburn School, Wednesday night.

The big-fact lead. The writer stops you with a startling first sentence and explains it in the rest of the story. For example:

Champaign has never had a hotter day.

We don't want to make a big thing about news-story leads, but we hope you will feel comfortable around them. Your best guide is your local newspaper. Some people find that reading leads aloud helps them get the "feel" of writing. Good leads tend to have a subtle rhythm.

If you have thought through your message and have clearly identified the main points the reader should know, the lead should almost write itself—perhaps not the first time, but with a little practice.

Building the Body

Writing a lead that gives the reader the gist of the story is much like laying the foundation and putting up the framing for a house. The rest of the building job follows a natural progression of steps.

With the house, a roof is nailed to the rafters, outside and inside walls are placed on the studs, doors are fitted in door frames and windows in window frames.

The body of a news story is built in much the same way. Needed details are added to the who, what, when, where, why, and how. What will be done with the money released for the Champaign County EOC? How was previously released money used? Was the amount released more or less than EOC anticipated?

Readers of the story on the sidewalk art fair may want to know if the paintings are for sale, if there is still time to submit entries, or if there is an age limit for participating artists.

Farmers will expect County Agent Herb Gully to explain how to measure the degree of corn-borer infestation in their corn fields. And they will certainly need to know what to do about the borers if there is a severe infestation problem.

As the writer, you anticipate reader questions, select information to answer those questions, and arrange the information logically within the body of the story. Let's look at another example.

Assume that you are an agricultural agent. Farmers are asking about a new wheat variety recently released by the USDA and the state college of agriculture. There were previous stories on the development of the new variety, and you have received additional background information from the college. You know the variety's advantages and disadvantages compared with other varieties being grown in the area.

From your experience, you know farmers want answers to three main questions: (1) Should they plant the new variety this year, and why? (2) Are there special considerations they should know before they decide? (3) Where can they get the seed and how much will it cost?

You can answer those questions in a brief news story. You simply think through the answers and put them down on paper. Your story might read like this:

Champaign County farmers who have fairly light and well-drained soil may want to seed some of their wheat acreage to the new Growgood variety just released by the USDA.

County Agent Herb Gully says the new variety will outyield old varieties on the light, well-drained soils of the county. Farmers with heavy soils where drainage is more of a problem should stick with present varieties until more yield trials have been completed.

According to Gully, the Growgood variety requires the same soil treatment and should be planted at the same rate as other varieties grown in this area. In a normal growing season, the variety will be ready for harvest a few days earlier than the standard varieties.

The supply of seed is limited, however, and interested farmers should apply for seed at Gully's office. The seed will cost $4.75 per bushel—about 75 cents more than regular varieties.

That story should answer the main questions that farmers might ask. Other details could have been added, of course. The writer could have explained how the variety originated, elaborated on its growth characteristics, and anticipated when more seed would be available.

Go over some of the stories in your local newspaper again. Stop after reading the lead and ask yourself if there are additional questions you want answered. Then read the story to see if the writer answers your questions. Note how he uses his lead to build the body of the story. Check *his* writing skill by noting the length of his sentences, his use of words, the way he ties his paragraphs together with transitional words and phrases. Has he given his writing movement by using specific, working, active verbs? Is he concise? Does he use personal references to give his writing human interest? Were *you* involved in the story?

WRITING THE SPECIALIZED STORY

We think of news stories as reports of "news happenings," and most news stories are just that. They give the details of something that happened—fires, accidents, floods, strikes, robberies, good and bad deeds performed, successes, and failures. The writer's job is to report *what* happened, *why* it happened, and *how* the happening affects people. That's why the newswriter on a newspaper is called a reporter.

Unless you are actually a newspaper reporter, your news-story writing may be more specialized. You probably will be concentrating on three types of stories: (1) the "advance-information" story about a meeting or some other event, (2) the "follow-up" story about that event, (3) the "subject-matter" story about the field of interest in which you are involved—agriculture, home economics, social welfare, community affairs, education, medicine, or the work of various civic groups.

The Advance-Information Story

The advance-information story has two primary objectives: to persuade people to attend an event, and to encourage their "involvement" ahead of time. Unfortunately, too many advance stories fail on both counts. They only serve as announcements, giving the date, time, place, subject, and speaker, if there is one. The reader must generate his own interest and involvement. Often he is unwilling or unable to do this, so he stays home. The good writer anticipates the interests and concerns of the reader and writes the story to appeal to those interests and concerns.

The following two leads demonstrate the difference:

Lead 1: A meeting on livestock outlook will be held next Wednesday evening at 8 o'clock in the Gordon High School gym. All farmers are invited to attend.

Lead 2: Gordon County farmers can learn how to hedge marketing risks in the face of skidding hog and cattle prices by attending the livestock outlook meeting next Wednesday at 8 P.M. in the Gordon High School gym.

Both leads give the facts of time, place, and subject. But the second lead adds purpose and reason to the facts. The writer knows that farmers are concerned about the livestock price situation and assumes that they are interested in doing something about their concerns.

We can look at another example:

Lead 1: The regular meeting of the Southside PTA will be held at 7:30 P.M. Friday in the main conference room on second floor. An interesting meeting is planned for all Southside parents.

Lead 2: Southside School parents will learn why some children can't read and what they can do about it when they attend the regular PTA meeting at 7:30 P.M. Friday. Parents should go to the main conference room on second floor.

The first example gives the reader a "promise" of an interesting meeting. The second gives the reader a reason for deciding for himself whether or not the meeting is worth attending.

Every advance story should contain all of the factual details of the event. The reader wants and needs to know where to go, when to go, and how to get there. But more important, he wants to know *why* he should go. What rewards can he expect for leaving the comforts of home and taking the time to attend a meeting, conference, or field day?

You cannot expect the speaker's name and title to provide sure-fire interest from the reader. Many writers assume that a long biographical sketch of the "star attraction" is enough to lure an audience. If the speaker is the President of the United States or a famous movie star, the writer may get by. But most of us are not as interested in the speaker as we are in ourselves and our own problems, needs, and interests. If you want me to attend your event, tell me how the speaker will help me.

The Follow-Up Story

When our job is to inform people about a meeting and we face the prospect of an empty hall if we don't succeed, we work pretty hard on advance-information stories. When the event is over, we are likely to give a sigh of relief and forget about our next-most-important job—to inform people about the event after it is over.

The follow-up story has three main functions: (1) to summarize the information presented at the meeting for those who, for many reasons, were unable to attend; (2) to reinforce the information and to provide a reference for those who did attend; and (3) to establish an environment of anticipation among readers who we hope will attend future events.

County Agent Herb Gully has the task of writing the follow-up story on the livestock outlook meeting held in the Gordon High School gym. Of the 1,200 livestock farmers in his county, 65 attended the meeting and he considered the turnout excellent. He doesn't have to worry about another livestock meeting for a year, so he writes the follow-up story as shown below, turns it in to his daily paper, and goes home to bed.

More than sixty county farmers attended the livestock outlook meeting Wednesday evening in the Gordon High School gym.

Those attending heard specialists from the University of Illinois College of Agriculture review current trends in livestock prices and present their views on probable price trends for the future. Supply and price outlook for hogs, cattle, and sheep were reviewed.

The farmers seemed to agree that this was one of the best meetings they had attended this year. There will be another livestock outlook meeting next year.

Herb recorded the fact that a meeting was held, and that's all. He thought his purpose was to get something to the editor of the paper, and he did. But he missed an opportunity to communicate with the 1,200 livestock farmers in his county—the 65 who attended the meeting and the 1,135 who did not. It is unlikely that he created much interest in next year's meeting. He could have started his follow-up story this way:

County farmers were advised at the outlook meeting Wednesday evening to hold their hogs and cattle off the market for at least thirty days. The downward price trend is about over, and the markets should reverse themselves before the end of the month.

One of the sorriest follow-up stories is the one that merely recites the details of the program. It reads much like the menu of the local restaurant. After an opening lead that tells the reader a meeting was held, the writer goes down the program something like this:

The opening speaker was Mrs. Mildred Dooley, who talked about stretching the food dollar by using meat substitutes. Mrs. Dooley explained how homemakers could cut their grocery bills 15 percent in this way.

Mrs. Dooley's talk was followed by a demonstration by Gordon Davis of the Meat Foundation on new cuts of meat that are coming on the market. Davis said the new cuts would be in local grocery stores next month.

Following lunch, the group heard Sally Jones of the Baking Institute, who gave her predictions on the future of ready-to-bake cake mixes.

The last speaker of the day was George Barnard of the Barnard Grocery Company, who showed slides of the grocery store of the future.

The meeting ended at five o'clock.

If you have not read follow-up stories similar to this, you have not been reading your local paper lately. If you write a follow-up story like the one above, the purpose of this chapter will not have been fulfilled.

The Subject-Matter Story

The subject-matter story is often called a "news feature." It is not based upon a news happening but upon the known or anticipated interests of a group of readers. Such stories are usually pegged on new information or they give a new twist to information previously reported.

Every newspaper carries a variety of subject-matter or news-feature stories. They touch a broad spectrum of personal interests including health, recreation, hobbies, education, social problems, family relationships, child care, agriculture, law, science, and the arts. Many such stories tell readers why and how to do something and are often called how-to-do-it stories—how to save money, grow better corn, stretch food dollars, buy carpets, talk to teen-age children.

This type of story challenges the writer, because the form is less rigid than that of a straight news story. The lead needn't be tied quite so closely to the five W's and the H. You can use more big-fact, surprise, and teaser leads, but don't try to be too cute or clever.

With the subject-matter story, you match your knowledge of audience with knowledge of subject. Knowledge of audience comes first. Even though you have information *you* want your readers to have, you think first of the information *they* want to have.

It works like this:

The reader wants to know: Is it necessary to water shade trees during the summer months?

The story lead answers: Homeowners who planted shade trees last fall or this spring should water them at least once every fourteen days during the hot summer months.

Or a different lead: Young shade trees, like young puppies, need frequent drinks of water when the weather is hot.

The reader wants to know: What is the best way to kill ants and other crawling insects that get into the house during the summer?

The story lead answers: It is easier to spray the foundation of your house to keep summer bugs out than it is to kill them once they are inside.

The reader wants to know: Is it wrong to let children snack between mealtimes?
The story lead answers: What a child eats is more important than when he eats, according to the latest studies on child nutrition.

The reader wants to know: Should I learn the teen-ager's special language in order to communicate better with my teen-age daughter?
The story lead answers: Your attitude, not your language, is the key to your ability to communicate with the younger generation. Talking as if you were a teen-ager doesn't make you one in their eyes.

As with any other news story, the body of the subject-matter story builds on the main idea expressed in the lead. It provides supporting information for the lead statement, gives additional details, and answers other questions related to the main idea.

The story on watering shade trees, for example, will tell how to water and how much to use. It also may include information about watering shrubs, hedges, and flowering plants.

In addition to telling the reader how to spray the foundation of his home, the bug story will answer his first question—how to kill the bugs that got into his house before he sprayed the foundation.

The anticipated question on between-meal snacks provides a basis for a more complete story on child nutrition. The teen-age language lead should take you into other mother-daughter relationship situations.

Nearly all subject-matter stories identify an authoritative source for the information in the story. Identify the source in the lead or in one of the early paragraphs. Use "tag" phrases at the end of a sentence, such as "reports Peter Miller, University of Illinois landscaping specialist." Or you can start a paragraph by revealing the source, like this: "Nutritionist Martha Thomas points out that milk, fruit, and other basic foods provide the child with the same calories, vitamins, and minerals when eaten at three o'clock as when eaten at the regular dinner hour."

WRITING A PERSONAL COLUMN

As an authority in your field, you may be asked by the local paper to write a regular weekly column. Before you accept, consider what a personal column can and can't do.

A personal column plays a unique role in the process of communicating knowledge and information to people. Unlike a news story, which should be objective, a personal column is subjective. The personality of the writer stays out of news stories; it goes into a personal column. A column permits you to visit with your readers. Personal pronouns are in. You can say "I think" or "I saw" or "I heard." The "you" approach is good style.

Most good columns are made up of bits and pieces of information related to a general subject area. There is little point in using a personal column for comprehensive treatment of a subject. You can do that with a news-feature story. Most good columns, too, bring the reader into the picture by asking questions, quoting responses, and crediting others with contributions.

The successful columnist has trained himself to listen and to observe. His column reflects what he has heard and seen.

The Things People Do, Say, and Think

As a writer of a column on education, you would listen closely to students, parents, and teachers. From this listening you would have tips for countless column items about new math, study habits, homework, speed reading, language difficulties, teaching methods, learning habits, student-teacher relationships, and a wide range of other subjects.

One of your column items might then start this way: "An eighth grader mentioned the other day that he couldn't study at home because his dad wouldn't let him have the radio on." With this introduction, your item might point out that different children have different study habits, so parents should not expect all children to study in the same way.

Observations of the Seasons

Many column writers take advantage of seasonal observations and base items in their columns on those observations.

The writer of a farm column sees dirty snow along the roadside in winter and uses the observation to discuss the dangers of winter wind erosion and what farmers can do about it.

Another farm columnist observes that the lower corn leaves in many fields are firing and realizes that some farmers will blame the lack of rain. The real reason is lack of soil nitrogen, so he points out the difference in his column.

The author of a home-and-garden column points out the need for better insulation in some houses by calling attention to the observation that snow melts quickly on the roofs of some houses and not on others.

The New and Different

The readers of your column assume that you know more than they do about the subject you are reporting. They expect you to keep them abreast of the new and different. Your column is the place to pass along new information that you picked up at meetings or read in the special publications coming across your desk.

Some Don'ts

While a column can be personal, it is not the place to practice soapbox oratory or to exploit your position on special subjects.

The farm-column writer is out of his field when he expresses opinions about labor strikes, political candidates, or race relationships. He is not an authority in those fields. Nor should the writer of a column on education speak too loudly about farm subsidies or the high cost of food at the local market.

The place for a columnist's family is in his home and not in the items of his column. The writer who must relate the latest "sayings" of his 3-year-old son, or mention daughter Susan's birthday party, or tell about the family's latest camping trip, is out of both things to say and readers.

A little humor goes a long way in a personal column. Use it sparingly if at all.

CHAPTER 14

Writing Direct Mail

The most effective way to communicate with a friend is to sit down and chat with him. The next-best way might be to visit on the telephone.

If neither of those channels is available, you could write him a letter. If you thought several other friends might be interested in what you had to say, you could make copies and mail one to each. You simply use the channel of *direct mail* to get a message to intended receivers. As the size of audience increases you change the technique of duplicating the message, alter the language code, and make some adjustments in the *form* of writing. The basic method of communication remains the same.

Communication by direct mail is big business in the United States and getting bigger. Business and industry spend millions of dollars each year acquiring mailing lists, designing direct-mail packages, and hiring skilled writers to compose messages.

You may not be involved in the "big business" of direct mail, but you can use the channel to communicate with your audiences.

The characteristics of the direct-mail channel help determine the form of writing. To use the channel, you need to take advantage of its strengths and avoid its weaknesses.

CHANNEL STRENGTHS

In discussing the strengths and weaknesses of direct mail, we must compare one channel with another. In a way this is unfortunate because it is a little like discussing the strengths and weaknesses of race horses in comparison with work horses. The strength of a race horse for racing is a weakness when it comes to plowing a field. A work horse is ideal for pulling a plow but not so ideal for winning a race.

Audience Control

The newspaper controls the audience for our news story. All members of our intended audience may or may not be subscribers. On the other hand, a message may be received by many for whom it was not intended. This may be good or bad.

With direct mail, we have complete control over who receives the message—at least who gets it in his mailbox. We can be as selective or as general as we choose. If we intend the message only for parents of children in high school, we can identify such an audience, place the names on a mailing list, and send the message to that audience only.

If our business involves getting information to farmers, we can identify and structure any number of audiences for direct-mail communication. One audience may consist of men who raise more than 200 hogs a year under a confinement system. Another may be dairymen who milk more than fifty cows—or fewer than ten. We can separate owners from renters, livestock farmers from grain farmers, and men over forty from men under forty.

By carefully building our mailing lists, we have both audience control and audience knowledge. By various means we can add personal, social, and economic information to the names on the mailing lists.

Message Control

With direct mail, we can say exactly what we want to say in exactly the way we want to say it. Our message does not have to be filtered through an intermediate "gatekeeper" such as a newspaper editor who may be forced to shorten, edit, or alter the form of the message to fit the available space.

Nor are we concerned about "unintended" receivers. If the message is intended to tell a special audience how to take advantage of certain income-tax provisions, we need not worry about "other people" getting the wrong idea.

Message Treatment

Because we control both the audience and the message, we can write in the "language of the reader." We can treat the message for innovators differently from the message for late adopters. Messages for low-income families can be treated differently from messages for those in the high-income brackets.

Timing and Sequence

The direct-mail channel permits us to communicate with our audience *when* we want to and as *often* as we want to. With other channels, we may or may not control the timing and sequence of our messages.

A teacher, for example, may want to communicate with parents of preschool children two weeks before the children enter first grade, then a month after school opens, and again at the end of the first term. An agriculturist may need to get disease- and insect-control information to fruit growers at precise times during the orchard season. Direct mail permits such timing.

Referability

We can design direct-mail messages for instant reading and for future reference. Normally, news stories do not provide the reader with lengthy background information, detailed instructions, or basic information for future reference. Direct-mail messages can have a high degree of referability.

CHANNEL WEAKNESSES

Mailing Lists

Direct mail is only as good as the mailing list. When we use the newspaper channel, the editor hands us a ready-made mailing list. It is ours for the using. With direct mail, we must spend the time (and often the money) needed to build precise and accurate mailing lists. We must locate and identify the specific audiences for specific messages, collect names and addresses, and record additional information about audience characteristics. We need facilities to record the information on mailing cards or plates. We must follow routines to keep the lists up to date, because people move away, change occupations, step into another social classification.

Mailbox Competition

On any day, mailboxes bulge with all kinds of mail—personal letters, newspapers, magazines, bills, notices, and direct-mail messages from a wide variety of senders. A direct-mail piece must be good enough to meet the competition in the receiver's mailbox. With the pressure from other mail, the receiver decides quickly after opening the envelope whether the message is worth reading, let alone keeping.

Minimum Facilities

We need only a typewriter and some paper to get our message to an audience via the newspaper. We need more facilities than that for direct mail. In addition to the typewriter and paper, we must own or have access to reproduction facilities and mailing systems. These may range from a simple spirit-duplicator to an expensive offset press, and from simple typed mailing stickers to elaborate addressing machinery.

WRITING FOR A PURPOSE

Direct mail can help achieve any one of a number of purposes. As with any writing, though, we must clearly identify that purpose first. Direct mail can help create an *awareness* of you, your organization, product, or service. It can stimulate added *interest* after awareness has been achieved through other communication channels. Direct-mail messages can help the reader *evaluate* products, services, or proposed changes in behavior, and can give instructions to guide him through the *trial* and *adoption* stages.

Many direct-mail messages, of course, attempt to take the receiver through two or three stages in the adoption process. This is especially true of the "trial" offers you receive in the mail. The sender tells you all about a new book, brand of perfume, improved coffee, and ends up by urging you to return the enclosed card for a free "trial sample." Sometimes the trial sample is enclosed with the direct-mail package. The sender is trying to take you through the awareness, interest, and trial stages as quickly as possible. His ultimate objective is to move you into the adoption stage.

Granted, you are not in the business of selling perfume, books, or improved coffee, but you are in the business of influencing an audience. Consider the direct-mail channel when the audience is relatively small, the message subject is specialized, and you need to control the communication process. In general your messages will fall into one of two categories: news-information or subject reference.

WRITING NEWS-INFORMATION DIRECT MAIL

When writing news-information direct mail, you expect the message to create *awareness* and *interest*. The message meets most of the criteria of a good news story and tells the receiver something new—something he didn't know before. It may be "news" about your services, the way you plan to do things, the benefits to the reader if he takes certain action. Or the message may help the reader change habits and improve practices.

The news-information message is current and timely. It suggests action now and not sometime in the future. It says "spray your apple trees next week" and tells how to do it. It says "save money by buying a part of your milk needs as powdered milk" and explains how much you can save and how to use the product. It invites the reader to "pick up copies of these free bulletins" and outlines other services of your office.

When writing, keep four points in mind: (1) win attention, (2) get to the point, (3) anticipate questions, and (4) recap the message.

Win Attention

Put yourself in your reader's shoes. He has just come home from the office, or in from the fields. He is tired. The car needs fixing. He is concerned about a lot of things—higher taxes, the price of cattle, student unrest, his son's report card. You have an important message that you want him to read, be interested in, and take action on. Obviously you must win his immediate attention. How?

Start with his interests and his problems—not yours. Let him know you are interested in him before you ask him to be interested in you. Tell him so in the opening sentence. That opening sentence is your "lead," and it may determine whether the reader will go through the rest of the message. Here is an example.

You want farmers to know about and try a new variety of wheat. So your first sentence might say, "We can't do much about inflated prices for farm machinery. But we know how you can inflate wheat yields to help pay for that machinery." Some other examples are:

Your message: You want parents to provide their children with better lighting for home study.
Attention: "If *you* didn't like what you *saw* on Johnny's report

card, perhaps it was because Johnny couldn't *see* what *he* was reading.

Your message: You want homemakers to try powdered milk.
Attention: "Would you like to know how to stop paying 40 cents for a quart of water?"

You can also get attention by using headline forms that give quick attention to your message. These headlines can be "big-fact" statements or leading questions:

> DIM LIGHTS—FOR DRIVING NOT READING.
> WANT A BIG RETURN ON A SMALL INVESTMENT?
> PAY FOR MILK SOLIDS NOT MILK WATER.

If you need more examples, good and bad, of how senders attempt to win attention, check your mail for the next few days. What did you stop to read, and what did you throw away?

Get to the Point

The best attention-getter in the world will be wasted unless you move quickly to the heart of your message. Your receiver has other things to read and other things to do. He can give you only a couple of minutes of his attention.

Apply every principle of good writing—easy words, short sentences, brief paragraphs, the "you" approach. If you have three things to say, enumerate your points. Your writing should be concise but not cute, brief but complete, enthusiastic but not rowdy. Write simply but do not insult the reader's intelligence.

Anticipate Questions

Write for the reader in the way that you would talk with him. But there is a difference: he can't ask questions. You must anticipate his questions. How much does it cost? Where can he get it? How does he do it? Are there negative aspects? Any tricks? In fact, you can pose questions as a means of getting into parts of your message.

Recap Your Message

If the message is of vital importance to him the reader may re-read it. Most of the time, though, you won't be that lucky. A once-over reading is all you can expect. So hit the main idea again at the end of the message—in a sentence or a brief paragraph. Studies show that, for any message, the reader retains longest the first and last parts of what he reads. There are all kinds of ways to wrap up your message:

In a nutshell, Growgood wheat costs 75 cents more per bushel than what you are planting now but it should boost your yields an average of five bushels per acre.

Those specifications again.

Saturday is the thirteenth. So remember to use the first spray in one week—on the twentieth.

Support Your Written Message

With a little imagination you can support your written message in a variety of ways. Good illustrations—drawings, pictures, charts—will help win attention and add meaning to words.

Use clear tape to attach a few grains of Growgood wheat to your wheat letter to show the farmer what the variety looks like. A small plastic bag of powdered milk may arouse interest in your message about that product. Enclose labels with information about new weed-control chemicals. Include "free passes" for services that you or your organization may have to offer, or "free tickets" for meetings you want your audience to attend.

A direct-mail message about home decorating might be printed on wallpaper samples. Use pieces of blotter paper for messages that tell readers how to "blot out losses" by improving farm or home practices. Messages on giant postcards may get more attention than those printed in letter form and enclosed in an envelope.

Before using any supporting device, though, make sure that it really adds to the message. You have received some "clever" direct-mail pieces, but you may have been more interested in the gimmicks than in the message.

WRITING SUBJECT-REFERENCE DIRECT MAIL

Subject-reference direct mail provides the receiver with information he can use now or file for future reference. It meets these criteria:

1. It is written for a special audience that needs specialized reference information on a single subject or a family of subjects.

2. The content is designed for both current and future reference. It does not cover information that will soon be out of date.

3. The format encourages easy and systematic filing for later reference.

4. In a sequence of mailings, each mailing relates to preceding mailings, providing a build-up of reference information.

We can use agriculture for an illustration of this channel:

Johnson County is a major livestock-producing county, and County Agent Gully has identified 400 major dairy producers, each of whom milks more than fifty cows. These dairymen comprise an audience of specialized farmers who need specialized information. The information is of only limited interest to other farmers in the county—even other dairymen.

Gully knows he cannot regularly visit all 400 dairymen. Only a small percentage will attend meetings during the year. The needed information is so detailed and complex that it doesn't fit the requirements of news stories. Direct mail is the obvious answer.

Having identified his audience, Gully next analyzes their problems. They fall into five logical areas: (a) breeding, (b) feeding, (c) housing and equipment, (d) herd health, and (e) marketing. With this breakdown he is now ready to design his subject-reference direct-mail service.

He provides free, or makes available at cost, a loose-leaf notebook containing five dividers—one for each of the five problem areas.

Next he designs a simple letterhead or masthead to identify the service and to flag it to the attention of the receivers. In addition to identifying the general service, each mailing piece also identifies the subject area. His first reference mailing on breeding, for example, carries the file heading "Breeding No. 1." Subsequent mailings on this same subject area carry consecutive numbers. The same procedure is followed for each of the other subject categories—feeding, housing, health, and marketing.

Whether you are in agriculture or not, consider the advantages of subject-reference direct mail whenever your purpose is to provide a relatively small, specialized audience with a continuing flow of information.

Your first mailing may include a special letter explaining the service, the subjects to be covered, and the frequency of mailings. You may ask the receiver to return a card if he (or she) wants to get future mailings. Your first objective is to win acceptance of the service. With acceptance assured, you can assume an initial interest in each of your subsequent mailings if they meet the receiver's needs and are easy to read and understand.

BUILD ACTIVE MAILING LISTS

Mailboxes are filled each day with direct mail that the receiver didn't ask for, doesn't want, and won't read. Somebody somewhere put his name on a mailing list, and he doesn't know how to get off. Make sure that "somebody" wasn't you.

Start building an active mailing list by carefully appraising where, when, and how direct mail fits your total communication effort. Are you convinced you can do something with direct mail that you can't do as well or better with other channels? Do you have a special audience with need for specialized information? Do you have the information? Do you own or have access to needed production and mailing facilities?

If direct mail can contribute to your overall communication objective, you need an active mailing list of people who want and need your information. Accept from the start that there is no easy way to build such a list. The job will take time and patience. Here are some steps to consider:

Step 1: Build a prospect list. Your office or organization may already have a list of people potentially interested in receiving your information. The list can be a starting point. You may be able to borrow prospect lists from other sources. Schools have lists of all people with children of school age. Public-aid agencies have lists of low-income families. The local dairy has the names of all farmers who sell fluid milk. Local builders can supply the names of new homeowners.

Step 2: Convert prospective receivers to active receivers. With your general knowledge of the audience, cull your prospect list. You may want an active list of dairymen who milk at least fifty cows, for example. Eliminate the names of farmers with fewer cows. You may cull your list for other reasons such as age, location, type of business. Seek help from friends and associates who have special knowledge of the audience.

After a first culling, send one or two mailings to the remaining names on the list. At some point, though, give your receivers a chance to have their names taken off the list. Some senders use the hard-line approach and ask receivers to return a card if they want to stay *on* the mailing list. Others ask for a return card only if the receiver wants to be taken *off* the list. You fool only yourself when you keep people on your list who don't want to hear from you. It is better to have 20 active readers of your message than 200 frustrated receivers.

Step 3: Recontact both active and nonactive lists. With certain types of mailing permits, you are required to check your mailing list at least once a year. Common sense calls for such checking whether it is required or not. Send a card or letter to those now on your list and ask them if they want to continue receiving your mailings. Recontact your prospect list to see if new names can be added to your active list.

CHAPTER 15

Writing Reports and Proposals

Reports and proposals are special forms of writing with similar characteristics. Both are associated with many jobs; both are often required by superiors; and both are usually resisted by those of us who must write them. A report communicates past efforts and accomplishments. A proposal communicates future plans and directions.

AN APPROACH TO REPORT WRITING

A colleague of ours refers to narrative reports as the "curse of a civilized society." Others consider them "necessary evils," with the word "necessary" questioned by many. Report writing often is a chore that is accomplished with the least possible effort in the shortest possible time. Such reports are easily identified. The filing cabinets of the world are filled with them.

Narrative reports should meet the same writing standards as other writing forms. Effectiveness depends upon: (1) writer attitude, (2) purpose, (3) knowledge of audience, and (4) writing skill.

Write for a Positive Purpose

Too often, reports are written for the wrong reason. They are written to satisfy the "requirement" of the system. And there are few systems today—private, commercial, government, or education—that don't require regular reports from professional employees.

We usually learn about the obligation early in the orientation period of a new job. The requirement is included along with others related to the "rules and regulations" of the organization.

Unfortunately, the reasons for the requirement may not be explained, so we assume the system wants to "check up on us." We are told to submit the report to a supervisor or some other administrative person. We are not told what is done with them. We are not sure the supervisor reads them, and we soon suspect he doesn't. We start with a negative attitude and write reports because they are required to satisfy the system.

There is no way to eliminate "requirement" as one of the purposes for writing a report, but that purpose should be the least important of all. There are three other, more positive, purposes for report writing:

1. *To measure ourselves.* If a report served no other purpose, it would be worthwhile as a means of taking stock of our successes and failures. By reviewing the record of the past, we can compare accomplishments with objectives, analyze the way we used our time, reexamine plans and strategies with reference to new situations, and restructure future plans on the basis of past experiences. We can ask: What worked and what didn't? Why? What kept us from doing what we planned to do? Why? How can future plans be better executed?

2. *To record for future reference.* Regardless of how long we have been in our position, or how many years we will yet serve, we are a *temporary* occupant. We probably were preceded by someone; we will be followed by someone else. We alone can record present actions and accomplishments. This record should

serve as a benchmark for those who follow. Our report, then, serves the future as well as the present.

3. *To inform varied audiences.* Next to ourselves, the official persons receiving our report comprise our most important audience. The regulations state that we must write a report, but what do *we* want the report to accomplish? Our report is a channel of communication with the receiver. For what purpose? What do we want the receiver to think, know, or do after reading the report? Can we report actions and accomplishments in terms of the receiver's wants, needs, and interests?

Unless institutional regulations restrict the use of the report, we can consider its value for other audiences.

If we work with advisory committees or councils, we may send copies, or at least excerpts, to those members. We may work closely with other groups and agencies having objectives similar to ours. The report might serve as a channel of communication with such groups.

We may hold a position with a public, tax-supported institution, such as a local, state, or federal government agency, a community school system, or a state college or university. If so, one of our audiences may be the general public. We can use the report as the information source for a news story or a series of news stories, to publicly report our work and accomplishments.

Report Accomplishments, Not Activities

Many organizations ask staff members to prepare two-part reports. The first part consists of a form for recording statistical information for a given time period. The statistics account for the way time was used and provide a record of activities—number of letters written, people visited, telephone calls placed and received, meetings held, people contacted, and so on.

The second part, often referred to as the "narrative summary," is too often written as a verbal translation of the statistical information. The writer merely uses sentences, paragraphs, and pages to recite again the information already covered by the statistical data. He may convince the reader that he was busy, and he may clearly account for his time. But he fails to achieve the true purpose of his communication effort. He does not report accomplishments in terms of program objectives. He tells what, without relating the what to the why. His report consists of little more than a narrative diary of his days and weeks.

We can break this traditional pattern of report writing by thinking of each report as a chapter in a book. We have long-range goals with specific work plans for accomplishing them. Our reports chart step-by-step progress in carrying out the plans that accomplish the goals. Each report has a unity of its own but relates to those that preceded it and to those that will follow. Ten years from now—or fifty years—a reader should detect the thread of continuity in the reports.

The following steps may help you organize the content of your report:

Step 1: Within the framework of long-range goals, identify the specific program objectives that concerned you during the reporting period. In terms of the "big picture," where did you focus your attention? Why?

Step 2: List, in order of importance, the major *accomplishments* for the reporting period. Clearly distinguish between activities and accomplishments. The extension agent's statistical form may record the fact that he held two meetings for dairy farmers during the month, made five visits to selected dairymen in the county, and wrote three news stories for local papers on dairy subjects. His narrative report should relate *what happened* as a result of those efforts. He may be able to report that ten dairymen enrolled in a new record-keeping system and that this sign-up takes him one-fourth of the way toward his immediate goal of having forty farmers enrolled in the program.

Step 3: Relate the significance of each accomplishment to your immediate and long-range objectives. The Extension agent's enrollment of farmers in a record-keeping program, for example, may be a part of his long-range objective for improving the efficiency of milk production in the county. He would point out that good dairy records are the key to improved feeding and management practices.

Step 4: Report actions taken to provide the environment for future accomplishments.

Step 5: Summarize changes in conditions and situations that may suggest adjustments in program objectives and plans of work. Concerning the extension agricultural agent, for example, the late spring rains may have reduced the threat of certain crop insects but may have increased the probability of a late harvest. The agent may need to shift his educational emphasis from insect control and redirect it toward steps his farmers might take to avoid losses from a delayed harvest.

Write for Interest and Impact

The requirements for good writing are the same for reports as they are for news stories, radio scripts, direct mail, or any other kind of writing. In fact, with the above outline you could write your report as a series of brief news or feature stories. Cover each major accomplishment (Step 2) as you would write the *lead* for a news story, with Steps 3 and 4 comprising the body of the story. The information covered in Step 5 could be a separate story.

AN APPROACH TO PROPOSAL WRITING

Regardless of one's field, there are always opportunities to "sell" a plan for a program, project, or a better way of doing things. By its nature, a proposal has a clearly established purpose and the receiver is aware of it. We *intend* to inform the receiver about a particular problem and to persuade him to approve and support a plan for solving it.

Almost always, the audience also is clearly identified: our associates, our supervisor, a special committee, or some other group in the organization.

With both purpose and audience identified, communication success depends upon the soundness of the proposal, the *form* in which the plan is presented, and our skill in writing.

The Proposal Form

The purpose of any writing form, of course, is to permit the receiver to interpret messages quickly, easily, and with as little loss as possible. The receiver of our proposal knows that we intend to inform and persuade, so the form should be open and direct. It should answer his questions and give him the necessary information for deciding to accept or reject. We anticipate his questions, provide the answers, and supply additional information to support a favorable response.

In broad terms, the receiver will have these questions: (1) Specifically, what are you proposing? (2) Why do you think your proposal is needed? (3) What is your plan of action, and how will the plan improve the situation? (4) What, if any, additional resources will be needed—time, money, people, facilities?

The proposal should answer those questions in logical order. The following form permits it to do this.

The title. With a few key words, identify the general subject. The title serves the same function as chapter headings in a book or the head of a news story. It tells the reader what the message is about.

The proposal. The receiver wants to know the exact nature of the proposal so that he can relate it to the "case" we will be presenting later. Answer his question with a concise two- or three-sentence statement that tells him what the plan will accomplish. If we can phrase the statement in one sentence, so much the better. It should serve much the same purpose as the news-story lead.

The situation. This section should answer the receiver's two-part question: *What is the problem, and why does the problem exist?* Here we sketch essential background information as it relates to the problem and its need for solution. Whenever possible, we show a relationship between the situation that prompts the proposal and the overall program objectives of the institution or organization.

The need.   We move from the general outline of the situation to a specific citation of needs created by the situation. There may be one or several needs arising out of the situation. Include all that are related to the proposal.

The objectives.   Having reviewed the situation and identified the specific problems that the proposal intends to solve, we return to the proposal itself with a listing of specific objectives. This section is an expansion of the original proposal statement, and the objectives can be listed in one-two-three order.

The plan of action.   We tell the reader as precisely as possible the specific plans for carrying out the proposal, relating the action play to the objectives.

The required resources.   The reader must have a realistic appraisal of "costs" if costs are involved. Under appropriate headings, this section presents information on needed resources —people, money, facilities. The proposal may not call for additional resources or may call for a shift in the way resources are used. If so, we review those adjustments.

Write to Persuade

The proposal form helps present information logically and efficiently. It provides the structure for stating the case and for answering the key questions of the receiver. Writing should be tight, precise, positive, and factual. It should clearly reflect our knowledge of both the subject and the audience.

The proposal may be read by those who know a great deal about the subject and by others who know considerably less. The writing should satisfy the needs of both. Our words and phrases should indicate awareness of the knowledge level of our intended readers while permitting the inclusion of information for other readers who may be less informed.

After writing a first draft, test it with the following questions:

1. Does the proposal answer the key questions of the receiver?

2. Does the writing recognize the receiver's knowledge of the subject, the general situation, and at least some of the needs associated with the situation?

3. Does the writing reflect an honest and unprejudiced picture without exaggeration and overstatement? Are the facts accurate and the estimates realistic?

4. Is the writing objective, simple, and direct, free of words and phrases designed to impress the reader? Does the writing permit the merits of the proposal to speak for themselves?

5. Does the writing meet high standards of readability?

An Example

While perhaps not a perfect model, the following proposal is one that was actually submitted to the director of the Illinois Cooperative Extension Service.

PROVIDING EDUCATIONAL INFORMATION
FOR DISADVANTAGED FAMILIES VIA MASS MEDIA

The Proposal

To expand the communication via mass media of educational information for economically disadvantaged urban and rural families as a means of helping such families make more efficient use of available earned or public-aid income.

The Situation

1. The growing demand for programs of continuing education in urban areas has placed heavy burdens on the staff of the Extension Service. Adjustments are being made in educational methods to make the most effective use of available resources.
2. Currently, the Extension Service is focusing major attention on the educational needs of the economically disadvantaged families in both urban and rural areas. Unfortunately, these families represent the "hard-to-reach" audiences. Such families have not participated in the traditional direct teaching programs used so successfully for other audiences.
3. The Extension Service, therefore, needs to greatly intensify its

efforts to reach large numbers of economically disadvantaged families directly via mass-media methods, for these reasons:

A. An increasing number of Illinois families are receiving public financial aid, and, in most cases, this aid is the entire source of spendable income for food, housing, clothing and other life necessities. An estimated 4 percent of the total Illinois population is receiving public assistance under the A.D.C. program alone.

B. An even larger number of Illinois families, both rural and urban, have earned incomes from all sources that are below levels considered essential for more than subsistence living.

C. Families in the economically disadvantaged categories often do not have the basic education to make effective or efficient use of even the low level of earned or public-aid income available to them.

4. Consumer information is available through the Cooperative Extension Service. This information covers the broad fields of housing, clothing, foods and nutrition, financial management, and family living.

5. Nearly all economically disadvantaged families own radios; the majority own or have access to television sets; and nearly all receive or have access to daily or weekly newspapers and other printed publications.

6. The management personnel of the public-media outlets have indicated an interest in using their outlets as channels for carrying properly designed and presented educational information to their listeners, viewers, and readers.

7. Research studies support the conclusion that public media, including radio, television, and the press, offer an effective and economical method for providing families with educational information that will permit such families to make more efficient choices regarding the use of available income. These public media also provide motivational reinforcement for other direct and indirect communication methods.

The Needs

1. Determine by preliminary investigation the kinds of educational consumer information most needed by economically disadvantaged urban and rural families.

2. Determine in consultation with the management of public mass media the general communication behavior of these families with respect to each particular outlet.
3. Determine the requirements for preparing and processing educational information to be transmitted most effectively via the various channels.
4. Initiate and maintain a continuing flow of educational information to the primary audience via the selected public mass-media channels and covering the broad subject fields previously identified.
5. Maintain close and continuing liaison with all groups and agencies concerned with the general social and economic welfare of these families so that the educational information program of this project supports, and is supported by, all other direct and indirect efforts to improve the economic welfare of the families involved.

The Objectives

1. To improve the living standards of the disadvantaged rural and urban families by providing educational information to help them make better use of available income.
2. To permit the Extension Service to reach a large and expanding audience with available information through mass-media channels with minimum expansion of staff and resources.

The Plan of Action

The following plan is indicative and minimal but not definitive. Specific plans would be based upon the investigations and consultations proposed.

Radio

1. Mail selected radio stations fifty to seventy-five brief scripts or commentaries per week covering all phases of consumer information. These would be designed for "break" presentations on music, news, variety, and women's programs.
2. Mail four to eight taped, public-service spot announcements on consumer education subjects to the same stations each week.
3. Encourage stations to establish "family service" programs and provide program materials for such programs.

Television

1. Provide selected television stations with the following weekly services: (a) three ten-second slide announcements; (b) one twenty-second filmed public-service spot; (c) one sixty-second filmed public-service spot.
2. Provide these stations with a monthly five- to ten-minute personal-experience filmed documentary on a family's accomplishments in making more effective use of income resources.

Newspapers

1. Initiate and maintain a weekly consumer education news service for weekly and daily newspapers reaching the economically disadvantaged families.
2. Provide newspapers with current and accurate market information.
3. Supply newspapers with illustrative mats and other pictorial information on consumer subjects.

Other

The public mass-media services would be supplemented by other communication efforts designed to reinforce the intended messages. Such efforts would include:

1. Posters and store displays.
2. Magazine feature articles.
3. Handout materials for meetings and demonstrations.
4. Simple folders and leaflets for use as follow-up reinforcement for radio and television broadcasts.

Required Resources

The following staff would be needed to carry out the proposed operational program and to accomplish the objectives:

1. Television editor-producer.
2. Radio editor-producer.
3. News service–publications editor.
4. Artist.

Budget

1. Staff		$50,000
A. Professional	$40,000	
B. Clerical	10,000	

2. Production		$36,000
A. Radio	$ 3,500	
B. Television	20,000	
C. Press	3,000	
D. Film	8,000	
E. Other	1,500	
3. Travel		$ 2,000
4. Communication		$ 1,000
5. Other expenses		$ 2,000
	Total	$91,000

CHAPTER 16

Speaking: The
Face-to-Face Channel

Most of us are more comfortable when writing than when speaking. We enjoy talking with friends in a social situation or with associates around a conference table, but run for cover when someone suggests that we "give a speech." Getting up in front of an audience is the hardest thing we have to do. Our hearts pound, hands get clammy, minds go blank, and tongues are tied. We are "speechless."

Actually, the structure and discipline of writing apply to speaking. We usually write first what we intend to speak, adjusting the *form* of writing to the *channel* of speaking.

Once we have developed writing skills, we can move more easily into the speaking arena.

THE FICKLE CHANNEL

In many ways speaking is a fickle communication channel. Skillfully used, it can carry messages that inform, entertain, persuade, and motivate the receiver to action. At the same time, it can accommodate *noise* that blocks or garbles the message. While we use the channel every day, we may not be aware of its strengths and weaknesses.

Strengths of the Channel

Audience interest. To a degree, at least, we may assume that our message is directed toward receivers who are initially interested. The audience made an effort to come and hear us. They expect to hear something and are receptive. They have tossed the challenge to us and are waiting to see if we have something worthwhile to say.

Audience involvement. The face-to-face channel has a built-in potential for getting the audience involved in the communication process. In fact, there is no way to avoid the involvement. The response is there—verbal or nonverbal, positive or negative. The task is to make the involvement strengthen the message and to avoid letting the involvement turn to noise that destroys the message.

Message flexibility. The news story cannot be altered once it appears in the newspaper, regardless of how the reader reacts to the first paragraph. The direct-mail piece is unchangeable after it is mailed. All decisions regarding message treatment are made *before* the receiver had a chance to respond. The channel of speaking, on the other hand, permits us to adjust the message to the response of the receivers. With skill, we can "edit" our speech as we deliver it.

Message support. Since the spoken word tends to be elusive, we can support the message with an assortment of "aids," including slides, movies, charts, graphs, models, and other visuals.

Weaknesses of the Channel

Low retention. We can say a great deal in a half-hour speech. But little of what we say may be remembered by the audience. As mentioned earlier, an audience may remember only a fourth of what we say two months after we say it. We may be lucky if they remember that much.

Nonreferability. Unless we pass out copies of our speech, there is no way for the audience to refer to what was said. If the message is received in garbled form it may stay garbled. There is no way for the receiver to go back over the language to straighten out the message.

Limited audience. Regardless of the importance of the topic, our skill as a speaker, or the other attractions of the meeting, most audiences, even large ones, number in the hundreds rather than thousands. We contact only a small fraction of those for whom the message may be intended. Other channels are needed to reach those who cannot or will not listen to a speech.

BEFORE YOU ACCEPT

The most serious mistake some speakers make—even good speakers—is to accept a speaking invitation before making sure there is a proper fit of the audience, the topic, and the speaker. This "lack of fit" usually spells failure for the communication effort, and the failure is expressed in one or more of the following ways: "He was a good speaker all right, but he surely missed his audience with that topic." "He may be an authority on finance, but the audience knew more than he did about the subject of new trends in education." "He must have thought his audience would be a bunch of teenagers instead of mature adults who know a little about the experiences he was talking about."

Know the Audience

Knowledge of audience is essential for selecting message content and determining message treatment.

What are the characteristics of the group? What is the average age? Will it be a mixed group, all men, or all women? What about the education level? What occupations are prevalent? What economic level will be represented? Is this a small town, big town, or rural group?

What does the audience already know about the topic? Are attitudes mostly favorable or unfavorable? Are there ways to avoid controversy? Or does the group expect argument?

How well does the audience know you? Are you an "insider" or an "outsider?" Have some in the audience heard you before? Was your previous reception good, poor, in between?

You can get most of the audience information by asking the person who invited you. Consult others who have spoken to the same or similar groups. They can help you anticipate attitudes and knowledge levels. There may be literature about the group that will provide leads on member characteristics and positions taken on various issues.

Check Your Topic

The person who invites you to speak may be especially interested in the topic *he* suggests. That doesn't mean your audience will be. The sponsor of a youth group may think the topic of "getting along with parents" would be just dandy. But the young people may believe the topic has been "talked to death." The purposes of the program planners may differ from the purposes of the audience. Make sure the topic and audience are in agreement. If they are not, then adjust the topic, propose a new one, or decline the invitation.

Ask these questions about the proposed topic:

1. Does it fit the needs and interests of the audience? The audience expects rewards for listening. Decide whether they will be rewarded.

2. Does it fit you? You may be competent to discuss a variety of topics, but is the suggested topic one of them? Do you have something to say on the subject, an interest in saying it, and the knowledge to say it convincingly? If not, toss the challenge to another speaker.

3. Does it fit the moment? If the suggested topic is complex and involved and you are the last speaker on a full day's pro-

gram, chances are the topic is wrong for the moment. It would be all right for the first session in the morning, perhaps, but not for the last session in the afternoon.

4. Does it suggest a purpose? The topic itself should suggest a purpose, and that purpose may be to entertain, to inform, to change attitudes, or to motivate the audience to action. Do you agree with the suggested purpose? Does it fit the audience and the occasion? Can you handle it?

5. Does it fit the time allowed? The speaker who attempts to cover the history of mankind in fifteen minutes is defeated before he starts. Defeat is just as sure for the speaker who is asked to fill an hour with a topic that can be adequately covered in ten minutes. In fact, success is doubtful for any topic that takes an hour to cover. Most audiences won't listen that long.

Know Yourself

We once knew a man who declined an invitation to be the dean of an important college. When asked why, he said that he had made a list of the requirements for a good dean and another list of his qualifications and interests. When he compared the two lists they didn't match.

Your reputation as a speaker may be enhanced rather than hurt when you decline a speaking invitation. Unless there is a good match between your knowledge, interests, and attitudes regarding a proposed topic and those of the audience, a polite "no" may be the best response to a speaking invitation.

Time is another consideration. If you are too busy to give a speech the advance attention it deserves, you gain little by accepting. Nothing turns off an audience more quickly than a speaker who starts out, "Well, I really haven't had much time to think about this subject, but I am willing to tell you what little I know." The speaker may be willing to tell, but the audience soon recognizes the truth of his admission.

Having run through the "before you accept" checklist, you are ready to organize the content of your message, decide the treatment, and relate treatment to content.

ORGANIZE THE CONTENT

As already discussed, a news story consists of the lead that gives the gist of the message, and the body that expands on the lead, giving additional details and supporting information. A speech has three parts—*introduction, body,* and *conclusion* —and you approach the organization task differently. With both a news story and a speech, however, you should be able to state the main idea or the main purpose of the message in one sentence. If you can't, you will have trouble writing the lead for the story. You will have the same kind of trouble building the body of the speech, because that's where you start.

Start with the Body

A speech, even a brief, ten-minute one, is much longer than the average news story, so more of the message load is carried in the body. Start there and arrange content in logical order.

Main headings. Regardless of the topic or the length of your speech, divide the message into two, three, or four main headings. Most ideas, even complex ones, can be organized into a few main points. If the topic needs more than three or four such main headings, you may be covering too much ground. Once past the fourth point, you may lose the audience.

You should need no more than three or four main pegs for your message on the importance of exercise, the advantages of new math, the case for going to the moon, or the importance of having labor and management work together.

Supporting information. Having identified and listed the main points, expand and elaborate on those points.

You can illustrate points with humorous or serious stories, anecdotes, and analogies. Use humor with caution. Tell funny stories only if you have the knack for storytelling and when the story helps explain or clarify a point.

If possible, capitalize on the experiences of the audience. Relate what they know and have experienced to what you want them to know. Parents may better understand the "fads" of the modern generation if you recall the fads of their generation. Young people may better understand the need for parental rules if you remind them of rules their own social groups impose.

Use meaningful evidence and data but avoid citing page after page of statistics. The audience expects you to interpret the statistics and to give them the benefit of your analysis.

When appropriate, provide historical background and show how it relates to the point you are making. Most of us are more willing to consider the new and different idea if we can relate it to an accepted idea that may have been new and different in its time.

When you move into the area of opinions, attitudes, and beliefs, call on supporting troops. Quote authorities in fields related to the topic. What do doctors say about fluoridation of water? What are the chemists' opinions? What are the attitudes of parents in cities where fluoridation has been adopted?

If the idea or issue is controversial, don't hesitate to give both sides of the case while explaining why "your side" is more sound and reasonable.

When the speech includes a proposed solution to a problem, explain how the proposal relates to possible alternative action. Show cause-and-effect relationships. Compare costs, difficulties, probable chances for success.

Test each piece of supporting information against the main heading that it supports. Does the evidence, the analogy, the quotation of authority clarify and support the main idea or does it merely pad out the page or the time period? Does the opinion of Dr. Jones mean more or less to the audience than the opinion of Neighbor Smith, who may be in the audience and available for nonverbal support with a nod of his head?

There are two kinds of content that make a good speech: the kind that was considered and included, and the kind that was considered and discarded. Your audience doesn't want to know everything that you know—only the best that you know.

Prepare the Introduction

The newspaper reader decides from the news-story lead whether he wants to read the rest of the story. Usually the members of your audience will decide from the introduction to your speech whether to listen carefully, casually, or not at all.

The introduction, of course, must reflect your personality, your purpose, your message, and the interests of your audience.

Headlines. Newspapers catch the reader's attention with a headline. Use the same approach in your introduction. Pick out the most important point or fact in your message, and drive it home in your opening statement. For example:

On world population problems: "In the length of time it took the chairman to introduce me, the world had thousands of new mouths to feed. And I would like to visit with you about that problem this evening."

On food buying: "The average housewife in this room threw away $10 in food money last week by not taking advantage of food specials advertised in the local papers. We would like to talk about ways of finding that money."

On air pollution: "The Los Angeles Times recently carried a picture of that city's skyline as seen from the suburbs. It was the first time in four months that the smog had lifted enough so that those in the suburbs could see the city. Unless we do something about air pollution, none of us will be able to see one another, let alone our cities."

Normally, the headline introduction should do more than catch the attention of the audience. It should serve as an idea "lead" for further elaboration within the body of the speech.

Quotations. Following the moon landing in 1969, many of the speeches on that accomplishment, or on space travel in general, opened with a quotation of former President John F. Kennedy's challenge that the United States should land a man on the moon and return him safely to earth before the end of the '70s.

While not all quotations can be that prophetic, many can be

used effectively and appropriately to introduce the main idea of a speech.

Thoreau's observations while at Walden have been quoted and paraphrased to introduce talks on conservation, air and water pollution, and quality of life.

Shakespeare has provided many speakers with opening lines. So have the writings and speeches of Winston Churchill, Franklin D. Roosevelt, Abraham Lincoln, Thomas Jefferson, and other statesmen, writers, and philosophers.

Use introductory quotations only if you are sure the listener can tie the quote to the main idea of your speech—never if you have to provide the bridge of meaning. The listener doesn't want you to help him "get the point."

The problem. The bold, head-on, "this is the problem" approach is often the best way to introduce your message, especially if your purpose is to motivate the audience to action. Here are some examples:

On city traffic: "Ladies and gentlemen, unless this city applies modern traffic-engineering principles to its traffic problem, we will soon be able to walk to work faster than we can drive."

On drugs: "Parents, and not the police, must assume major responsibility for curbing the growing use of drugs by our teen-agers. It is our problem, not someone else's."

On education: "The plain truth is that our community has lost ground in the race for quality education during the past ten years. Our schools are overcrowded; our teachers are underpaid; and our school debt is going up."

A story. As mentioned earlier, an introductory story or anecdote can be effective *if* the story relates to the rest of the speech and *if* you have talent for telling a story, either serious or humorous. Telling a story just to be funny may detract from the message. The audience may still be thinking about the story—and others like it—as you try to move them into the main topic of your speech.

The serious man who handles humor poorly fails when he

tries to make his introduction "funny," and then never uses humor again in his speech. He seems to be saying, "See, I can be a funny guy, but let's get on with the business."

Summary. Some speakers use an introduction similar to the "summary lead" on a news story. They briefly mention the two, three, or four main ideas they plan to discuss. Such an introduction is especially suitable for audiences that already have a keen interest in the subject.

The Conclusion—a Wrapup

We hope that your audience has listened carefully and intently throughout your speech. From what we know about listening, though, this may be too much to count on. The attention of at least some members will have wandered during the speech.

Your conclusion gives you a chance to win back their attention and reestablish ideas that may have been missed earlier.

In planning the conclusion, review again the main purpose of your message.

If the primary purpose is to inform, the conclusion can be a brief recap of the main points. Enumeration is appropriate.

If the purpose is to change attitudes, the conclusion should briefly review and restate your case.

You may want to motivate the audience to action. If so, the conclusion should clearly spell out the desired action. Don't leave the members with the unspoken question, "All very well and good, but what are we supposed to do about it?" Use your conclusion to suggest what they might do about it.

You may have spoken on a controversial subject, knowing you were bound to spark a few flickers of irritation and resentment. If so, use the conclusion to reduce tensions. Leave the audience with the feeling that there are usually two sides to every question after all.

CONSIDER THE TREATMENT

Having selected the content of your speech and organized it into a logical pattern of introduction, body, and conclusion, consider message treatment for easy listening, impact, and interest.

Relate to Purpose

Language and the way you use it should clearly reflect the purpose of the message. Speeches that entertain first and inform second need a lighter, less serious, more humorous treatment than speeches designed to change attitudes or motivate to action. Some humor and some lightness may be appropriate for any kind of speech, however.

Use Audience Interests

You want to get a new traffic system adopted by the community. The audience is interested in safety for children on their way to school. Use that interest to support the proposal.

You want farmers to adopt an improved soil-fertility program for their farms. They are concerned about rising taxes and the high cost of machinery. Treat your message to accommodate their concerns and show how *your* program will help solve their problems.

Whenever possible, treat your message to reflect one or more of the basic needs of people—security, response, recognition, or new experiences. Reducing air pollution will protect health and security. The new shopping mall downtown will bring recognition to the city and its merchants.

Aim for Easy Listening

The listener, like the reader, wants you to use easy words instead of difficult ones, short sentences instead of long ones, short paragraphs instead of long ones. Specific, active, working verbs give movement and impact to your speaking as much as to your writing. Use them.

The listener, too, will translate your message better if you use words that are concrete rather than vague, specific rather than abstract. He will grow as bored and tired with wordy speaking as he will of wordy writing. Keep your spoken sentences direct, concise, and to the point. Chop out extra words and meaningless phrases.

Keep in mind that the listener, unlike the reader, can't go back over a sentence or a paragraph if he missed the meaning. Sense those passages that may be difficult to grasp. Build in a certain amount of repetition for the sake of clarity, but don't overdo it. When actually speaking, watch the audience for nonverbal signs that the message is not coming through. Back off, slow down, and use a slightly different approach.

THE FINAL FORM

When you get up to speak, the sheets of paper in your hand may represent an outline of your speech, a collection of notes and reminders, a rough draft, or a completely written presentation. The final form may depend upon several factors—the length and complexity of your presentation; the need for speech copies for future reference; the formality of the environment; and your skill, confidence, and experience as a speaker.

Unless you are an exceptionally gifted speaker, you will be on the safest ground if you write a complete version of your presentation even though you may never present it as written. It is hoped that you won't.

By writing the complete version you can check the content and organization, see how the pieces fit together, and add or take out supporting information. Writing permits you to tighten your sentences, eliminate vague references, introduce desired rhythm and movement. And you can practice your delivery with the complete script in front of you.

Having written a speech, many speakers tend to read exactly what they have written. The speaking sounds exactly like what it is—someone reading a speech. The audience wishes the speaker would hand out copies and let them read it to themselves.

There are several ways to avoid this. You can practice often enough so that you have committed the speech to memory. Have the written version in front of you for security in case your memory fails.

As an alternative, make a new, detailed outline of your written version, including key words, phrases, transitions, and quotations, and follow the outline rather than the written speech. A skillful speaker often uses a combination of these techniques. He keeps both a written version and an outline in front of him. He uses his outline until he comes to a particular section that needs careful emphasis and then reads that section almost as though he were quoting himself.

When you read a prepared speech you fail to take advantage of the channel strengths. You may miss the nonverbal feedback from the audience—the signs that tell you the audience is lost, that the message is not coming through. There is little opportunity to involve the audience or to make them a part of the communication experience. The environment of sender-receiver cannot be changed until you finish reading the last sentence of the last paragraph on the last page. By then, the audience may be interested only in getting out of the meeting room.

Writing a speech helps ensure that you are saying *what* you want to say. Speaking from an outline permits the audience to help guide *how* you say it. You then have the best of both worlds.

CHAPTER 17

Speeches for Special Occasions

Usually we do our best with the major speeches we give. Too often, though, we let down when giving a brief speech for a special occasion. There are all kinds of special occasions that require brief speeches, of course, but three are most common.

During a year we may have frequent opportunities to introduce a featured speaker on a program. At other times we may present some person with an award, a prize, or some other form of recognition. In a third situation we may receive an award or honor requiring a response of appreciation.

Our skill and grace in speaking effectively during such special times may add much to the success of the occasion.

SPEECH OF INTRODUCTION

You probably have sat in an audience and felt sorry for a speaker who had to pick up the pieces after a shattering intro-

duction. Often without realizing it, the person making the introduction assumed one of the following roles and left the speaker
to recover as best he could.

The Apologizer

The speaker is a substitute, and the program chairman takes
pains to let the audience know they are getting second-class
goods. He starts out something like this:

> I know your program states that our next speaker will be Dr.
> Lawrence Bentley, and many of you came here especially to hear
> him. But, as you might guess from looking at the speaker's table, Dr.
> Bentley had to cancel at the last minute and won't be with us. We
> were able to find a substitute, though, and I know you won't mind
> listening to Mr. Frank Gardner. Here's Mr. Gardner.

In another instance, the chairman has a feeling that the group
is a little tired of listening to speakers at every meeting. Since he
shares that feeling, he apologizes for having a speaker at all. His
introduction expresses his sympathies for the audience along
these lines:

> When your program committee met after last month's meeting, we
> considered two or three different types of programs for this month's
> meeting. We thought we had a good movie lined up, but it wasn't re-
> turned to the booking office in time for us to use it. Then we consid-
> ered a debate on the topic of driver education in schools but couldn't
> find anyone to take the negative side. We do have another good
> speaker lined up for tonight, though, and Mr. Frank Gardner is
> going to talk on the subject of air pollution.

The "Thunder-Stealer"

The "thunder-stealer" is the fellow who says he doesn't like to
give speeches and then ends up giving one every time he introduces the real speaker. He announces the subject and then ram-
bles off in two or three different directions for ten or fifteen minutes before remembering that his only purpose was to introduce
the speaker. He spends another five or ten minutes apologizing

for rambling, and then introduces the speaker without telling the audience who he is.

His other device is to give half the speaker's speech for him. In the process of assuring the audience that the topic is an important one, he covers most of the main points the speaker plans to make. In some extreme cases, the speaker has little left to say except "I agree."

The "Builder-Upper"

The chairman is interested in making points with the speaker and forgets the audience. He overplays the buildup. He goes into the speaker's background from the day he was born, reciting his every accomplishment, his employment record, and almost what he ate for breakfast.

By the time the introduction is over, the audience is so tired of the speaker that they are indifferent to his message.

The Funny Man

The chairman is a perfectly nice fellow, but some of his friends have told him that he can tell funny stories. He needs an audience, and one is right there waiting to hear the featured speaker. He thinks he does the speaker a favor by using the introduction to "warm up the audience" with a few of his latest tales. He may be successful, but the audience may still be laughing when the speaker tries to present his message on the dangers of air and water pollution—not a particularly humorous topic.

The Squelcher

The squelcher has heard too many "builder-uppers" give speeches of introduction, and he is determined to live by army rules—name, rank, and serial number are enough. His introduction is short and sweet, putting the speaker in his place something like this:

All of you have a copy of the program, so you can see that our next speaker is Mr. Karl Bentley of the University of Illinois. Mr. Bentley.

The Confider

The chairman has heard the speaker several times before, and wants to impress the audience with his "inside information" about the speaker's talents and techniques. If the speaker is known for his skill in giving humorous and entertaining presentations, the confider wants the audience to be on the alert for those "funny stories," so the following introduction puts the speaker on the spot:

> Folks, I'm about to introduce one of the funniest speakers you have ever heard. You might as well start laughing now, because you are going to be laughing the rest of the evening. I promise you that. This fellow can tell more jokes in less time than any fellow I know. Here he is now—so let's bring him on with a round of applause. Mr. Jokester himself, John Sober.

We have exaggerated a bit to make a point, but not much. You have heard speeches of introduction that are almost as bad—or worse—so it is fairly easy to build a list of things not to do when making introductions.

Don'ts

1. Don't apologize for the speaker if he is a substitute, or for having a speaker instead of some other kind of program.

2. Don't steal the speaker's speech by covering parts of it in your introduction or by talking about related or unrelated topics until the audience is tired of listening.

3. Don't embarrass the speaker by giving him a big buildup or by revealing the techniques he uses to make his speech entertaining or dramatic.

4. Don't tell funny stories about the speaker—or funny stories at all—if he is expected to talk on a serious subject.

5. Don't claim that your speaker "needs no introduction" and then spend fifteen minutes introducing him anyway.

6. Don't fail to establish a receptive link between the speaker and his audience so that he can move to his message immedi-

ately rather than spend time repairing the damage you may have done.

The speech of introduction should open the communication channel between speaker and listeners. It has no other purpose. It should gently but firmly shift the listener's attention away from whatever he might have been thinking about toward the speaker and his topic. You can do this by answering the three basic questions that the listener is likely to ask.

1. *Who is the speaker and where did he come from?* Give the listener a brief but complete and straightforward answer to that double question. Repeat the speaker's name and title even though it is listed on the program. Most audiences like to know where the speaker grew up and went to school and where he spent most of his professional life. Pick important points and be brief.

2. *What qualifies him to speak on the topic?* The topic and the speaker's qualifications are usually explained at the same time. You need not give the complete biographical history of the man, but select the significant experiences and accomplishments that relate to his qualifications for discussing the topic. The fact that a man played major-league baseball for five years is important if the topic is sports. It may mean little if the topic is urban renewal or agricultural productivity.

3. *Why should I listen?* A part of the audience may have come to the meeting to hear some other speaker who is appearing on the same program. They are not sure they have a real reason for listening to the speaker you are about to introduce. Your task is to relate the speaker and his topic to their fields of interest. Even when the speaker is the only one on the program, many in the audience have an initial "convince me that I should listen" attitude. Your challenge is to convince them.

The speech of introduction may not answer the above three questions in that order, but it should answer them—briefly, briefly, briefly!

While the introduction may take no more than a minute or so to present, it should take longer than that to prepare. As with any other speech, you will be on the safe side if you write it out in advance. If you have the opportunity, check the introduction with the speaker to make sure that the facts are correct and the approach is appropriate. If you plan to use humor, tell a joke, or refer to a particular local situation, let the speaker know in advance. He may want to adapt his own opening remarks to the setting you have provided.

In making the introduction, speak clearly, distinctly, sincerely, and enthusiastically. Above all, speak briefly.

THE PRESENTATION SPEECH

In many ways the presentation speech requires more skill and grace than the speech of introduction. There is danger of embarrassing both the receiver of the award and the audience, especially if there has been competition. You must recognize and compliment the contributions of the winner without detracting from the efforts of the losers.

Think about your presentation in terms of what the audience wants to know, and what the receiver does and doesn't want you to say and do.

Audience Questions

Often the presentation is an unannounced part of a larger meeting or program. The audience may or may not know that a presentation will be made or an honor bestowed. In any event, they would like to know why you are using this particular moment to make the presentation. If possible, relate the reason to the program or event.

If there was competition for the award, concentrate on the record and accomplishments of the receiver. Acknowledge the contributions of those who didn't win, but don't attempt to explain *why* they didn't win. The audience wants to know why the receiver won the award, not why others didn't win it. Be as specific as possible. Use facts, figures, dollars, numbers, and citations.

Whenever possible, show how the contributions of the receiver will open doors for future accomplishments of others. Stick to the accomplishments and contributions that relate to the award. The audience is less interested in the unrelated activities that merely prove the receiver is a worthy and talented individual.

If there is a donor of the award, the audience wants the donor identified and credited. Your purpose, though, is to honor the receiver and not the donor.

Finally, unless the name of the receiver has been announced in advance, save his name until last. The audience appreciates the suspense, and the receiver doesn't have to sit through your speech with everyone looking at him.

Receiver's Wishes

The receiver of the award has a few wishes of his own, and your presentation should respect them.

More than anything else, the receiver wants you to refrain from overenthusiasm and exaggeration. He hopes his record will speak for itself without flowery adornments and embellishments. In fact, he would prefer that you concentrate on the record and not on him.

Comparisons with others were made at the time his record was chosen for the award. The comparisons need not be made again in the presentation speech.

Finally, the receiver clearly understands that it is appropriate, even expected, for him to respond by expressing his appreciation for the award. He would prefer that you *not* ask him to "say a few words," and thus give the impression that he might forget to do so.

Your Pleasure

Respect the receiver's wishes and answer the questions of the audience—with pride and pleasure. Again, it is wise to write your speech ahead of time, even though you will not read it. Writing it permits you to check off the points you intend to cover, to make certain the information is correct and complete and the treatment appropriate.

When you speak, communicate pride, pleasure, enthusiasm, and sincerity. Speak clearly and loudly enough for everyone to hear you. Speak briefly, but avoid the impression that you are hurrying to get the presentation over and done with.

If the presentation includes a plaque, scroll, or some other tangible item, hand the item to the receiver with the concluding remarks of your presentation. And once you have started to hand it to him, give it to him. Don't pull it back as you remember a couple of other items you want to mention. With your concluding remark, shake the receiver's hand, offer your personal congratulations, and then step out of his way so that he can express his appreciation without having you look over his shoulder.

THE ACCEPTANCE SPEECH

The shoe is now on the other foot. You have received a special award, and the audience expects an appropriate response.

The fellow who made the presentation provided the proper setting for your acceptance. He was discreet, accurate, and sincere. He seemed genuinely glad that you were chosen for the award. Now it is your turn, and the checklist for your speech should include both the words to be said and those to be left unsaid.

Words to Say

After addressing the audience, express appreciation to the person who made the presentation. Thank him for his words but not for the award unless he was also the donor.

Thank the donor next. Be sure you clearly understand who the donor is. If there is more than one, name them all. Most donors, however, do not expect or want lavish praise. Such overpraise, in fact, may irritate the audience.

In most cases there will be others who made it possible for

you to achieve the award, and these people, too, should be recognized with sincere expressions of appreciation. Whenever possible, acknowledge the good work of others who may have tried for the prize and failed. There often is only a shade of difference between winning and not winning.

If the award includes money, a scholarship, or travel opportunity, indicate briefly how you will use the award and how it will help you accomplish other objectives.

Always end your speech by repeating a brief, sincere statement of appreciation.

Words Not to Say

Your record as reviewed by the person making the presentation should speak for itself. The audience will be embarrassed for you if you review in detail the work you did and the success you achieved to win.

Nor does the audience want to hear a long, detailed report on the history of the project or program that led to the award. If such historical review is needed, it should be given in the presentation speech.

Listeners may welcome a bit of humor on your part, especially if the humor is directed at yourself. But they will be bored if you insist on telling them about all of the "funny things" that happened to you, your family, and your friends on the way to winning the award.

Your audience will be disappointed, too, if your words seem to suggest that the award has been one of your lifelong ambitions and that now, having won it, you have little interest left in the race. They would rather believe that the award offers new challenges for you.

The Final Test

Usually the award will not come as a surprise, so you should have plenty of time to write your speech in advance. It is to be hoped that you will not read the speech you have written, although you may want to practice it enough times so that the important parts stick in your mind.

When you read it over, ask yourself if it is the kind of speech that you would like to listen to if you had been the loser instead of the winner.

CHAPTER 18

Radio: Mass-Media Channel for Speaking

We interrupt this program to bring you a special weather bulletin. And now for the news. . . .
Here's the latest hit record by the Fearsome Foursome.
It will be cooler tomorrow with a 20 percent chance of rain in the afternoon.
Blue-chip stocks rose today, with the Dow-Jones average. . . .
We have a report of a lost collie dog, last seen at the corner of Green Street and Prospect Avenue. Anyone seeing. . . .
Here's your farm report for today.
Strike three, and the batter is out of there.

The sounds of radio come to us wherever we are—in the living room, in the kitchen, in the car, or on the beach. The sounds may even come from the pocket of a shirt or the palm of a hand. Radio—the mass-media channel of sound, talk, soft music, loud music, news, weather, markets, sports, the lost dog, and the found cat. Radio—the constant companion of many, the bringer of news "when it happens wherever it happens," the extender of our voice, and the multiplier of our listeners. MAYBE.

Radio is nothing more than an electronic system for transmitting sound over distance. It has the potential for connecting the sender with hundreds, thousands, and even millions of receivers. But radio in itself is neither effective nor ineffective, good nor bad, worthwhile nor worthless. Its value depends upon our skill in using it.

When used for the right purpose and with the right message, radio can be one of the most effective communication channels.

Many years ago a colleague, Richard B. Hull, of Ohio State University, clearly identified the informational role of radio with these words:

> The peculiar genius of radio is the genius of speed and immediacy. It can be an electronic Paul Revere. Radio can educate, but it cannot teach in the normal sense of classroom teaching. Radio can suggest and motivate, but it cannot detail and reason. Radio can create attitudes, but it cannot philosophize and explore. Radio can generalize, but it cannot qualify and specify. In short, radio can motivate, stimulate, sell, induce belief, create and change basic attitudes—and in a hurry.

Since Hull made those observations, there have been changes in the way radio is used. But the characteristics of the channel —the peculiar genius of radio—have not changed. Radio is still fast and still personal—intensely personal. But it is also fleeting. Messages are spoken and disappear, to be replaced by new messages. Skill in using the channel depends upon understanding its strengths and weaknesses.

CHARACTERISTICS OF RADIO

Strengths of Radio

With radio we can reach thousands of people quickly, but each listener is often alone, just as the newspaper reader is alone with his newspaper. When we write for radio or speak on radio, our message can be, and should be, direct, informal, and personal. We are not sending our message to "everyone out there in radioland." We are not giving a speech to 500 people in a meeting hall. We are visiting with one person or two or three persons who are listening to us on a particular radio receiving set. The electronic system duplicates the one-to-one sender-receiver environment hundreds or thousands of times.

Print-media channels communicate only through sight. Radio communicates only through sound, but the sound includes the spoken words and a reflection of the speaker's personality. In print, words can be friendly or threatening only in the way they are selcted and used. On radio, those same words are enhanced by the way they are spoken.

Radio is constant and continuous during the hours the station is on the air. News bulletins, weather warnings, special announcements can be flashed any hour of the day and any minute of the hour. The message need not be set in type and held for the next edition. It can be reported now—this instant.

Radio can and does repeat its messages. News flashes may be repeated several times during the morning before the story receives more complete treatment on a regularly scheduled news broadcast. Weather warnings often are given every few minutes during times of severe storms. Public-service announcements are aired several times during the day.

Finally, radio can be a constant companion and, within certain limits, we can listen wherever we are and whenever we want to.

Weaknesses of Radio

We have already suggested some of the weaknesses of radio, and they are included in the observations of Richard Hull, mentioned above. In some ways, the weaknesses are almost a reversed reflection of the strengths.

Because radio communicates only by sound through the sense of hearing, a message cannot be amplified or supported by stimuli to other senses. A newspaper can use words to describe the havoc of hurricane Betsy and include pictures to make the message even more meaningful and dramatic. Radio, of course, cannot make use of pictures. We can send charts and graphs to amplify our direct-mail message and even include the scent of some new perfume, but we can't with radio.

We can subscribe to two or three newspapers plus that many more magazines, and read them all when we have time. Not so with radio. Our set may receive thirty stations and all thirty may be broadcasting good programs, but we can listen to only one of them. We miss the other twenty-nine programs unless they are repeated later.

People listen to radio casually. Often they combine listening with other activities—reading, eating dinner, doing the dishes, building a boat, talking with family or friends. If a listener misses something on a radio program, he can't go back and relisten to that part as he might reread a paragraph in a newspaper story.

The radio channel is a one-way channel. The listener can't ask questions as he can with face-to-face speaking channels. Nor can we, the sender, check the response to the message by watching for nonverbal signs from the listeners. We have no way of knowing at the moment whether our message is getting through.

KNOW YOUR RADIO STATION

We can use the channel of radio only if the radio station management is convinced that our message is worth communicating and that we are the logical source for the information. The station management, like the newspaper editor, is the gatekeeper for his particular channel. He decides when and how to open the gate for messages, and when and how to close the gate.

Everything we said about knowing your newspaper editor and understanding the newspaper business applies to radio stations. Unless you are an advertiser and purchase radio time, you ask the station to *give* you time for your message. Unfortunately, the station has other sources of messages, and more messages than time to air them. Unlike the newspaper that adds pages as it sells more advertising, the station cannot add time. It has a fixed broadcast day of so many hours, and there are only sixty minutes in each of those hours.

Like the newspaper, the radio station must make money to stay on the air. All income must come from the sale of "time" to advertisers. There is a potential price tag on every minute of every broadcast day. The price varies with the time of day and the power of the station. Just as the newspaper has space that isn't sold, so does the station have time that isn't sold. You have an opportunity to use that time if you have information that the station's listeners want to hear.

If you plan to use local radio, then, visit the station and get acquainted with the management, the staff, and the programming procedures. At the same time, give the station personnel a chance to get acquainted with you, your organization, and your work.

Station Personnel

A visit will acquaint you with station personnel and their responsibilities. Small stations, like small newspapers, have small staffs, and each staff member may wear two or three hats, with duties ranging from selling advertising to hosting a kiddies' program. Larger stations have larger staffs with more specialized assignments. In general, though, all stations handle the various functions among the staff members as follows:

Station manager. This man (or woman) may or may not own the station. He may be active in the programming side of the business, or he may concentrate on business management activities. On small stations, the manager may double as the chief announcer, chief engineer, or head advertising salesman.

Program director. The person with this title, regardless of other titles he may have, decides what does and what doesn't go on the air. He works within the policy framework established by the station management, which may decree that the station will be mainly a "talk" station, or a "music" station, or a "community-service" station. Within that framework, the program director selects programs, approves general content, and has a voice concerning nearly everything that is transmitted by the channel. The program director is the person to see if you want to direct your information to one of the station's regularly scheduled programs or if you want to suggest a new program.

News director. Nearly every station devotes considerable air time to news broadcasts. There may be three, four, or more news programs each day, ranging from five to fifteen minutes each. Some stations have brief newscasts every hour or every half-hour and break into regular programming to report special news breaks. The news director runs this part of the station's broadcast day, and he is the man to check with if you plan to supply the station with news and feature items. He can tell you when he wants news copy and how it should be prepared. He will advise you on the kinds of items that will get used and the kinds that won't. Find out if the news can be called in or whether it must be written and mailed. Some stations have excellent facilities for recording phoned-in reports and they prefer this method of reporting. Others depend on regular news announcers to voice all news material.

Public-service director. Some stations, especially the larger ones, designate one staff member as the public-service director. This man or woman plans and may host the station's public-service programs, including those on community affairs, community schools, and telephone call-in programs. Such programs may be aired on a regular basis or produced as "specials" at the discretion of the station.

The public-service director, if there is one, also selects the public-service spot announcements. Most stations have more such announcements than they can use, pouring in from health organizations, religious groups, educational institutions, conservation societies, and agencies of state and national government.

Other specialized staff. The station may have a number of other specialized-program staff people, depending upon the size of the station and its programming patterns. A number of stations still have full-time or part-time farm program directors. Some have persons who are responsible for women's programs, sports broadcasts, or special music programs.

FIT MESSAGES TO PROGRAM STRUCTURE

The listing of station personnel probably suggests the kinds of programs that might carry your messages. You can learn more by visiting the station and by listening to the station throughout the broadcast day.

With nearly all stations, you should be able to fit your message into one or all of four general program categories: (1) regular and special news broadcasts, (2) public-service spot announcements, (3) public-service programs, (4) your own show.

Your choice of program carrier will depend upon the policies of the station, the type and complexity of your message, and the characteristics of your audience.

CHAPTER 19

Writing Radio News and Spots

"The peculiar genius of radio is the genius of speed and immediacy."

Radio means different things to different people, but it means one thing to nearly all people: news.

We "hear first" on radio and later turn to television newscasts for a visit to the scene and for visual elaboration. We read newspapers for additional details, new versions, printed confirmation. The radio alerts us, tips us off, gives us clues; television amplifies and dramatizes; newspapers elaborate and confirm.

We "hear first" on radio, because we are exposed more to radio. We can have it with us in every room in our home and take it with us wherever we go.

Radio is fast and immediate, but it "cannot detail and reason." Radio scans back and forth over the news landscape, spots the news as it breaks, and brings us the headlines in the form of news "flashes" or special "interrupt bulletins." Later, on regularly scheduled news broadcasts, it goes over the "front page" of the news and gives us the gist of the happenings much in the manner of news-story leads.

There is not time to go into detail, and the listener doesn't expect it. Five, ten, even fifteen news stories may be covered in a five-minute broadcast. The story that would take three or four minutes to read in the newspaper is boiled down to a minute or even thirty seconds for the radio newscast.

Local radio also reports the local scene. The community station has radio wire services, network affiliations, and other news sources to help it report state, national, and international news happenings. It must depend upon its own staff, often small, to report what's happening down the street, across town, and in other towns and rural areas covered by its signal. The station will welcome your "news" and help you carry your messages to your audience, if you prepare your communication properly and put it in their hands promptly—while it is still news.

NEWS CHARACTERISTICS

The channel does not determine the characteristics of news. The audience does. Radio news is the same as newspaper news, or television news, or the news that is passed back and forth whenever people gather and communicate with one another.

As mentioned in earlier chapters, news is what we, the people, want to read, hear, know about. It is made up of those things that are new, that happened or are going to happen, that affect our lives, directly or indirectly. News includes the reports of the unusual and different. It tells us what people are doing, saying, thinking about. News often includes messages that tell us *why* to do things and *how* to do them—why and how we should diet, exercise, read more books, take a vacation, drive safely, stop destroying our environment, plant trees, learn to swim, or vote for the next school-bond issue.

For the farmer, news is the report of rain last night, the anticipated price for cattle next month, the advice on new chemical weed-killers.

For the teen-ager, news is the listing of the latest hit records, the reviews of coming movies, the instructions for applying for admission to college, the points of view on new draft laws.

Whenever we respond "I didn't know that before," we are talk-ing about news regardless of the channel. When we prepare news for radio, we should ask this question: "What information do we have or can we gather that station listeners would like to hear?" Having identified those messages, we prepare them in the *form* that the radio channel can best transmit and the listener can best receive.

RADIO NEWS FORM

When we write for newspapers, we write for the hurried reader. When we write for radio, we write for the casual listener. The re-ceptiveness of the receiver and the characteristics of the channel determine form and style.

Alert the Listener

The news story counts on the boldface head or headline to capture the attention of the reader. The lead gives him the gist of the story as quickly as possible.

With radio, the first spoken words of the message must win at-tention by saying, in effect, "Now hear this, hear this." Give the listener at least a split second to screen out the "noise" in the communication system. He is tuned to the newscast, but he has been looking out the window at the snowstorm, or thinking about problems at the office, or wondering what his wife is pre-paring for dinner. If the key to the message is in the first ten or fifteen words, it may slip past him, because he really wasn't lis-tening. First win the listener's attention, and then give him the key to the message.

Suppose the message is written like this:

Prospect Street, between John and Church Avenues, will be closed to all traffic tomorrow so that workmen can install new traffic signals near Southside School.

The Street Department expects the work to be completed by Thursday, but the street cannot be opened to traffic until the work is completed.

There is nothing wrong with that story, but the listener had just started to light his pipe and missed the first seven words. He picked up the message at the start of the phrase "will be closed tomorrow," and the rest of the message didn't help him a bit. He did get the message the next day when he came to the barrier on Prospect Street.

The message could have alerted his attention by using a spoken headline that said something like this:

You may need to take a new route to work tomorrow.

The Street Department will be installing new traffic lights near Southside School. Prospect Street will be closed to all traffic between John and Church Avenues.

The writer used the important word "you" to catch the listener's attention. If the listener wasn't tuned in for the first sentence, he got a second chance, since the writer took care of the *why* before the *what*. He delayed the key to the message a few fractions of a second.

If you listen carefully to the news, you will notice the variety of ways in which radio newswriters alert attention. Here are some examples from one night's newscast:

There was another American plane hijacked to Cuba last night.

There's more bad news for cigarette smokers.

Police are following new leads in the latest Mafia murder.

The St. Louis Cardinals are in the trading market to put some hitting power in their lineup for next year.

More fighting has been reported along the Suez Canal.

Authorities have come up with a new source of funds for the anti-poverty program.

Each opening sentence alerts the listener to the subject of the message before giving him the first of the key points.

The second sentence of the hijacking story gave the name of

the airline, the plane's destination, and the number of passengers.

Having alerted the cigarette smokers, the message revealed the results of a new study on smoking and heart disease.

The St. Louis Cardinals had just traded popular Curt Flood and Tim McCarver to the Philadelphia Phillies for the controversial but hard-hitting Richie Allen.

The Suez Canal fighting was in an area that had been relatively quiet for almost a year.

The state governor had authorized cities to use general reserve funds for the anti-poverty program.

When you write for radio news broadcast, use opening words that provide the same attention-getting function as the heading on the news story. Follow the "alert" with the key points of your message.

The Lead Is the Body

The form of the radio news story is similar to the form of the newspaper news story. The listener expects you to give him the five W's and the H—Who, What, When, Where, Why, and How? But with radio copy, the proportion of lead to body is reversed. Or, put another way, the expanded lead *is* the body of the story, as there is little time to elaborate on the main points or to provide lengthy details.

Compare the two ways that a news story on community improvement was handled—one by the local paper and one by the local radio station:

Newspaper Treatment	*Radio Treatment*
MORE STORES REMODELING ON EAST SIDE	(No head to get attention)
Two businesses in the 100 block of East University Avenue have started work on the remodeling of their store fronts as part of the	East University Avenue is getting its face lifted. The Old Fashioned Tavern and Dave and Harry Locksmiths are

Newspaper Treatment	*Radio Treatment*
beautification plan for their block. The Old Fashioned Tavern, 106 E. University, and the Dave and Harry Locksmiths Shop, 116 E. University, have begun work proposed by the Champaign County Development Council Foundation. The CCDCF has described the block as the optimum area for demonstrating what can be done toward rehabilitating old buildings.	putting up new store fronts. Both are in the 100 block.
	The new look is a part of the city's beautification program sponsored by the Champaign County Development Council Foundation. You can see the change in about three weeks.
The Old Fashioned is having the large sign removed . . . (the rest of the paragraph describes the changes that will take place, gives the name of the contractor, the cost, and the expected date of completion).	
(The final paragraph gives more information on the CCDCF and its plans for future improvements.)	

The newspaper story used nearly 200 words to report the gist of the message and elaborate on details. The radio copy left out the details but reported the gist of the message with 57 words. The newspaper was aware that not all readers would complete the story but it provided the details for those readers who were interested. The radio newscast gave the main points and assumed that more-interested listeners would turn to other sources for details.

The Writing "Style"

Good writing is good writing, regardless of channel or form. But there are subtle differences between radio news style and newspaper news style. The above example suggests some of those differences.

Radio is a more personal channel than newspapers. So the

writing is more personal and informal. The writer can write (speak) more directly to the listener. The tone is more conversational, more casual.

For newspapers, easy words and short sentences are important. For radio, they are essential. The reader can ponder a difficult word in writing and even take time to look it up in the dictionary (but don't count on it). There is no time to ponder a difficult word spoken on radio. Sentences are not only short but terse, even incomplete.

Newspaper writers seldom uses contractions. Radio writers nearly always do. The news story says, "Police were not able to convince the demonstrators." Radio copy says, "Police couldn't convince the demonstrators."

Newspaper style generally calls for crediting the source of information at the end of the sentence. The story says, "Soybean prices are expected to level out during the next two months, according to Stanley Potter, agricultural economist." Radio news style generally calls for identifying the source at the start of the sentence. So we write, "Agricultural Economist Stanley Potter expects soybean prices to level out during the next two months."

Newspaper writing is for the eye. Radio newswriting is for the ear. When read, it "sounds" like talking. Hard news on radio usually calls for an objective style. The "you" approach isn't appropriate for reporting wars, disasters, murder trials, and other happenings that would be front-page copy in a newspaper. But the "you" approach is appropriate for radio news-features and the kinds of items that make up "page 3" of the radio newscast. The "you" approach is suggested even when not actually used.

Radio copy, even more so than newspaper copy, must suggest movement and action. The simple, direct sentence is always better than the long, involved sentence. Avoid as many modifying clauses and phrases as possible. Turn a modifying clause into a separate sentence.

Example: Victor Palmiere, a former official of the Kerner Commission that studied racial disorders and civil unrest, accused the administration today of attempting to placate the South on integration and of appealing to racial prejudices with its "forgotten American" theme.

Rewrite for radio: Victor Palmiere accused the administration today of placating the South on integration. Palmiere is a former official of the Kerner Commission that studied racial disorders and civil unrest. He said the administration was appealing to racial prejudices with its "forgotten American" theme.

One long sentence was chopped into three. The modifying clause identifying Palmiere was made into a separate sentence. The two charges against the administration were separated.

Practice your radio newswriting skill by rewriting some of the stories in today's newspaper. Go through the story first and note any words that might be difficult for the listener to understand when spoken on the air. Select substitutes that give the same meaning.

Circle all long, complex sentences, especially those with one or more modifying or dependent clauses. Follow the rule of putting one idea in one sentence when you rewrite.

Check the sentences that list the news source at the end of the sentence. Rewrite by starting with the source.

Finally, read your rewritten effort aloud. Ask yourself if it reads the way you would talk.

WRITING PUBLIC-SERVICE ANNOUNCEMENTS

Smokey Bear tells you to "put out that campfire and break burned matches before throwing them away." You hear his message right after the station break.

The special message from "your Heart Association" is tucked between two numbers of your favorite music program.

The United Fund invites your contributions immediately following the morning market summary, and the invitation is repeated several times during the day.

There will be other public-service messages during the day— from the Boy Scouts of America, the Savings Bond Division of the U.S. Treasury Department, the Society of the Blind, the League of Women Voters, and the local cooperative extension service.

In the language of the trade, these messages are called "public-service announcements," or, more simply, "public-service spots." The radio station, *as a public service,* permits worthy, nonprofit groups and organizations to use its channel for communicating brief messages to its listeners. The station schedules the messages at various "spots" during the broadcast day, so the combination of purpose and timing leads to their identification as *public-service spots.*

If you are associated with a worthy, nonprofit group or organization, public-service announcements offer an effective way to reach your audiences with certain kinds of information. If you are uncertain whether you qualify, check with the station manager, program director, or public-service director. None of these men will promise to use your stuff, but they can tell you whether you and your group qualify for "free" public-service time. They will also tell you how they want the announcements prepared and presented.

Most stations, however, will have these minimum requirements:

Source. The message comes from a recognized, nonpolitical, noncontroversial, not-for-profit group or organization. Your group may be local or may be organized on a state or national basis. It should have a broad public purpose.

Message. The message should be in the public interest. The public benefits when forest fires are reduced, heart disease is conquered, or youth is served by expanded youth groups. It also benefits when people drive more carefully, when children observe bike-riding rules, and when community citizens are informed of the dangers of water pollution.

Time. Most public-service announcements run either thirty or sixty seconds. Some run shorter, but few run longer. They correspond to advertising commercials and often are used because the station has saved time for commercials that were not sold. The station "fills" the time with a public-service announce-ment in much the same way that a newspaper fills out the end of a news column with a one-paragraph "news filler."

Form. Stations use both written announcements read by the station announcer and tape- or disc-recorded announcements played by the station engineer. The station can tell you which form it prefers. In any case, the writing comes first.

Fit Message to Time

The average person speaks at a rate of 100 to 125 words per minute. With a sixty-second spot announcement, you have that many words to use. No more. For a thirty-second spot, cut the number of words in half.

You may insist that no message of importance can be spoken in a hundred words, much less fifty or sixty. But if you think about it, you know that advertisers spend millions of dollars for the privilege of selling cars, soap, perfume, and hundreds of other items with messages that are spoken in 125 words or less. And Smokey Bear has made most of us pretty aware of forest-fire dangers with fifty- or sixty-word messages.

Writing public-service announcements requires the distillation and application of just about everything that's been said about writing, especially writing for radio. And the distillation works in this way.

1. Have a single, clear purpose, and select only one—repeat, only one—main idea to support that purpose.

2. Make every word a working word and throw out every word that does not contribute to the meaning of the message.

3. Spend the first of your few words to alert the listener.

4. Write to and for the listener. Use the "you" approach if at all possible.

5. Repeat directions or instructions if the listener must have them to take the requested action.

6. Write, edit, rewrite, and edit again. Then practice reading the message aloud—to yourself or to a critical friend.

Here are two examples:

Are you and your family going on vacation this summer? Your local, friendly burglar hopes so. And he's waiting for your signal that you are away from home. You can tell him in many ways. Let the newspapers pile up on the front porch. Pull the shades so he knows you're away during the day. Make sure no lights are left on. The Crime Prevention Society says such help makes the thief's work much easier.

It's not often that you can get something for nothing. But now you can. The Champaign Chamber of Commerce has ordered 500 shade trees to help make the city beautiful. You can have one free for your home. To reserve your tree, call 000-1788 and give the girl who answers your name and address. That's all. Just call 000-1788 and tell the girl you would like to have one of the trees. You only have to pick the spot and do the planting.

CHAPTER 20

On the Air

Program directors know that on-air participation by qualified authorities adds interest and variety to their programming schedules.

Your on-air appearances may be regular or irregular and may involve one or more of these broadcast situations: (1) voicing news and information features for regular station newscasts; (2) voicing public service announcements; (3) presenting five- or ten-minute features on regular station shows; (4) hosting your own complete show.

Before agreeing to appear regularly on radio, ask yourself three questions:

1. *Are information sources adequate?* Radio gobbles up information at a fantastic rate. The station expects you to give its listeners something worthwhile each time you use their channel. Make sure your reservoir of information is big enough to fill a daily or twice-weekly broadcast segment. If it isn't, adjust the frequency of appearances to fit the supply of information. Don't run out of things to say after the first few weeks of broadcasting.

2. *Do I have the time?* Radio is a demanding taskmaster. The adage "the show must go on" applies to radio. If your presentation is scheduled for 10:13 A.M. each Tuesday and Thursday, you or your recording must be at the station at 10:13 A.M. each Tuesday and Thursday. Broadcasts can't be handled "at your convenience."

A set series of broadcasts is not for people who must be away from home base for long periods or who face unpredictable and unavoidable demands on their time.

3. *Do I have the skill?* Radio depends entirely upon your voice and delivery skill to carry your message. An inadequate voice or ineffective delivery distracts the listener and interferes with the reception and interpretation of the message. In public speaking, a less-than-adequate voice is supported by the physical appearance and gestures of the speaker. The speaker may also use visual aids and other devices. On radio, voice carries the whole load.

If you are unsure of your radio ability, seek the critical judgment of a professional in the field.

Relatively few people have such poor voice quality that they should altogether avoid radio. At the same time, few people are "natural" radio performers, born with a voice for radio. Most people have adequate voices and can develop the skill to speak on radio.

VOICING YOUR MESSAGE

You may make your presentations "live" at the station or record them ahead of time for broadcast. The task is the same except for differences in physical environment.

If you record in the studio, the station handles the engineering details. If you record in your office or elsewhere, you need a broadcast-quality tape recorder and a relatively noise-free and acoustically adequate place for recording. (For some subjects, background sounds can contribute desired "atmosphere.") Most good tape recorders are simple to operate. Check with station personnel, though, on questions of make, model, and operating procedures.

The Friendly Listener

When we first appear on radio or make a recording, many of us have a faulty image of our audience. We know the station has "thousands of listeners." When we think of such numbers, our hands perspire, our mouths get dry, our voices tighten, and we speak as though we *were* addressing thousands. We assume a different personality.

Think of your audience not as thousands of faceless people but as one or two friendly listeners in the familiar and comfortable surroundings of their own homes. By tuning you in, they have invited you to visit with them for a few minutes. They are not particularly aware that others are listening. They don't care. Neither should you.

Be natural. Visit with one or two of your favorite people. Visualize them listening to you in an environment familiar to both of you. Perhaps it is your favorite coffee shop, the living room of their home, or the backyard. Visit with them in that environment and anticipate the kinds of nonverbal responses they might give you. Ignore the microphone. If you don't, you will be talking to it instead of visiting with friends.

Unless your message is grim, smile when you talk. Your listeners can't see the smile, but they can feel it in your voice. A smile helps you relax and smooths your delivery.

The Effective Delivery

If you think of your audience as one or two friendly listeners, the other suggestions for effective radio speaking make sense.

Be enthusiastic. You are speaking for a purpose. You want listeners to understand and believe you. Be as enthusiastic about your message as you want your listeners to be. Convey your enthusiasm in your delivery, the same as when you talk with a person face to face.

In face-to-face talking, we usually express our enthusiasm and conviction with a wide assortment of facial and body gestures. We open our eyes in amazement, smile, grimace, and shake our heads. We point, clench our fists, shrug our shoulders, hold our hands apart, and make all sorts of gestures to emphasize and dramatize. Many effective radio speakers use the same facial and body gestures in front of the microphone even though the listeners can't see them. The gestures and body involvement are reflected in the voice, and they help convey interest and enthusiasm.

If you doubt this, go off by yourself and try it. First, try reading a piece of copy with your hands resting quietly on the table or in your lap. Make your voice do all the work. Then try the same piece again, but help your voice by using your hands, shifting your body, shrugging your shoulders, and wrinkling your face. Which approach seems best to communicate your message?

Use variety. A message that is not well written can seldom be well spoken. But even good writing does not assure good delivery. The best message can be dull and monotonous unless the speaker's delivery gives it sparkle and variety.

Learn to use pauses. Pauses help pace your delivery. They give you time to breathe and give your listeners time to think. If you pack too many words into any time segment, both you and your audience will be fatigued.

Give punch to your speaking by emphasizing key words and phrases in much the same way that you underline such words and phrases in your writing. In fact, it is a good idea to underline those key passages in your written copy. Otherwise, you may speak each sentence in the same way and produce a sing-song effect.

Change your speaking pace. Slow your delivery for certain passages, especially those that carry key meanings. If you must give details or instructions, speak slowly enough for the listener to fix them firmly in mind.

Change the pitch of your voice occasionally. This takes practice, but you can learn to do it, and it gives variety to your delivery. Pauses, changes in tempo, and changes in pitch also serve as punctuation marks in your delivery. They help the listener follow you as you shift direction and move from one part of your message to another. Avoid the common error, though, of dropping your voice at the end of every sentence. This too results in a sing-song delivery—strong beginning, weak ending; strong beginning, weak ending; up, down; up, down—like water dripping from a leaky faucet. After a couple of minutes the listener may treat you like a leaky faucet and turn you off.

Practice delivery. If you have written in the natural style of talking, you should be able to speak in the same style—but not without practice. Without practice, the act of reading tends to interfere with naturalness. The mind focuses on words rather than meaning. The listener hears words instead of meaning.

Practice by reading copy aloud. You can then tell if a phrase or a sentence sounds natural. Eliminate words that are hard to pronounce. Try different tempos, and mark your copy for points of emphasis. Concentrate on the meaning of the message.

If you have a recorder, use it for your practice sessions. Try a variety of deliveries. Find the most natural and comfortable style. Don't worry about sounding strange or foolish during practice sessions. No others need listen unless you want them to.

Be your own critic. If you record your presentations in advance, tune in to your own broadcast. Do you sound friendly, natural, sincere, enthusiastic? Do you come across as though you are talking with a friend, or do you sound as though you are making a public speech? Have you emphasized the right words and phrases, or does the whole message seem to run together on an endless belt? Do you like the person who is talking?

INTERVIEWING A GUEST

The interview is one of the most effective ways to present information to listeners and is a widely used technique on many radio shows. Too often the technique is poorly handled.

You change roles when you interview. You may know quite a

bit about the subject, but your guest is the authority. You represent your listeners as the seeker of knowledge. Anticipate the kind of information listeners want, and plan the interview to permit the guest to provide it.

With modern radio, interviews are brief. You may have only two or three minutes to cover a bit of information—seldom more than five minutes—unless you are the host on a special "talk" program.

Planning the Interview

Four elements are involved in a radio interview—you, your guest, the message, and the audience. The first three must get together in advance before the fourth can be served. Meet your guest in person or by telephone to discuss the purpose of the interview, the amount of information to be covered, and the kinds of questions you plan to ask.

Regardless of the formality or informality of this planning session, it can determine the success or failure of the actual interview. Check off the points the two of you will discuss.

The guest wants to know how his appearance fits in with the overall objectives of your series of presentations. He can assume that other programs have preceded his and others will follow. Let him know how he fits in.

Tell the guest what you hope to accomplish with the interview. Explain your purpose in terms of audience interests. Unless the guest is an experienced radio performer, he will undertake a broader range of topics than the interview can cover. Help him focus on the one, two, or three points you hope to make. Make sure he understands the time limit and the need for dealing in specifics rather than generalities. At the same time, make sure you fully understand the boundaries of your guest's knowledge. Such understanding will keep you from asking questions he is not prepared to answer.

While a good interview is never scripted in advance, both the host and the guest should know the route the interview will follow. It should have a logical beginning and ending. Tell the guest how you will open the interview, discuss the key questions you probably will ask, and let him know how you will clue him on available time as the interview nears the end. Assure him that you will avoid "surprise" questions.

The Interview

The listener has invited you into his home. You have brought a guest, and your first task is to introduce him properly. Your interview will not be scripted but you may want to write a short opening statement to introduce both your guest and the topic. Such prepared openings help you move quickly and smoothly into the interview without groping for the right way to get started. The opening statement should take only fifteen or twenty seconds and might go something like this:

> We have been visiting with you this week about the growing dangers of air and water pollution. This morning, our special guest is Dr. James Glissendorf, a wildlife specialist with the Illinois Natural History Survey. He has been studying the effects of water pollution on the nesting habits of wild ducks and other waterfowl. Welcome, Dr. Glissendorf. May I open our discussion by asking you to explain the cause of most of the water pollution in this area.

Always open the interview with a question or request that permits the guest to take the lead in the discussion. When appropriate, follow your opening question with supporting questions that show you are following his line of thought while giving him an opportunity to expand on his first answer. With the above example, a supporting question might be: "If industrial wastes are the chief cause of pollution, what are some of the other causes?"

When shifting the discussion and moving to new areas, make the transition smoothly. Let both the guest and the listener know that you are shifting directions as you ask the next question, perhaps something like this: "I want to come back to the causes of pollution in a moment, Dr. Glissendorf, but I wonder now if you would describe what happens to wildlife when pollution is severe?"

In phrasing your questions, rely heavily on those that ask how, what, or why. Avoid questions that can be answered with a "yes" or "no." Also avoid questions with implied answers, leaving the guest with little to do but agree or disagree. Don't, for example, ask Dr. Glissendorf a question such as this: "As I understand it, Dr. Glissendorf, most water pollution from industrial wastes could be avoided if the plants would install adequate filtering systems. Is that correct?" If the statement is correct, you have posed as the authority, and your guest becomes a head-nodder. If the statement is incorrect, you have placed the guest in the embarrassing position of either correcting you on the air or leaving the wrong impression with the listener.

The "two-in-one" question is almost as bad. You ask, for example: "Is there a way that industries could reduce water pollution, and, if so, why don't they do something about it?" By the time your guest has replied to the first part of the question, he, the listeners, and probably you have forgotten the second part. Always try to break your big question into a number of smaller ones, so your guest can answer more precisely.

As the interview nears the end, give your guest verbal or visual clues, or both. It is perfectly acceptable to mention the remaining time when phrasing the last or next to last question. "We have time for only two quick questions, Dr. Glissendorf. Here's the first one."

Reserve the last ten or fifteen seconds of your interview for a brief but unhurried closing statement that includes a "thank you" for the guest. Here again you may want to have your closing statement written in advance to assure a smooth ending. The following would be suitable for the above interview:

It's been a pleasure visiting with you, Dr. Glissendorf, and I know everyone listening feels better informed about the seriousness of our water-pollution problem. Thank you for joining us. Our guest has been. . . .

When you are off the air, take a few moments to review the interview with your guest. Make sure he is satisfied with the presentation.

YOUR OWN SHOW

The local station may ask you to host your own show if there is wide public interest in your subject. Extension county agents often host daily or weekly farm shows. Extension home agents have regular programs for homemakers. Your special field may have similar public appeal. If so, the station might welcome a regular program.

Normally, you will have a ten- to fifteen-minute time segment, with the frequency depending upon your schedule, the availability of information, listener interest, and the station's other program commitments. The show may either be sponsored or offered as a public service.

Select a Format

Given a fifteen-minute time block, first decide on the basic format for the show—the way in which you intend to spend each of those fifteen minutes. The format is the standard outline for the show.

Choice of format depends upon the subject areas, the availability of talent, and the interests of listeners. You can eliminate two formats rather quickly. First, you do not want to talk alone for the entire fifteen minutes, regardless of how skillful you are. You will soon run out of material, and the listeners will run out of interest. Second, fifteen minutes is probably too long to fill with an interview with one person. Listeners want programs broken into smaller bits and pieces. They expect a variety of information and a variety of voices.

Panel discussions. Many subjects are ideally suited for the panel-discussion format. If your field is health, you might host a panel of doctors, for example, for a continuing series of discussions on community health problems. Each week you and the guest panel of two or three specialists discuss one area of health —the common cold one week, heart disease the next, and so on. You could use the same panel members each week, or a new panel, or a combination featuring a regular member and one or two new members.

A teacher, a member of the school board, and a parent might make up a panel for weekly discussions on education. Local professional or amateur artists might be your guests for a wide-ranging series of discussions on art.

When hosting such a show, your tasks are to introduce the panel members, introduce the subject, open the discussion with a lead question, make sure all panel members have a chance to participate, and finally take the show off the air. Host a true discussion, not a series of questions and answers with you posing the questions and the different panel members giving the answers.

Panel and authority. A slightly different discussion format features a single authority and a panel of questioners. The "Meet the Press" program uses this format, with a panel of newsmen interviewing a prominent figure in the news.

Your show on health might feature a local doctor discussing various health issues with a panel of local citizens.

Parents might form the asking panel for discussions with the superintendent of schools on issues of education.

Your role is the same. Keep the discussion moving. While the authority has the technical knowledge, panel members will also have points of view that interest your listeners. Provide the environment for the expression of those views. After the authority has touched on a point, take a reading from one or more members of the panel. Avoid petty arguments with the authority, but don't be afraid to air different points of view. Not all of your listeners think alike. There is no reason to assume that your panel members do.

Friendly debates. A third format might feature two guests who participate in a friendly debate. Your objective is not to stir up controversy but to provide a platform for both sides of a question to be heard. Programs on community affairs are particularly suited to this format.

Careful advance planning is essential. Meet with your guests ahead of time to agree on the ground rules and the procedures. You may want to give each guest an opening minute to outline his position. After that, you keep the discussion alive with probing questions and requests for clarification.

You serve as the thermostat. A good debate should produce a little heat, but try to avoid those raging personality fires. A touch of humor often helps. If a particular question generates too much heat, shift the discussion to a different question, or moderate the tension with a comment of your own that summarizes the best points of both sides.

As host, always reserve the final moments for yourself. Take a half-minute or a minute to sum up the discussion, thank the guests, and end the program on a moderate note.

Audience participation. Many subject areas are ideally suited to formats featuring audience participation. You alone, or you and a guest authority, open the show on a particular topic and then invite listeners to phone in questions or comments regarding the topic. The participation of the listeners may be "on the air," or someone at the station can take the calls and relay the questions to you. You then repeat the question or the comments for the benefit of other listeners.

In either case, the program must be produced "live" at the station. If the listeners' questions or comments are to be broadcast, the station generally has facilities for recording and delayed playback, to screen out inappropriate calls. The success of the format depends upon the level of audience interest in the subject, and listener willingness to phone in questions.

The variety show. Often the variety show is the ideal format to match subject with listener interests. Agricultural leaders, for example, know that farm audiences are interested in programs that feature weather, markets, farm news, and farm information. The format for a fifteen-minute farm program usually includes those areas of interest. The time period might be broken down as follows:

1 minute:	Sign on, opening greetings, comments on the features for the day.
2 minutes:	The weather situation. Weather review, short- and long-range forecasts, the effect of the weather on farming conditions.
3 minutes:	The market summary. Yesterday's market review, anticipated livestock receipts for the day, and price outlook.
3 minutes:	Farm news report. Local, state, and national farm news, including announcements of farm events of local interest.
5 minutes:	A farm feature. Timely interviews with agricultural specialists or farmers, an on-the-scene recording from a farm fair, machinery demonstration, or other farm event.
1 minute:	Closing announcements and sign off.

The sequence of elements in the format can be changed, of course, and so can the time allotment for each element. But once a sequence has been established, follow it for each program. The listener likes to know that you will cover the weather at a certain time during the fifteen minutes or that the markets will always follow the weather, regardless of whether those items are reported at the beginning of the show, the end, or in the middle.

The set format also makes it easier for you to plan your show and to select the amount of information you need to fill the various time segments.

The variety-show format fits other subject areas equally well. The format for a program on education might feature segments on (1) local school news, (2) educational news from various sources, (3) answers to questions sent in by listeners, and (4) a featured interview with a specialist in the field of education. The same segments could be adapted for programs on health, recreation, home building, youth organizations, and a variety of other subjects.

Promote Your Program

Many people tend to be "station listeners" rather than "program listeners." Their sets may receive twenty or thirty stations, but they leave the dial set to only one. They like that station's program offerings, and they stick with it.

This listening habit works to both your advantage and disadvantage. Your program will have a certain number of automatic listeners, since they are already tuned to the station. Unless your show completely turns them off, they probably will keep you tuned in. You have the chance to turn casual listening into active, interested listening.

You also have an opportunity to attract new listeners to your program. But before the nonlistener can become a listener, he (or she) must know that your program is on the air. It's up to you and the station to let him know.

The station, of course, may do a certain amount of on-air promotion. They may "plug" your show during station breaks and at other times during the broadcast day. The objective is to make sure the regular listeners stay tuned in for your show. The station may also use newspaper advertisements, posters, and program listings to promote your show.

You have additional opportunities to contact potential listeners. Mention the show at your meetings or other events. Plug it in one of your direct-mail letters. Follow the advice offered by one of the top broadcasters in the country a few years ago. When asked how he built such a large audience for his program, he answered, "One at a time."

SAVE TIME WITH TAPES

If you plan to use radio regularly, buy a dependable, broadcast-quality tape recorder. The recorder will free you from the time schedule of the station, permit you to record news and features on location, and let you handle interviews in a less formal environment than a station studio.

With a little practice and a small investment in tape-editing equipment, you can edit a tape recording in much the same way that you edit a news story. By cutting and splicing, you can re-arrange paragraphs on the tape, take out whole sections if the tape is too long, erase mistakes and flubs, and even transpose sentences. The end product is often a better production than a live broadcast.

If you are unfamiliar with makes and models of recorders, seek the advice of the engineering staff at the radio station. They can also advise you on the station's quality standards, tape speeds, and recording techniques. Some makes and models feature accessories that permit them to operate on battery power as well as from standard electrical outlets. Battery conversion is desirable if you plan to record in the field, away from sources of electrical power.

Avoid the temptation, though, to purchase a so-called multiple-use recorder—one that you can use for office or automobile dictation, stereo playback, and so on. When you use your recorder for such purposes, it may not be available when needed for making broadcast tapes.

Once you purchase a good broadcast-quality tape recorder, you can, of course, use it in other ways. Interviews made originally for broadcast may also be used to add variety to meetings and conferences. Or you can use the recorder to improve your own speaking and delivery skills, and you may find it useful to help teach others such skills.

The Channel of Television

We were there. Transported by the wonder of television to what was then Cape Canaveral in Florida, we waited, watched, listened, and hoped as the thin pencil of a rocket blasted the first American astronaut into suborbital flight. The next year we were there again in the early hours as another rocket sent John Glenn into the first orbits of the earth, and we were there seven years later, late at night, as Neil Armstrong became the first man ever to set foot on the moon.

From the safety and security of our living rooms we have participated in national conventions, watched a hurricane smash into a city, and observed a riot from the edge of the crowd. At other times we have looked into the heart of a blast furnace, seen a tiger stalk its prey on the plains of India, and watched delicate surgery in a hospital operating room.

Everyone born in the twentieth century understands something of the impact of television. It has been called the "master" channel and the "monster" channel of communication. It can be either, both, or neither, depending upon the way the channel is used. It has the potential for great good or great evil. It has been credited with tremendous educational accomplishments. It has been charged with warping the minds of the young.

When used effectively, television can teach more people in less time than any other educational method, including the teacher in the classroom. It can also lure the mind away from education and the real world and into the world of fantasy and make-believe.

CHANNEL CHARACTERISTICS

Television's impact, of course, lies in its ability to transmit the language of sight and sound simultaneously from sender to receiver. Unlike public speeches and motion pictures, where sight and sound are also transmitted simultaneously, the receiver is given the message in his own environment. Television has the intimacy of radio and the believability of personal participation.

Television can show who, what, why, and how, as well as tell. Spoken and visual language reinforce the message. Through still and motion pictures, the receiver is transported to the scene of the happening—the walk on the moon, the making of a watch, the division of a human cell. Animated drawings show how a rocket engine works or how blood circulates in the body.

Television commands an attentive audience. Some people claim they can read and watch television at the same time, but there are few such people.

Television, then, can inform, inspire, motivate, and educate. But the channel has limitations.

Because television demands attentive viewing, it is highly competitive. You can't take it with you as easily as you can radio. Nor can you put the message aside for later attention as you can the newspaper or magazine. Television demands the viewer's time and attention now, at this moment, when the message is being transmitted. In a few years, when home video recorders become more common, this limitation may be removed.

Television is also competitive within the environment of family viewing. There may be three, four, or more radio sets in a home, and all may be portable. Each member of the family can listen to the program of his choice. The same home often has only one television set, and the choice of programs results from family compromise. The "vote" usually favors entertainment over education or information.

Television productions are expensive compared with the other mass media. The cost per person contacted may be low, however, when compared with face-to-face channels. Time spent in planning and preparing a message for radio must at least be tripled in planning and preparing that same message for television, unless you are content merely to televise a radio-type interview.

Television viewers tend to be critical. They are accustomed to the best talent the world has to offer. They are entertained by the stars of Broadway and Hollywood, lured by news and entertainment spectaculars costing thousands of dollars, taken on journeys to the moon and to the depths of the sea. When they switch on their television sets, they expect a professional presentation. The day of the bumbling amateur on television is over— if it ever existed. The viewer has too many choices to be entertained, informed, and instructed by highly skilled and competent professionals.

This does not mean that you should avoid using television. It does mean that you should not be a performer on camera unless you are willing to develop the kinds of talent television viewers expect of on-camera performers.

Most television stations have larger staffs than radio stations do, but the key positions are similar. Nearly every station has a station manager. On the program side, there will be a program director, news director, and perhaps a public-service director.

The majority of stations have network affiliations, and a large share of the program hours are filled by the networks. But nearly all stations produce a variety of local shows, with news programs heading the list. They may also produce community public-service programs, local documentaries, and variety shows that include many features—news reviews, public commentary, and educational items.

Nearly all stations carry visualized public-service spot announcements, and, like a radio station, the television station may have one staff member who is responsible for selecting the announcements and spotting them into the day's program schedule.

If you plan to use television, there is no substitute for a visit to the station to acquaint yourself with the staff, the organization, and the station's programming operations.

Become acquainted with the station's facilities and capabilities. Does the station produce all of its local shows in color? What news visuals can it use? Does it prefer slides, still photos, silent or sound film clips? Is the news staff large enough to cover all of the news events, or does the station welcome news and news-feature contributions? How does it want such contributions prepared? Who should receive them? What are the deadlines?

As with radio, the most logical outlets for your television material probably will be the station's news programs and public-service spot announcements. If the station produces community-service programs, local documentaries, or variety shows, you may be invited to appear on those shows or to prepare segments for them.

PREPARING TELEVISION NEWS

Television requires the same basic newswriting form as radio. There is the same need to alert viewers with the opening statement. If the viewer misses a key name or point at the start of the message, he cannot go back and re-listen or re-look. Television, like radio, can present only the top of the news, so the writing must be tight, direct, and uncomplicated. Television newswriting, in fact, must be somewhat slower paced than radio news, since the receiver must register the message with two senses— sound and sight. His sensing mechanism darts back and forth between the two, and if it lingers too long on sight, part of the audio message may be lost. When the writing is visualized, therefore, it must provide "seeing" spaces.

Not all television news is visualized, of course. Some of the news is read by the station's newscaster without visual support. Such news follows the form and style used for writing radio news copy.

Whenever possible, though, visualize television news copy. This is not as difficult as it may seem.

Think Visually

With radio, you think verbally—in terms of what you want to tell the listener. With television, think visually—in terms of what you want to show the viewer as you explain it. Because nearly all stations have color transmission, you show in color. This places obvious restrictions on visual alternatives.

Unless you are a professional filmmaker, or can afford the services of one, your best visual medium will be 35mm color slides. They are relatively inexpensive, flexible, and easy for the station's news staff to handle. When preparing slides, keep the following technical suggestions in mind:

Use horizontal slides rather than vertical. The station's projection mechanism can't handle vertical slides, and they don't fit the proportions of the television screen.

Shoot your picture so the visual message is confined to the center two-thirds of the picture. Of the total picture, only the center two-thirds will appear on the home screen. If the key to the message is outside of this area it will be lost to the viewer.

Slightly overexposed slides are better than underexposed ones. When taking slides expressly for television, open the shutter an extra one-half f-stop.

When covering events for television, anticipate the kinds of pictures that make news. Viewers are interested in people—people in action, doing things, demonstrating something, showing how. Think about the event in terms of those kinds of action shots. A picture of a speaker standing at the rostrum doesn't convey much action. Catch him when he is pointing, or clenching his fist, or doing almost anything except just standing. At best, pictures of speakers are undramatic, but if the speaker is the source of your message, viewers like to see the source.

If something is happening at the event, show that. Don't show the backs of people watching something happening. Show the happening itself—the new machine at work, the tree being planted, kids trying out the new swing at the park dedication, the farmer taking a soil sample.

Plan at least half of your pictures in advance. Reserve the other half for the unusual and unexpected.

Combine Picture and Message

While television news, especially news features, cannot be as immediate as radio news, the station wants your visualized report as quickly as you can get it to them. Color-film processing takes more time than black-and-white processing, but strive for twenty-four-hour service. The station can tell you where to get such service, or it may have its own processing facilities.

When you have your processed shots, select those that best visualize the message. Ideally, you should have one picture for every fifteen or twenty seconds of spoken copy. A one-minute report can handle from three to five pictures, depending upon the subject and the details of each picture.

Blend your writing to the visual, but avoid obvious references. The viewer should be able to associate the visual with the spoken message without clue words from you. Reference phrases such as "This next picture shows . . ." or "Here you can see . . ." or "This is a slide of . . ." irritate the viewers and interfere with the flow of the message. The visual will introduce itself on the screen if your message is keyed to it.

The physical preparation of the script shows the newscaster and the director how the audio and visual (video) messages should be tied together. Divide your news-copy paper into two columns with the right column about twice as wide as the left one. Head the left column "Video," and the right column "Audio." Write your message on the right, and use the left to indicate where the visuals should be inserted in the continuity.

The newscaster has one copy of this double-column script, and the director in the control room has another copy. The director follows both columns to know when to have the news-caster on camera and when to punch the button that replaces the newscaster's image with the called-for slide. The newscaster also follows both columns to know when he is on camera and when he is off.

Number and identify each slide. The slide number and identification also should appear in the video column opposite the sentence in the audio script where it is to be shown.

The following script shows how the message and visuals were tied together for on-air presentation:

HUMAN MOSQUITO BAIT MAY HELP
TO CONTROL ENCEPHALITIS

Video	*Audio*
Medium shot of Cliff Scherer and boys in background	Here in this two-thousand-acre swamp in southern Illinois important work is being done in an attempt to control the dreaded sleeping sickness disease—encephalitis.
Close-up of boys collecting mosquitoes	These fellows are acting as human bait so mosquitoes can be caught.
Shot of veterinarian in laboratory	The mosquitoes are frozen and sorted according to sex and species. These samples are then sent to the University of Illinois College of Veterinary Medicine where they are checked for the encephalitis virus. Researchers believe that birds and other warm-blooded animals act as a reservoir for the disease.
Medium shot of boys collecting mosquitoes	But it takes the pesky mosquito to carry the disease to humans. In case you're wondering, these fellows volunteered for this job. The mosquitoes are captured before the boys are bitten.

Video	*Audio*
Close-up of Cliff Scherer and boys	Researchers are checking many possibilities to learn more about the encephalitis disease and how it's transmitted to man. These boys are making a big contribution to help all of us be safe from the dreaded "sleeping sickness" disease.

PREPARING PUBLIC SERVICE SPOTS

Public-service spot announcements must be visualized. And the competition is keen.

Television stations receive far more acceptable public-service offerings each week than they can use. They also receive some unacceptable ones. The minimum requirements for acceptable spots are about the same as for radio. The source should be a recognized, nonpolitical, not-for-profit group or organization; the message should be in the public interest; and the length should be from thirty to sixty seconds. In addition, television demands high-quality visualization. Check with the station to learn the specific requirements.

Find out whether the station will accept color slide–script spots with the message read by an off-camera announcer. Some stations do, but many want the announcement on 16mm sound, color, motion picture film, or video tape.

Slide-Script Spots

If the station accepts slide-script public-service announcements, your production problem is simplified. Technically, you go about the task the same as when preparing a thirty- or sixty-second news report. For a thirty-second spot you need two or three slides, while a sixty-second spot requires four or five.

Television spots, like radio spots, can have only one clearly identified purpose. In a single short sentence, write what you

236 : *Communication: Methods for All Media*

want your viewer to know, think, or do. Have only one main idea to support your purpose. Here are some examples:

Purpose: Persuade mothers to keep medicines out of the reach of young children.
Main Idea: Children are naturally curious. They like to put things in their mouths, so if they can reach pills or medicines, they will put those things in their mouths.

Purpose: Keep children out of the yard when mowing with a power mower.
Main idea: Children like to be around where daddy is working, but a power mower can pick up and throw stones, sticks, and pieces of broken glass at a velocity of 100 miles per hour.

Purpose: Convince farmers to always turn off the power on a machine before cleaning and adjusting it.
Main idea: Time spent turning off power on the machine is infinitely small compared to the time lost if a hand or foot is injured.

With the purpose and main idea identified, use your double-column copy paper with headings of video and audio to "think through" your message and visuals. Do you plan to use positive or negative appeals? Will your visuals be actual picture slides or slides of prepared art work?

Actual photographs could easily visualize the spot on keeping medicines away from children. The first couple of shots could show a child drinking milk and eating cake, with the message stressing that children "think most anything is good to eat." The next shot could show a child on the floor reaching for pill capsules from an overturned pill bottle, with the message explaining that "to a child, brightly colored pills look just like candy." The final slide could show the mother placing a bottle of pills or medicine in a high medicine chest out of the reach of children.

Both picture and art slides could be used to visualize the power-mower message. The first photograph might show the "danger" by having a child running alongside the mower. The second could be art work showing the velocity of a thrown stone or stick. The third could show the child safely looking out the window at the lawn-mowing operation.

As with television news copy, write the message to support the visuals without referring to them. The viewer will make his own association.

During the planning stage, describe in the video column the needed photographs or art work. Outline the key points of the message in the audio column. Consider two or three different approaches during the planning process. The idea for a visual may suggest an approach to the message. Or the message may suggest new ways to visualize.

Once you have determined the final combination of visuals and message, use the outline to schedule your photographs and to write the final script. Provide the station with the set of slides and at least two copies of the final double-column script.

The Filmed Spot

Many stations prefer "sound on film" for public-service spots. The spot is either 16mm motion-picture film or video tape. The audio is either "voice narration," often called "voice over," or "lip-synchronated." With voice narration, an off-camera voice presents the message as the film progresses. There are no shots of people actually talking. With lip-synchronated sound, the people in the film do the talking. Lip movements and voice sounds are synchronized.

In general, narrated films are less complicated to produce, because the film is shot first and the narration is added later through an optical or magnetic process. With lip synchronization, both the film and the sound must be shot at the same time, and the processing lab fits the sound to the lip movements.

Motion-picture film, of course, can be shot anyplace. Video tapes are usually made with television cameras and a video recorder in a television studio or commercial video-tape studio. In either case, you probably will have professional services for the actual shooting and production. There is little need to cover the technical aspects of such production here. Be familiar with the limitations of such productions, however, before you decide on the type of public-service announcement.

Once you are familiar with the capabilities and limitations of films and video tapes, plan the filmed spot announcement as you would a slide-script spot. Use the same double-column copy paper to relate your audio message to your filmed visual progression. Describe the scenes in your motion picture in the same way you describe the slides in the slide-script presentation. Experiment with various sequences of scenes as you fit message to scene and scene to message.

As you arrive at the final combination of scenes and messages, assign time limits to each scene and each bit of message copy.

With the message "always turn off the power on machines" as an example, you might decide on a five- or ten-second opening shot of a farmer operating a corn combine in a field of corn. The message explains that "harvest time is a critical time and farmers are always in a hurry to get their corn harvested ahead of bad weather."

The scene could then shift to a close-up of the revolving gears, belts, and wheels of the corn combine in operation, with the message explaining the "five most dangerous areas" of a corn combine. This scene-message combination might take another five or ten seconds.

If the appeal is negative, you could next show a sequence of scenes of the farmer stopping his machine, moving to one of the five dangerous areas, and attempting to remove a corn stalk or some obstruction from the mechanism without turning off the power. If the sequence is done well enough, you need only a few words of message to underline the danger.

The next sequence might show the man on his front porch, with a hand or foot bandaged, looking at his unharvested cornfield. The message would point out the loss the farmer suffers because he tried to save a minute.

The positive appeal, of course, would show the farmer following the correct procedures.

The video column of your script can be used as a shooting

outline by the filmmaker. He will know the scenes you want, the way you plan to use the scenes, and the approximate length of each. Once he has shot and processed the film, he can then edit the work print to the exact footage needed to fit each time segment called for.

The final step is to voice the narration of the message so that the processing laboratory can combine audio and video on the final print.

CHAPTER 22

You Are on Camera

You may have opportunities to appear on television as a guest or as the host of your own show. And you probably won't start out as a "natural" performer, nor will you become one by reading this chapter. Skill and naturalness come with practice and experience. You may feel more comfortable when making your first appearance, however, if you are familiar with the studio environment and some of the techniques of on-camera presentation.

THE STUDIO ENVIRONMENT

Regardless of how many television shows you have watched, you may be unprepared for the strangeness of the television studio environment. Most studios will be smaller than anticipated. And the small space will be crowded with one, two, or three movable cameras; microphones; batteries of bright overhead lights; strings of cables; and odd assortments of furniture, studio props, projection stands, studio monitors, and people—many people.

Production Facilities

Cameras. Some stations may shoot your show with one camera, but most will use two or even three, if the show is complex or has more than one stage setting. A one-camera show is less confusing at first, but production is more restricted. Know ahead of time how many cameras will shoot your show.

Each camera is movable, and the cameraman shifts it from one location to another for the best shot. The director in the control room and the floor manager guide the camera movement.

Regardless of the number of cameras, only one will be "on" at any given time, and the "on" camera will show a red tally light on the front. When you are speaking to the audience look at the "on" camera.

Microphones. The studio has different types of microphones, and the type used depends upon the kind of presentation.

Most commonly used is the lavaliere microphone, usually referred to as the "neck mike." It fastens around the neck and permits a fair amount of body movement. It is used when there are two or three participants on a show or when the presentation calls for limited seated or standing movement.

If the presentation calls for considerable movement between stage settings, the studio may provide a "boom" microphone. The mike is suspended from a long, movable boom operated by a technician and can follow you around the set. The boom mike frees you from the trailing cord of the neck mike, but your movements must permit the boom technician to keep up with you. If you are talking as you move from one position, the trailing mike may lose your voice.

For talk shows, when participants are sitting at a table, the standard table microphone is used. The table mike restricts body movements, of course, since you must face the mike. It is difficult to turn to another participant without losing voice volume.

Studio monitors. In most studios you will notice one or

more TV monitors. The monitors help the production crew produce a smooth show. They are not there for you or the other show participants to look at. In fact, they may be turned so that you can't see them. We mention them only because they are a part of the studio environment.

If your show includes slides or film clips projected from the control room, you do watch the monitors to follow the progression of the film or slides, especially if you are "voicing" the narration over the visuals.

Presentation aids. Some studios will have a rear projection screen, usually located at the rear of the set, and slides, films, or other visuals are projected on the reverse side. When using the rear-screen technique, both you and the projected visual can be on camera at the same time. The projected visual can either serve as background or play a key role in your presentation. You can point to a particular feature of a slide or to the action being shown on a film clip.

The studio may also have one or more "flip-card stands." With the floor model, the card holder is mounted at camera height on a movable stand. Visuals, either photographs or art work, are mounted on cards, usually eleven by fourteen inches, and the cards are arranged on the holder in proper order. A member of the production crew flips the cards on cue from you, and the director switches the action between the camera that is focused on you and the camera that is on the cards.

The table-model flip-card stand rests on the table, and you can either flip the cards yourself or have someone flip them for you.

Teleprompters are standard equipment in many studios, and you may use them for some of your presentations. Copy is written or typed in large type on a roll of paper and unrolled on cue by a teleprompter operator. You need considerable practice and experience in using this device. The inexperienced person often looks and sounds unnatural, and viewers are sophisticated enough to detect reading from the teleprompter.

Film projectors. Slides, motion pictures, and video tapes are projected from the control room, and this projection equipment is not in the studio itself.

Studio Staff

There may be from four to six or more production staff members in the studio when you are on camera. They are not your audience, however, and you need be aware of only one or two people.

The director is in the control room, and you may not see him once the show is on the air. But he is the "man in charge" and has complete control of the show's action.

The floor manager is the director's "man in the studio." He sets up the studio before the show and carries out the director's instructions when the show is on. By hand signals he will give you the "start" cue, all other time cues during the show, and other instructions for a smooth presentation. He is *your* director in the studio.

Try to ignore the other members of the production crew in the studio—the cameramen, the boom-mike operator, the man or woman who is turning the flip cards. They will concentrate on their assignments and assume that you will concentrate on yours.

PERSONAL APPEARANCE

Unless you are an entertainer, you want the audience to be more interested in your message than in you, but your personal appearance can influence the way the viewer receives your message. While you can't change the shape of your nose, your height, or your weight, you can follow some tips that will put you on camera looking your best.

Unless you have perfect coloring for television, assume that at least a touch of makeup will improve your image, especially on color television. Most stations have the proper supplies, and you can get instructions from a member of the station staff. Makeup should be applied at the studio anyway, so there is little need to do it yourself ahead of time.

Both men and women should strive for a natural, well-groomed hair style. Men should avoid a too-close haircut immediately before a show to avoid a "scalped" appearance. A bald spot will show whether you want it to or not, so give it some makeup attention. Most women should avoid unusual hair styles and the "fresh from the beauty parlor" look.

Men will do best to stay away from extremely dark or extremely light colors and coarse pinstripes or plaids. A pale-colored shirt is better than a white one. Avoid loud colors and patterns. Select a solid-color tie that contrasts with your shirt. Wear clothes that make you feel comfortable.

Women should choose conservative colors for outfits that are smartly styled and tailored. Avoid frilly dresses, large prints and plaids, and outfits that have large masses of deep color or white. Also avoid unusual or extreme styles that may encourage the viewer to pay more attention to your dress than to you or your message.

YOUR PRESENTATION—NATURAL AND EASY

Your appearance on television may be "live" or filmed in advance. Presentation techniques are the same.

You have something to show and say to an audience of friendly people who have invited you into their homes. They are relaxed and comfortable, and they expect you to be the same.

Your audience is fairly sophisticated about television. Even though most of them have never been on television, they know something about cameras, microphones, teleprompters, and cue cards. They will not object if you make occasional natural references to *your* environment such as you might in saying, "Could we bring the camera in a little closer, so I can show the folks exactly how this gadget works?" Nor are they concerned about an occasional mistake or slip of the tongue. They have seen and heard such mistakes and slips before.

You will not go on camera "cold." Whether yours is a filmed or live presentation, you will review the presentation with the director and have at least a "walk-through." You may have one or more complete rehearsals, depending upon the length of the show and the complexity of the presentation. The director and floor manager need to check out lights, camera placements, microphones, and movements of participants. There should be enough advance review and practice to assure a smooth presentation but not so much that all of the freshness of the final on-camera performance is lost.

Use the sessions to check your appearance, your visuals, and your movements on the studio monitors, but forget the monitors during your presentation.

The Art of Being Interviewed

Being interviewed as a guest authority is a relatively easy introduction to the mysteries of television. But your role consists of more than appearing at the studio at a certain time with some answers to predetermined questions.

Planning. As the person with the answers, you work with the show's host in relating your knowledge to the interests and needs of the audience. This takes us back to the basic fundamentals of good communication. Your host should give you a fair idea of the audience characteristics. He knows whether his viewers are mostly men or mostly women, and he has some idea of their general knowledge of your subject. He can also explain the relationship of your presentation to his previous shows and to the future shows he has planned.

This audience knowledge, coupled with your knowledge of the subject, should permit the two of you to agree on specific content and the best approach for presenting the information. As with radio, the interview should be informal, but its progress should be structured. Know the types of questions your host will ask and the order of the asking.

With this background, concentrate on the information needed to answer the questions. If precise facts and figures are called for, have some notes in front of you or have the information written on cue cards off camera.

246 : Communication: Methods for All Media

On camera. Once the camera's red tally light goes on and the floor manager gives the "start" cue, place yourself in the hands of your host. You are his guest, and the audience expects you to respond to him and not to them.

For most interviews, forget about the cameras. Look at your host and not at your audience. Assume that the audience is listening to you and your host and watching over your shoulder. Respond naturally to your host's questions, using a conversational voice tone.

Let your answers be brief but complete. Avoid giving the entire "load" in one answer.

A picture or a simple chart or drawing may help illustrate a point. Have such visuals close at hand, either lying on the table in front of you or on a small card holder at the edge of the table. You and your host should agree in advance how such visuals will be cued in. He may say something such as, "I think the viewers would be interested in seeing that chart you were showing me a few minutes ago." You can then hold up the card or turn to the card holder to show the viewers. If both you and the illustration are on camera, it is desirable to look at the camera, since you are then talking directly to the audience instead of to the host.

Slides used to illustrate a point will be projected from the control room on cue from you or the host. You can glance at the studio monitor as you explain the illustrations.

Most interviews take place at a table or in suitable studio chairs. In either setting, find a comfortable position but don't assume that you must sit perfectly still throughout the interview. Some shifting of body positions is natural, and the audience expects it so long as you don't appear to be nervously fidgeting every second. Use natural movements and gestures, but avoid meaningless ones such as touching your tie, smoothing back your hair, tapping your fingers on the table top, or playing with pens and pencils.

Your host will close the interview and thank you for your participation. Respond naturally and maintain the atmosphere of the interview until the floor manager assures you that you are off camera. The camera may remain on you and the set until there is transition to an off-camera presentation. Don't start taking off your microphone or gathering your notes until you have the signal to do so.

Making Audio-Visual Presentations

While interviews are commonly used on television, they fail to take full advantage of the channel's ability to visually support and dramatize the message. Television is best used to *show* what, why, or how. Whenever possible, therefore, use your television appearance for an audio-visual presentation.

Go through the same planning process to determine what you want your audience to know, think, or do, and to select your message. Decide how to support your message with effective illustrations. Finally, organize your presentation to blend audio and visual segments.

Visual check list. Choice of visuals depends upon subject, availability, cost, and convenience.

Whenever possible, the audience likes to see the real thing. When presenting information on the proper procedures for starting vegetable plants or potting flowers, for example, use the containers, the soil, and the other materials the audience will use. If there are steps in the procedure that take place over time, use two or three setups. Show the audience how to start the seedlings, how to transplant them to larger pots in two weeks, and how to transfer them to the garden site in another two weeks.

When discussing the need for safe storage of medicine and drugs, have the actual pills and capsules on hand. Show the audience how they resemble the candy samples you hold in your hand. Show a well-designed storage cabinet or container with a suitable lock.

Use plants to show effects of disease, air pollution, or improper cultural practices. Have lamps and lighting fixtures on hand if your message deals with proper lighting for the home.

Models and mockups can be used effectively when an object is too big or too complex to handle in the studio. Use models to explain principles of landscape design, park renovation, the workings of complex machines or production systems.

Unfortunately, some models can be relatively expensive and time-consuming to construct. You may be able to borrow the one you need from a local source.

Many subjects, of course, can be effectively illustrated with 35mm color slides. Slides are relatively inexpensive and easy to use. They can either be projected directly from the control room or onto the rear-projection screen.

If motion is essential for interpreting and understanding the message, consider using 16mm color film clips or segments. Motion-picture film is especially valuable when showing how something works. The station may have facilities for producing the needed films. Silent film is acceptable, unless the sound of the action is essential to understand the message.

Drawings and other art illustrations mounted on cards can be used either alone or in combination with other visuals. Normally, the audience will have only a few seconds to look at the illustrations, so keep all art work simple and uncluttered. Make a visual impression but don't try to tell the entire story with one visual.

On some shows, the standard chalkboard can be used effectively. In most cases the board will be green, and you will use colored chalk. You or someone else can put the drawings and messages on the board ahead of time, or, if you have the skill, you can write and draw while making your presentation. Practice maintaining contact with your audience while using the board.

Flannel boards, magnet boards, and Velcro boards also can be used, but their use also requires skill and practice.

Regardless of the technique, make sure the visual can be seen and understood by the viewer. Viewer frustration sets in when you show him something that he either has to strain to see or can't see at all. Eliminate the visual if you have to tell the viewer what he is supposed to see.

Check with the station on preferred color combinations for art work on visuals. Station personnel can also give you tips on letter size and spacings. If you use visuals prepared for other purposes, take them to the studio ahead of time to make sure they will project and transmit on television. In fact, preview all visuals on camera whether they were prepared for another purpose or for the show itself.

Presenting your show.   Practice is the key to a smooth audio-visual television presentation.

Start with a working script. Again this script can be outlined on double-column paper with audio and video headings. Use the audio column to sketch the verbal progression of your message and to indicate the approximate amount of time for each segment. Normally, you will not write out a great deal of what you plan to say, but you will indicate key phrases and sentences that can serve as cues to visuals and camera selection.

The video column identifies the visuals and may include notations on how the visuals will be used, with phrases such as "holds up card," or "moves from table to model on stand."

The working script is used primarily by the director in the control room in calling for the right shots with the studio cameras and for the projection of off-camera visuals. The floor manager may also have a copy of the script, but he depends upon specific guidance from the director. You may also have a copy on the table in front of you, or the main outline may be on cue cards out of camera range. Ideally, you have practiced the presentation enough so that the progression is clearly in mind. Use the script only as a crutch.

You need not do all of your practicing in the studio. Start at home with a make-believe studio. For realism, place two medium-sized mirrors on stands or chairs at angles on your "set" to simulate studio cameras. Show your visuals to the mirrors and practice gestures and movements that you will use in the presentation.

Television cameras tend to exaggerate movements, so avoid quick, abrupt, and jerky motions. Give the cameraman time to move with you when you move. Be sure he is on target before discussing a visual. If the object must be moved for a better viewing angle, rotate it slowly. Don't put it down or remove it from the camera position until the viewer has had time to look at it.

Practice the technique of switching your attention from one "taking" camera to another. Lower your eyes for a moment and when you look up, be looking at the "on" camera. Avoid the impression of darting your eyes directly from one camera to another. Practice this technique in front of your two mirrors.

Maintain maximum eye contact with your audience by looking into the lens of the "taking" camera. If this seems unnatural, talk "through" the camera to the cameraman on the other side. Show him your visuals and explain their meaning so that he will understand you. If there are times when you must turn away from the camera to show or demonstrate something, keep those times brief and reestablish eye contact as often as you can.

Keep microphone placement in mind. Don't lean away from a table mike or walk away from a boom mike. If you are using a neck mike with a trailing cord, keep movements to a minimum. Few things are more distracting than to catch your mike cord on some object as you move to a new position on the set.

Remove most of the rough spots from your presentation through home practice. Go through a final rehearsal at the studio with the director, floor manager, cameramen, and other studio personnel.

In the final analysis, however, you carry the final responsibility for the success of your presentation. If you are unsure and unenthusiastic, there is nothing that the director or the cameramen can do about it. And the best visuals in the world probably won't save you. Know your subject and the mechanics of presentation well enough so that you can concentrate on getting your message across to the viewer.

CHAPTER 23

Communicate with Pictures

The camera, in skilled hands, is an invaluable tool for effective communication.

There is much truth in the adage that "seeing is believing." News pictures dramatize and confirm the news happening. We may read that fire completely destroyed the local lumberyard but *seeing* a picture of the blazing building or the fire-scarred ruins confirms the seriousness of the loss. A story may report that a thousand marchers gathered in front of the courthouse. The picture permits us to make our own estimate.

Pictures can do more than dramatize and confirm a news happening, however. Regardless of channel, good pictures can help achieve almost any purpose of communication. They can arouse interest and curiosity, create moods and impressions, furnish evidence, show how, tell why. Pictures can compare, contrast, or show change over time. They can do these things on television, in newspapers and magazines, as part of a direct-mail offering, and as visual support for speeches and conference discussions.

Good pictures can do those things. Poor pictures only inject "noise" into the communication system. They may distract rather than attract the reader or viewer.

251

Good pictures depend more on what goes on inside your head than on what goes on inside the camera. Many people try to substitute quality cameras for quality thinking. An expensive camera, like an expensive automobile, will only take you where you decide to go. Quality cameras and technical skills will help you take effective pictures only when you have decided where you want to go in the process of communication.

THE PURPOSE OF PICTURES

All communication intends to influence the receiver in some way. The sender of the message has a purpose, or a combination of purposes, for communicating: to inform, motivate, persuade, instruct, or entertain.

Pictures code messages visually so that receivers can accurately decode and interpret them. Pictures provide a visual rather than a verbal language for communication.

To Report Happenings

Newspapers and television report "news happenings." They inform the reader or viewer about *what happened*. When you cover such happenings, anticipate the activities that will make good pictures, and have an advance plan for taking them. Your primary audience includes those people who did not attend. Show them what those who were there saw, did, and learned.

If a group of parents tours a new school building as part of the dedication ceremonies, use pictures to show some of the features of the building. The audience may be interested in the modern chemistry laboratory, the self-study carrels, or the new recreation center. Show those features with pictures. Include some of the parents in the picture but avoid merely showing a crowd of people in a room.

Advance planning is especially needed for meetings featuring a series of talks. A picture of the speaker at the rostrum is the least informative. A crowd shot of people listening to the speaker is no better. If the speaker uses visuals, frame the picture with the speaker using his visual either during his presentation or when he finishes. Consider an informally posed shot of the speaker discussing his visual with one or two members of the audience following his address.

If there are exhibits or displays at the meeting, use them in your pictures. The exhibits are there to inform the attending audience; use them to inform the audience who could not attend. Add interest and action by having one or two people pointing out some interesting feature of the display.

Even though you know you can use only one or two pictures, take two or three times that many. Make your final selections after the pictures are processed. Don't try to save a few pennies on film and processing by taking only the one "best" shot. The day may be over before you find it.

To Arouse Interest in Events

You write advance news stories about your events to interest people in attending. You provide information to answer reader questions: (1) Why is the event being held? (2) What do I have to gain by attending—what rewards can I expect? (3) Who are the participants—the speakers, the audience?

Pictures can help answer those questions and arouse audience interest. Too often, advance pictures show the speaker, if there is one, but fail to show the problem or the reason for the meeting.

If your organization has called a meeting to discuss opportunities for improving the community's park system, take pictures of the park problems you hope to improve. Show broken swings, bare ground that should be covered with grass, kids drinking from a sprinkler pipe when they should be drinking from a fountain. For a positive approach, visit a neighboring community with a good park system and show how that community has improved its parks.

Use pictures of city blight to arouse interest in your conference on urban renewal. Picture some of the highlights that farmers will see on the scheduled farm tour.

Use candid shots of children playing in the street to

accompany your advance story on a meeting to plan better community recreation facilities.

One county agent used a picture of an out-of-state egg truck delivering eggs in his town to publicize a county meeting on opportunities for increasing egg production in the county. Another used a picture of a herd of top-quality cattle grazing legume-grass pasture to dramatize the benefits of soil fertility, a subject scheduled for discussion at his next farmer meeting.

To Motivate and Change Attitudes

Obviously you don't need events as an excuse to communicate with pictures. Pictures can be most effective when the purpose is to motivate and change attitudes of the audience whether there is a meeting or not. Pictures showing the need for park improvements will interest people in attending your meeting. Those same problem-identifying pictures will motivate people to support your park-improvement campaign when no meetings are planned.

Shots of junkyards, littered streets, dilapidated buildings, and abandoned automobiles can create favorable attitudes toward a community cleanup program.

You can use words to tell about the dangers of air pollution, but a picture of black smoke billowing from a smokestack will add force to your message.

A picture of a local stream clogged with tin cans, junk, and other debris will present your message on water pollution better than several hundred words.

One Midwest soil-conservation specialist shot a simple but dramatic picture of a rampaging, silt-loaded river breaking out of its banks after a heavy rain. The picture ran in all of the local papers with this caption: "Is your farm in there?" Five words and a picture vividly demonstrated the need for improved soil conservation practices in the county.

Pictures, of course, can identify solutions as well as problems, and your appeal thus would be positive rather than negative. A picture of a farmer standing in a gully on an eroded hillside hits the need for soil conservation from a negative angle. A shot of a farmer mowing a grass waterway plays up the positive.

Pictures of the problem help to establish an acceptance of the need to "do something." Pictures of somebody doing something about the problem may motivate others to similar action.

Before-and-after pictures identify the problem and also show the solution. They show the rewards for action and suggest that others can have similar rewards by taking similar actions.

Pictures can also compare and contrast the results of alternative actions. For example, in comparing the effectiveness of chemicals to control weeds, you could show a treated field and an untreated field. If your subject dealt with solutions to a landscaping problem, you might show the same yard planned for a family with teenage children and for a family with preschool children.

To Show How

You can tell someone how to do something. But if you can "show" him how, your teaching is more effective.

Whenever instruction is the key purpose for communicating, ask how much of your instruction can be given in pictures. How much of the messages can be visually coded?

Pictures can show the audience how to plant a tree, lay out a flower bed, cut out a dress pattern, grow seedlings, check for corn borers, take soil samples, repair a light cord, ride a bike safely, wear dresses to appear slimmer, reupholster furniture, landscape a yard, or build a flower box.

Television, of course, offers the ideal channel for showing and telling how. But how-to-do-it pictures also have a place in newspapers, magazines, and direct mail. Again, planning is the key. Describe each picture needed to illustrate your message before taking the camera out of the case. Avoid taking pictures first and then writing a message to fit the pictures.

Most of your teaching pictures will be close-ups. You can't

show how the husking rolls of a corn combine work by standing twenty feet from the machine. Get in close and take only that portion of the machine that helps tell your story.

SLIDES—PARAGRAPHS IN A PICTURE STORY

A good picture with an appropriate caption can tell a brief story by itself.

A series of 35mm color slides permits you to tell a more detailed and complete story either on television or at meetings and with other person-to-person channels. Each slide is a visual paragraph in the picture story.

Plan the slide series the same way you plan your news-feature story. Write in one sentence exactly what the audience should know, think, or do after they have seen the series. Next, outline the main points needed to achieve that purpose. Then list the number and kinds of pictures you will take to support each point. If you can get the point across with a single picture, stop with one.

Visual specialists often use a technique called "story boarding" to plan their slide sets. The technique is simple and makes sense. You may want to use it.

All you need is a supply of plain three-by-five inch cards and a convenient place to arrange and rearrange the cards as you plan the picture story. Sketch a rectangle on the left of each card the same size as a 35mm slide—1½ inches by 1 inch. (You may be able to buy story-board cards from a local photo supply shop and save yourself the effort of sketching in the rectangles.)

Start identifying your specific picture needs on the cards. Sketch a rough drawing of the shot you want in the rectangle on the left and briefly describe it in the space to the right. To complete the card, write below the sketch the message that might go with the picture when the series is presented.

You need not be an artist to use this technique. The sketch is only a rough guide for a picture idea. But the combination of sketch, brief description, and suggested message will tell you if, where, and how each particular picture fits into the planned series.

When cards are completed for all pictures in the series, start arranging them in possible sequences on a desk or table top. The visualized cards may suggest an approach different from the one you originally had in mind. The "No. 6" picture in the series may work out better if placed in the "No. 2" position. Or perhaps it should come later in the "No. 12" spot. The arranging and rearranging of the cards may reveal missing links in the story. You may need to add a shot or two. On the other hand, you may find that a couple of the planned shots tell almost the same story, so you take one of them out.

Sometimes you may see that one shot works so well it should be repeated again for emphasis or in summary. The story-board technique is especially helpful if others are working with you on the series. By glancing at the cards and the arrangement sequence, your associates can criticize the planned approach before you take a single picture. If you are planning the series but an associate will be taking the pictures, the final cards become guides for the photographer.

If you are producing a series of slide sets, consider using a simple display board for the cards. Staple or tack inch-wide strips of medium-weight cardboard to a three-by-four foot sheet of plywood, fiberboard, or heavy cardboard. Place the staples or tacks about three inches apart along each strip to form slots for the story-board cards. You can then hang the board on a wall and rearrange your cards by moving them from one slot to another.

Once you have completed the planning process, set up a shooting schedule for getting the right picture at the right place at the right time. Patience is a virtue any time and patience is essential for good photographs. Wait for the right shot. If the story calls for a picture of a herd of cattle eating grass, don't settle for a shot of cattle looking at you, just because you are in a hurry and want to get home to dinner. The story deals with the appeal of good pastures, not the appeal of good photographers. Once you have taken a picture you will be tempted to use it in the series even though it doesn't do the job.

When you show a substitute picture, you tend to make excuses. You say, "Well, those cows don't seem interested in the pasture, but I can assure you they like it." Or you say, "This machine wasn't working the day I was there, but I hope this picture gives you some idea of how it works when it is in operation."

Season of the year and time of day are obvious considerations. You can take snow scenes only in the winter and spring planting pictures only in the spring. If you need pictures of flooded streets to show the need for a better community drainage system, spot a location ahead of time that will give you the most dramatic angle. Then be ready to run when the rains come.

While each picture should support a specific point, strive for variety. Use close-ups whenever possible. Try for the unusual angle for special impact. Experiment with lights and shadows to bring out dramatic features. Take the shot called for on your story-board card, and then try two or three other approaches to see if there is a better way to shoot the action.

PICTURE TOOLS AND TECHNIQUES

Photography is one field where there is an abundance of literature and teaching aids on equipment and techniques. Much of it is free and can be obtained from any good shop that sells cameras and photo supplies. Most bookstores also carry a variety of "how-to-do-it" books and pamphlets on photography.

With little effort you can provide yourself with free or inexpensive references on camera selection, basic steps to good photography, using indoor and outdoor flash, taking close-ups, using different lenses and filters, taking time exposures, the secrets of night photography, using floodlights, and almost any other photography subject you can think of. We could not possibly review the wealth of technical information in a single chapter—or in a half-dozen chapters. And there is little need to do so, since the information is yours for the asking at the nearest camera shop.

Start Small—Grow Big

We can, though, offer some general suggestions and observations about cameras and camera equipment.

1. Select a camera for your primary photography job. If most of your assignments will be black-and-white news and news-feature pictures, buy a camera designed primarily for that purpose. If most of your pictures will be 35mm color slides, choose one for that purpose. Generally, you will be happier with one medium-priced camera for each task than with a single, more expensive camera that will do both.

2. Allow for improved skill. Consider a camera that will challenge your picture-taking ability. Anticipate that you will improve your skills to the level of the camera's capabilities.

3. Buy only from a reliable manufacturer. Make sure you have a place to turn to if you need repairs or replacement parts. Consider the trade-in or resale value of reputable makes and models.

4. Look for ease of focusing. Some models have brighter viewfinders and simpler focusing mechanisms than others. Try out the various kinds and pick the mechanism that feels most comfortable to you.

5. Check the lens. Lens quality helps determine the technical quality of the picture. If you anticipate the need for interchangeable lenses, buy a model with this capability even though the initial cost is higher. For the average assignment, a moderate lens is more useful than a telephoto lens.

6. Consider an automatic diaphragm. This is an added-cost feature on the basic camera. You focus with the diaphragm open, but it closes to a preset aperture for correct exposure when the shutter is snapped.

Ten Tips for Good Pictures

Until you complete your file of photographic references, follow these ten tips for improving your picture-taking skills:

1. *Recognize total perception.* You have selective percep-

tion. For any scene, you see what interests you most—what you want to see. If you are late for an appointment as you hurry down a street, you *see* the clock on the corner, and screen out other views. Your friend on the same street has a headache and wants to buy aspirin. He *sees* the sign for the drugstore but doesn't see the clock on the corner. The camera has total perception. It sees and records, without selection, all images seen by the camera lens. Unless you recognize this, your shot of the street scene to show the clock may actually end up with the drugstore sign as the main feature. When you look through the viewfinder, make sure you see the whole scene and are satisfied to have that scene recorded. If the scene is not what you want, move closer or change your angle so you and the camera are seeing the same thing.

2. *Concentrate on centers of interest.* The center of your picture is not the main "center of interest." Actually, there are four interest centers in each picture. To locate them, use a sheet of paper the same size as your photo print. Draw two lines vertically and two horizontally to divide each dimension into equal thirds. The centers of interest are where the vertical and horizontal lines cross. Compose your picture so that the main feature is at one of those four intersections.

3. *Stress unity of action.* Let each picture concentrate on one message—one focal point or one piece of action. Avoid side actions that compete with the main attraction. If there is a small child in the corner of your shot of the aware presentation, you can be sure the child will steal the scene from the action of the presentation.

4. *Avoid clutter.* Clutter detracts from the unity of action. You may have to "police" the scene to remove unwanted objects. When photographing people, stay away from flowery drapes as background. As pretty as they may be, they provide clutter, and your print may show a beautiful rose growing out of the head of your main speaker. If a chair, table, or floor lamp is not needed in the scene, move it out of the way.

5. *Move closer.* The camera lens tends to lengthen distance.

What seems close to you shows up rather far away after the shutter is snapped. Move in on the scene—closer than you think you should so long as you don't leave out a key part of the picture. Close-ups achieve unity of action and help avoid clutter.

6. *Add depth to flat shots.* Outdoor medium-distance shots tend to be flat. Try to use a familiar foreground object to achieve the feeling of depth and dimension. Your shot of the landscape design will have more depth if you "frame" it with something in the foreground—the edge of a tree trunk, the corner of the house, or the leaves of an overhanging tree limb. Keep your foreground objects away from the centers of interest.

7. *Keep up the angles.* We normally see things from a standing, eye-level position. But there is no need to take all of your pictures from that angle. Some pictures will be more dramatic and convey the message better, if you look down on the action. Stand on a chair or the top of your car to get the shot from a higher point of view. Other scenes may require you to get down where the action is. Your position may seem awkward at the moment, but the pictures will be better. Head-on shots become monotonous, too. You may get a more effective angle shot by turning your subjects slightly.

8. *Manage the horizon.* Except for close-up shots, the horizon plays a role in most outdoor pictures. Adjust the angle of your shot to avoid a half-and-half effect, with the horizon dividing your picture in the middle.

9. *Encourage close harmony.* People, especially Americans, seem shy about getting too close together. When taking pictures of three or four people, move them "uncomfortably" close together. They won't seem that close when the print is developed. Have them doing something besides looking at the camera. Then move in close to concentrate on faces.

10. *Use lights and shadows.* Lights and shadows can be used to show contrast, create moods, and focus attention on your subject. Don't be afraid of shadows unless they block out a part of the message you want to get across. When that happens, use outdoor flash or reflected lighting to remove the shadows.

CHAPTER 24

Other "Visual Aids"

Pictures are only one of a wide variety of visuals that add interest and impact to written or spoken messages. We commonly refer to such visuals as "visual aids" to suggest such a supporting role. There are times, though, when the visual plays the leading role, and written or spoken words lend support.

Actually, the assignment of either leading or supporting roles is academic and not particularly important. It is the combination that is important. With few exceptions, we communicate most effectively when we use a combination of verbal, audio, and visual symbols.

We have discussed the role of photography and other visuals in the mass-media channels of press and television. We will concentrate now on use of visual aids in face-to-face communication— meetings, seminars, workshops, and other formal and informal teaching situations.

A THREE-PURPOSE FUNCTION

Good visuals take time, effort, and usually money to plan and produce. They require effort and skill to use. Unfortunately we may use lack of time, skill, or money as reasons for not using visuals. Often, the real reason is lack of conviction that visuals are worth the effort. They are, for three reasons:

1. *Good visuals attract and hold the receiver's interest.* We mentioned earlier that audiences at meetings have leftover listening time. The receiver can hear words at a faster pace than the speaker can send them. With straight talk, the receiver may lose interest in what's being said. Visuals help refocus his attention on the message.

2. *Visuals help the receiver interpret meaning.* Visuals can simplify complex concepts and principles, show comparisons and contrasts, demonstrate processes and procedures, and point out relationships. Some studies have shown that good visuals permit us to "teach" as much as 35 percent more material during a given amount of time than we can teach without visuals.

3. *Visuals increase message retention.* It is impossible, of course, to assign a precise value to the "memory aid" of visuals, although many studies have tried to do this. Some studies show that visuals can increase message retention by as much as 50 percent. All agree that the contribution of visuals is significant, with the precise value dependent upon the type of message, the kinds of visuals, and the characteristics of the audience.

To achieve this three-purpose function, a visual should (1) be appropriate and have a clearly defined purpose in the presentation, (2) be simple, accurate, and attractive, and (3) be visible.

A visual without a purpose may be worse than no visual at all. Some people tend to "throw in some visuals just to brighten the presentation." Such visuals may arouse interest, but the interest may be in the visuals themselves and not in the message. Make visual planning a part of your overall presentation plan. Once you have identified the messages, consider the specific ways that visuals can help the audience understand and remember those messages. If a visual doesn't contribute to interest, understanding, or retention, don't use it.

Simplicity and accuracy are obvious requirements of good visuals. In general, each visual should present or clarify only one idea, and the receiver should be able to "get the idea" at a glance. If the receiver must spend more than five or ten seconds figuring out what the visual is saying, or if it must be supported by a long, detailed explanation, the visual fails its purpose. Think through the presentation again, and use visuals that are easier to grasp and understand. While visuals need not be made by professional artists or graphic specialists, they should be neat and attractive, with art work carefully done and lettering that is neat and readable.

Visibility is perhaps the most important characteristic of a visual aid. Too many visuals are simply not visible. Either the object or image is too small for the size of the audience or there are too many details for the audience to see clearly. Audience size is the key factor in determining the kind of visual to use. A visual seen by only the favored few in the front rows distracts rather than aids.

Some people are reluctant to use visual aids because of difficulty in choosing one type of aid over another. It seems easier not to use any than to make choices. Other people select or stumble onto one type of aid and use it to the exclusion of all others. They use all slides, or all charts, or all posters, and ignore other techniques that might be more effective for a particular message or a particular audience.

We can simplify the task of choosing a suitable visual technique by classifying the variety of visual aids in terms of their basic characteristics and the way in which we would use them in a presentation. Most aids then fall into one of the following three categories: (1) display visuals, (2) active visuals, and (3) projected visuals.

SELECTING AND USING DISPLAY VISUALS

As the category suggests, display visuals are completely prepared visual units that require little or no manipulation during the presentation. They tend to be static rather than active and are often referred to as "static visuals" or "static graphics." They can be effective when used with relatively small audiences.

Actual Objects and Samples

If you want to show a small audience of home gardeners how a certain disease affects a tomato plant, a plant may tell the story better than any other visual. If your message deals with characteristics of different types of carpets and floor coverings, use samples of the various types to get the message across. You can best talk about the advantages and disadvantages of various kinds of home fire extinguishers when you have a selection of the extinguishers on display.

Actual objects add realism to the presentation, but they must be big enough to be seen easily while on display, or suitable for passing from one member of the audience to another. If actual objects are available and suitable, always give them first consideration.

Models

Consider using models when actual objects are too small to be easily seen or too big for easy transportation. Models can provide a dramatic visual impact when small objects are reproduced in giant size and when large objects are miniaturized.

Most models, however, are relatively expensive and require a fairly high degree of professional skill to design and produce. They are most effective when a three-dimensional form is needed to clarify the message. Take-apart models are effective in showing how a machine or system functions.

Maps

Maps have a multitude of uses as effective display visuals. They have a place whenever the message is related to location, distance, or area. Use maps to compare and contrast economic growth, population movement, production characteristics, rainfall, weather movements, building sites, soil types, water resources, natural and artificial drainage systems, recreation areas, and almost anything else related to space. A map can show the world or a part of a city block. Maps can show the audience "where they are" in terms of social, economic, and geographic factors and in comparison with "where other people are" relative to those same factors.

You can easily obtain basic outline maps for almost any area of interest. With words, figures, symbols, and other visual devices, you can convert such basic maps into effective display visuals.

Charts and Graphs

Well-designed charts and graphs can present statistical and other complex information quickly, easily, and effectively. The distinction between a chart and a graph is largely academic, and most people use the two terms interchangeably. In general, charts present information as a single-dimensional concept, while graphs show change on a two-dimensional basis. For example, a chart would show average corn yields by areas of the state or nation in a given year. The single dimension is average yield at a given point in time. A graph would show yield trends over a period of years with the two dimensions—time and yield—being related.

Line graphs are most commonly used to show trend relationships over periods of time. One line on the graph, for example, can show the trend of hourly wages during the last ten years, while a second line can show the trend of food prices, housing, automobiles, or other types of purchases.

Bar graphs also can show trends but are more commonly used to show changes in relationships between two or more factors.

Pie or circle graphs and charts are effective in showing the parts of a whole. By dividing the pie or circle into segments, you can show where the consumer spends his food dollar, how the government spends its income, or the uses made of cropland in a county or area.

Charts and graphs should be used as headlines are used in a news story. They should highlight the main feature but not tell the details.

Posters

Posters or display cards can also highlight the main features of a presentation. Think of them as headlines or chapter titles. If the message contains five main points, prepare a poster or display card for each of those points, using a simple illustration and a few key words on each card. Reveal the cards one at a time as you come to the particular point in the message.

Use one or more posters as "summary cards" at the end of the presentation to list the four or five points for the audience to remember. Use key words or phrases rather than complete sentences. Simple illustrations help the audience remember the words.

Special Considerations

Most display visuals require a minimum of manipulation. They can be prepared in advance and placed where wanted before the presentation. Posters, charts and graphs, maps, and most other display visuals should be "hidden" from the audience until they are referred to. Premature display of visuals encourages the audience to get ahead of you. Reverse the visuals on the display stand or lay them face down on a table until you are ready to use them. Whenever convenient, keep actual objects or models out of sight or covered with a display cloth. The act of "revealing" the visual can be an effective part of the presentation and serves to refocus the audience's attention.

Use display visuals for groups of twenty to forty people. Don't use them for audiences larger than fifty or seventy-five people.

SELECTING AND USING ACTIVE VISUALS

Active visuals permit a high degree of manipulation. Part or all of the component units are prepared in advance, and you reveal or build up the visual story as you go along.

Chalkboard Visuals

The chalkboard is one of the oldest, yet most modern, and often most poorly used visual aid available. Old-fashioned blackboards have been replaced by permanent and portable greenboards, yellowboards, and boards of many other colors. White chalk has been supplemented by chalks of many hues and shades.

With some advance planning and a minimum of chalkboard skill, you can produce dramatic visual effects with this versatile aid—with only a modest investment in time and effort.

Use the chalkboard for formal presentations, illustrating and highlighting the main points as you present them. With practice, almost anyone can illustrate with stick figures and simple designs. If you completely lack artistic skills, have a friend lightly sketch illustrations on the board in advance. Then trace over the sketch at the appropriate time. In fact, you can have the entire presentation lightly sketched in advance, including both the key words and the illustrations. This saves time, avoids mistakes in spelling, and permits a neater presentation.

The chalkboard is probably best used when the audience is actively involved. Key conclusions of group discussions can be recorded, changed, rearranged. Sketches can be made of possible organization plans and the sketches can be changed as new ideas are registered.

Chalkboard visuals and words can be used to record, explain, emphasize, clarify, or challenge. With a sketch and a word or two, you can register an idea or a concept, raise a question, or record an answer.

Newsprint Pads

The newsprint pad is the first cousin of the chalkboard. You can buy large pads of newsprint stock at most newspaper offices or paper supply houses. They have advantages over chalkboards.

As you build the visual message, you simply turn the page for more space rather than erase the board. You can combine a formal presentation with a visualization of the results of informal discussions. Some of the pages can carry precompleted visuals, and others can be left blank or partially blank for visual buildup during the presentation and discussion. With colored chalks, crayons, or felt-nibbed pens, visibility may be better than with chalkboards.

Both chalkboards and newsprint pads will accommodate about the same audience size—ideally, fewer than fifty to sixty people.

Visual Buildup Boards

A visual technique called the flannel board became popular in the 1950s. It is still widely used, and has been joined by magnet boards, felt boards, Velcro boards, and boards covered with other materials that permit visuals to cling to the display surface. You use the same visual technique regardless of the material used on the display surface or as backing for the visual units.

Buildup boards are ideal for formal presentations when showing the step-by-step development of an idea, concept, or process. Visual units—pictures, drawings, words, symbols—are prepared in advance and arranged in order of presentation. You then build up the visual story during the discussion.

Advance planning, careful selection of visual units, and practice are all needed for an effective presentation. Pictures, sketches, and diagrams must be simple and free of distracting detail. Words should be bold, active, precise, and few. Each visual unit should relate to all other units in the final display.

Colleagues in the visual field have identified and labeled some of the "sins" to avoid in making buildup-board presentations. The following are the most serious:

Visual waving. The speaker picks up the visual unit before he is ready to place it on the board. He waves it in the air, jabs it at the audience, reveals part of the sketch or the wording, or gives the viewer an unwanted glimpse of the backing or adhesive.

Discarding. The speaker uses visual units prepared for some other occasion and does his editing as he goes along. He sorts through his array of visuals, selecting some and discarding others, leaving the audience more intrigued with the discarded visuals than with the message.

Overkill. The speaker is not sure the visual will convey the point so he explains the visual before displaying it and repeats the explanation for emphasis. The audience becomes irritated by the continuous repetition. The opposite sin is committed by the speaker who tries to make a key point while displaying his visual. The audience is caught trying to see the visual and misses his words.

Troweling. The speaker carefully places his visual on the display board but seems unsure that it will stay there. He repeatedly smooths it with his fingers, presses it with the palm of his hand, and conveys his lack of confidence to the audience.

Blocking. After placing the visual on the board, the speaker either talks to the board or continues to stand in front of the visual when he turns toward his audience. In either case, he has effectively blocked the audience's view of the visual.

Effective use of the buildup board technique assumes a degree of showmanship. Your movements are part of the visual process. Watch your audience for feedback signs that tell you when to increase or decrease the pace. If some members of the audience have difficulty seeing the display board, hold your visual units for them to see before placing them on the board.

SELECTING AND USING PROJECTED VISUALS

There are few display or active visuals suitable for audiences of more than fifty to seventy-five people. For large audiences, use techniques that project an enlarged image of your visual.

Slides and Filmstrips

You are familiar with slide and filmstrip presentations, of course, and appreciate the versatility and adaptability of this visual technique. For most situations, slides are more flexible and easier to adapt to local situations than filmstrips, but both are convenient, practical, and easy to use.

If you have prepared charts, graphs, posters, maps, and other display visuals for use with small discussion groups, photograph such visuals and project them as slides for larger audiences.

Motion Pictures

There are many commercial and educational sources of 16mm color-sound motion pictures covering a wide variety of topics. You may be able to borrow or rent prints that will contribute to your presentation.

Super-8mm camera and projection equipment is becoming increasingly popular and relatively inexpensive. If you have an interest in motion-picture photography and a need for visuals that show motion, investigate the potentials of this technique. You may not want to go into complete color-sound productions, but you can use the 8mm camera to produce silent color film clips and segments to add variety and dramatization to your presentation.

Overhead Projection

With the overhead projector, you project the visual image over your shoulder onto a raised screen a short distance behind you. The size of the visual transparency or "slide" depends upon the size of the machine's horizontal projection platform. Most platforms are ten by ten inches.

The overhead machine will project any transparent material in color or black and white, and all manufacturers provide detailed instructions for making and using transparencies. Most office copying machines will reproduce black-and-white transparencies on special projection paper. The process for making color transparencies is slightly more complicated and requires special equipment.

Overhead projectors also are equipped with rolls of transparent paper that permit you to use the machine as a projected chalkboard. The paper rolls over the projection platform, and writing is projected onto the viewing screen behind you. With the overhead-projection technique, you face the audience. You can view the visual on the projection platform without turning your back to the audience to look at the screen. By using acetate overlays, you can build up the visual by adding and taking away visual features.

Opaque Projection

In general, the opaque projection technique is less versatile than slide or overhead projection, but it has certain specific advantages.

With opaque projectors, you can project any visual image from a flat, opaque base. Original art work, illustrations from books and magazines, and pictures can be projected directly without being converted to a 35mm slide or an overhead transparency. With the opaque projector, you can turn to a variety of sources for ready-made visuals. Make sure, though, that you don't infringe on copyrights.

COMMUNICATE WITH COLOR

We live in a world of color, and wise use of colors can increase the effectiveness of visuals. Colors can create moods and atmosphere, focus on highlights, and stimulate viewer interest. By themselves, colors tend to have special meanings for most people. We think of blue as a cool color and red as a hot color. This color-meaning list shows the feeling each color generally conveys:

Black—formal, neat, rich, strong	Orange—festive, gay, harvest
Blue—cool, melancholy, depressed	Yellow—warm, light, ripe
Purple—royal, rich, imperial	Green—fresh, growing, youth
Red—love, anger, hate, heat	White—pure, clean, neat, fresh

Color combinations affect legibility. Studies show that black on yellow is the most legible, and blue on red the least legible combination. The ranking from greatest to least legibility runs like this: (1) black on yellow, (2) green on white, (3) red on white, (4) blue on white, (5) white on blue, (6) black on white, (7) yellow on black, (8) white on red, (9) white on green, (10) white on black, (11) red on yellow, (2) green on red, (13) red on green, and (14) blue on red.

In choosing color combinations, keep in mind that cool colors such as light green, blue, and grey tend to recede and are best suited for backgrounds. Use bold or warm colors such as black, red, yellow, and orange for emphasis.

In general, light colors make objects appear larger, while dark colors tend to reduce the size of objects. Heavy, dark colors tend to pull the eye downward; when used at the top of a visual, they give it a top-heavy appearance.

Consider lighting, too, when selecting color combinations. If you plan to use your visuals at night under artificial lighting conditions, check your color combinations under those conditions.

If your visuals will be used on television at some time, check with the station on preferred color combinations.

USE LEGIBLE LETTERING

Good visuals should contain few words, and the words should be legible to every member of the audience. Legibility depends upon the size and characteristics of the lettering. Estimate the distance between the last-row viewer and the visual, and use the following guide to determine needed lowercase letter height:

Letter Height	Viewing Distance
¼ inch	8 feet
½ inch	16 feet
1 inch	32 feet
2 inches	64 feet

Use equal spaces between letters. The normal rule calls for the space between letters to equal the width of the letter stroke. The width of the letter stroke should be about one-fourth to one-fifth of the letter height. Use simple, clean letters without serifs. Lowercase letters are easier to read than all capitals. Except for selected points of interest, use the same letter style for the entire visual. Combinations of letter styles create clutter and confusion.

CHAPTER 25

Exhibit Your Message

People like to window-shop. That's why merchants pay such high rent for choice locations where foot traffic is heaviest. They spend thousands of dollars for plate-glass windows and thousands more for effective displays. They use their windows to communicate with prospective buyers.

You have something to sell whenever you communicate. You are "selling" a product, an idea, a practice, or a bit of information. You can display and exhibit your message as a supplement to the other communication channels.

There is no easy way to define an exhibit. The Museum of Science and Industry in Chicago is filled with exhibits. Some are as simple as the round ball of special metal that you lift to prove the tremendous weight of the metal. Others are as complex as the model underground coal mine, complete with elevator shaft, coal cars, mine lamps, gas warning signals, and other details.

An exhibit can fill a building at a world's fair or fit on the corner of your desk. It can cost $10 million or 25 cents. It can be simply something to look at, or it can be complete with buttons, knobs, levers, spinning wheels, flashing lights, and all sorts of gadgets for the audience to push, pull, or turn on and off. The message of hunger in the world can be told with an exhibit featuring a picture of a single starving child. It can be told more fully with a larger, more detailed exhibit that shows trends, explains why, and suggests solutions.

We will discuss here the kinds of low-cost exhibits that you can design and build with a minimum of professional help. Your investment should be high in imagination and ingenuity but low in cost of materials. Although the same principles apply regardless of cost, you will be money ahead to seek the services of an exhibit specialist for a complicated, high-cost display.

THE GAME IS THE SAME

An exhibit, whether large or small, simple or complex, is a person-to-person channel of communication. All principles of the communication process apply. The viewers are the receivers of the message. The exhibit in its environment of room, window, or county fair is the channel. You select the message and code it in visual, verbal, and perhaps audio symbols.

The Audience—Who and Where

The store owner knows that all sorts of people pass by his windows. While he would like to attract as many viewers as possible, he designs his window display for a special segment of the total audience. When he features modestly priced teen-age fashions, he directs his message toward teen-age girls and their mothers from middle-income families. He is not much concerned about the interests of the rich.

Be equally precise in your audience identification. If your exhibit is in a public place, many people will pass by it. But of all the passers-by, which ones do you most want to pay attention to your message? Are they young, old, middle-aged? Are they parents, homeowners, professional people? What do they know about you, your organization, and your subject? As with any other channel, the audience should determine message selection and treatment.

Environment is equally important. Exhibits are effective only if they are seen by the intended audience and only when the environment gives people the seconds or minutes needed to receive the message.

You may consider using an exhibit for a special occasion or event—a meeting, community fair, home-and-garden show, or field day. The event selects the audience. You must decide whether that audience will be interested in your subject and message. If not, save your time and money. Avoid being lured by the planners of the event who may urge you to be "represented" with an exhibit. If your subject doesn't fit, only the planners will know you are there. The audience won't.

Think about two other factors when considering exhibits for special events and occasions. First, will the audience response to your exhibit justify the time and expense of building it for one-time use? This question poses a difficult dilemma. You may have a better exhibit if you design it specifically for this one event. The approach, however, may limit its use for other occasions. If you design the exhibit for multiple use, you may reduce its effectiveness for the special event.

The second factor is competition—as to both kind and amount. For most special events, your exhibit will be but one of many and the expected audience may or may not have time to see all of them. With limited time, the audience pays attention to those that interest them most. Decide whether your exhibit will be one of the attention-getters. If the event features extravagant displays and free entertainment, your exhibit may be lost in the crowd. You might attract more people more effectively by getting permission from a downtown merchant to place your exhibit in one of his main street windows.

Don't underestimate the value of display windows, either downtown or in suburban shopping centers. If your subject is noncommercial and noncontroversial, many store owners will provide window space for exhibits on subjects of community interest. Exhibits on 4-H, Boy Scouts, Girl Scouts, and other youth programs are welcome almost everywhere. Most machinery dealers would gladly donate display windows for a week or two for an exhibit on soil and water conservation. Home-beautification exhibits are natural for lumber companies, hardware stores, and flower shops. If you want to reach homemakers with sewing information, a logical exhibit spot would be a local store that handles fabrics and sewing supplies.

People, of course, do more than walk past store windows. They go inside, and many businesses have lobby and display areas suitable for small, well-designed exhibits. Consider locations such as banks, savings associations, real-estate offices, local airports, railroad stations, medical centers, automobile salesrooms, and other professional and business establishments.

The Message—What and Why

Some studies show that you may have as little as sixty seconds in which to communicate your message. That's an average figure, of course, and it won't apply to every exhibit in every environment. But don't count on much more time than that. The world is filled with things to see and do, and people are in a hurry. Your exhibit must stop them, "speak" to them, and let them move along before the second-hand reaches sixty. That's not much time, but it is the length of most radio and television commercials.

Exhibit planning starts with message purpose. Again, what do you want the viewer to know, think, believe, or do after he has given you sixty seconds of his time? How will the viewer benefit from knowing, thinking, believing, or doing what you want him to? Answer those two questions before you start thinking about designs, shapes, sizes, materials, or specific message content.

You want the viewer to contribute to the United Fund, vote "yes" on the school-bond issue, wear safety belts, equip his home with fire extinguishers, follow soil-conservation practices, stop littering the streets and highways, join in the community-beautification program. Why? If you can't translate your purpose in terms of the viewer's interests, wants, and needs, chances are the viewer won't make the translation for you. With only sixty seconds to spend, he doesn't have time.

The Appeal

The what and why of purpose may suggest the appeal. The purpose may relate to problems the audience recognizes and wants to solve. The appeal is then easily identified. You need only say, "Here is how you can solve your problem." An exhibit at a home-and-garden fair that shows and tells how to control lawn weeds appeals to the built-in needs of the audience. An exhibit at the same event on "wise use of pesticides to prevent personal injury" will not have the same built-in need for an appeal peg.

Most people are patriotic and community-minded. But most people also are self-oriented. An appeal to patriotism or the "good of the community" will not be as effective as an appeal to self-interest. This may be unfortunate, but it is true. Parents will pay attention to an exhibit on the need for higher school taxes when the message relates to better education for their children. The appeal to nonparents must be in different terms—perhaps the longer-range benefits that a better school system will bring in terms of higher property values, more job opportunities, a lower crime rate.

Consider exhibit design and construction only after you have identified the audience, selected the message to fit the viewer's interests, and chosen an appeal that satisfies his wants and needs.

DESIGNING AND BUILDING SIMPLE EXHIBITS

A complete news story includes the headline, the lead, and the body. Most exhibits have a headline, a message, and "visual content." The headline, with help from the visual content, attracts attention and stops the viewer. The combined visuals and words communicate the intent and purpose of the exhibit.

Design planning starts with visual content, moves to message, and then to headline—almost the reverse of planning a news story. The reason is logical. The visual content should carry most of the communication load. Message should be related to visuals, and the headline serves the important but single function of attracting attention.

We said that exhibits come in all shapes and sizes, and they do. But most exhibits will have three dimensions—height, width, and depth. Think of your exhibit area as a stage setting with a background and foreground.

The Visual Content

When considering the design for any exhibit, determine first whether the visual content can feature actual, real-life objects— soil, plants, water, tools, products, or even animals. Go with the real thing whenever you can.

Grow plants in soil, with different soil treatments as your visual content, for an exhibit on the values of soil-testing and proper fertilizer application.

Use glass jars of clean and dirty water to show what happens when streams and lakes are polluted.

Exhibits on flower-growing should feature growing flowers. Why settle for a drawing or a sketch? If your message deals with control of weeds in lawns, grow the weeds in flats or pots, and use them in your exhibit.

Use actual bottles, cans, containers, and storage cabinets to show how to store medicines and household chemicals safely.

When the environment is suitable and your message deals with the care, feeding, or management of animals, use live animals in your exhibit if facilities are available for proper care.

If it isn't possible to use the real-life object, turn next to models and replicas. Any variety store is filled with models of real-life objects—animals, machines, cars, houses, fruits, flowers, vegetables. Some are even life-sized and hard to distinguish from the real object.

If you can't buy models and replicas, use imagination and ingenuity and make your own. Green sponge rubber can be shaped and cut into trees, shrubs, and bushes for a landscape design. Stained corrugated cardboard makes a realistic plowed field. You can do great things with modeling clays, plastics, and other materials.

Three-dimensional visuals, especially real objects, add depth and realism to your exhibit. When they are unavailable or inappropriate for your subject, turn to other techniques for your visual content.

Black-and-white and color photographs can have tremendous visual impact when handled properly. For some subjects, a dramatic giant blowup of a single, story-telling picture may serve as the major visual content for an exhibit. The picture should be truly big—3 feet by 4 feet or larger—and it should tell a story with only a word or two of caption.

Picture these possibilities:

Topic	Picture	Caption
Air pollution	Black smoke billowing from industrial chimneys	Breathless beauty?
Urban blight	Rats in a junkyard	Neighbors!
Soil conservation	Muddy water rushing down a sloping field	Land in motion.

Use two blown-up photographs in your exhibit to compare, show contrast, present before-and-after situations, say "this or that." A series of three or four pictures can tell a step-by-step story.

If your budget permits and the equipment is available, use an automatic slide projector and a shadow-box arrangement to project a continuous slide showing for visual content. Remember that the "show" can't take more than thirty or forty seconds, so use no more than ten or fifteen slides.

The visual content for many subjects may require drawings, sketches, and designs. If they are simple and dramatic, maps, charts, and graphs can serve as effective exhibit visuals. They must be understandable at a glance with a minimum of verbal explanation. For some subjects, humorous cartoons and drawings will attract attention and get a message across.

The Message

The exhibit message has one objective—to underscore, explain, or clarify the visual content. If people can read the message while walking slowly past the exhibit, you have done a good job. If they have to stop and spend two or three minutes reading the fine print, the message is too long and too complicated.

Try to restrict the message "reading time" to ten seconds. Five seconds is better. Say what you have to say in twenty-five to fifty words, no more.

The Headline

The headline has two functions—to catch the attention of the viewer and to identify the exhibit subject. It should shout but not offend. DIRTY AIR IS DANGEROUS. KEEP YOUR FARM OUT OF THE RIVER. RATS MAKE POOR NEIGHBORS. 4-H NEEDS YOUR HELP. VOTE *yes* FOR BEAUTY.

Use fewer than ten words in your headline. The fewer the better.

Setting the Stage

Think of your exhibit design as a stage setting, with your main visual content as the "principal actor." Focus attention on the visual message—the object, model, picture, or poster. Usually, this will mean the foreground of a three-dimensional exhibit but not "center stage."

Design your exhibit so that the visual "flow" is from left to right and from top to bottom. People read from left to right and from top to bottom, so they are used to looking at things in that way.

Such an arrangement then calls for the headline to be at the top, left of center, of the background. The major visual content should be in the foreground, off center to the upper or lower left, while the supporting message can be located at the right of center foreground or background. Strive for informal rather than formal balance of the exhibit elements.

The left-to-right design must be switched, of course, if the exhibit is located in a controlled traffic pattern that moves the audience from right to left. In that case, arrange the elements from right to left so the viewer can follow the exhibit flow without moving against the traffic pattern.

Attention-Getters

A well-designed exhibit with an important message will stop most people who are interested in the subject. Heighten attention and interest with lighting, movement, and sound.

Basic lighting is essential, of course, for any exhibit. The audience must be able to see all of the exhibit elements without interference from glare or dark shadows. Outdoor exhibits may require shading, while nearly all indoor exhibits, even those in store windows, require supplemental artificial light.

Add emphasis through focus lighting, intermittent lighting, and color lighting. Small spotlights can focus the viewer's attention on the visual content, the message, or both. Use spotlights to create light-and-shadow contrasts for mood and atmosphere. With inexpensive timing devices, alternately illuminate and darken exhibit areas, and use alternating "signal" lights to direct attention from one part of the exhibit to another.

There are various ways to achieve movement or the illusion of movement in an exhibit. Alternating or sequence lighting can give the impression of movement. Use small, hidden electric fans for subtle effects of movement.

All exhibit supply houses have a wide range of small electric motors that rotate turntables, pull and release springs, and move pendulums. You can adapt inexpensive electric trains for special exhibit features.

In certain environments, you can add sound to the exhibit through the use of continuous tape recordings. You can record and play a brief message, make use of appropriate sound effects, or play background "atmosphere" music.

It's best to avoid mechanical and electrical devices and systems, however, unless you or someone else can be readily available to service and maintain the system. If the exhibit depends upon movement devices, and the devices fail, you are out of business. The same is true of devices that contribute lighting or special sound effects.

Audience Participation

There are various ways to design exhibits that encourage audience participation. A simple technique calls for a panel of key questions in one area of the exhibit, with the answers on a panel in another area. The viewer is invited to answer questions before looking at the answer panel. With a little sophistication, the answers can be placed on a backlighted panel, remaining invisible until the viewer presses an "answer" button. With a little more sophistication, you can design a series of questions and answers with duplicate "ask" and "answer" push buttons.

Exhibits can also be designed so that viewers can activate special movement and lighting devices. In other designs, the viewer can be invited to "tune in" for the recorded message. He either picks up a telephone instrument or pushes a button to activate the playback mechanism of a continuous-tape playback unit.

Audience-participation exhibits are best suited for longer-time installation in environments where people have more "waiting" time. Since such exhibits permit the participation of only two or three people at one time, they tend to restrict audience flow. If the units are "busy," most people will walk on by and not wait for their turn.

CHAPTER 26

Meetings: Desirable
or Deadly

Meetings can be effective channels for communication. But many are not. Too frequently, they are more deadly than desirable—for a variety of reasons.

Objectives are vaguely defined or not defined at all; audiences are polite but indifferent and uninvolved; speakers are poorly prepared or prepared for the wrong audience; presentations are boring; and the environment is so distracting that communication is almost impossible.

For many subjects, the meeting channel is capable of carrying a message to only a small fraction of the people who might benefit from the information.

Meetings consume huge chunks of time on the part of planners, speakers, and members of the audience. The time-cost per person reached at meetings is usually higher—much higher—than for any other group or mass-media channel. The cost may be even higher than for some person-to-person channels. If you doubt this observation, use your own experience to arrive at some figures. Select a message to communicate. Then estimate the number of people you might reach and the time involved in presenting the message via meetings, direct mail, newspapers, radio, television, or even telephone calls. Include all time costs —yours and those of the audience and the speakers.

In short, the purpose of many meetings, when truly identified, can be achieved more effectively by using other communication channels.

Why, then, are so many meetings held if they fail to achieve purpose or when there may be better ways to communicate? Here are some possible reasons:

1. *Habit.* Many meetings will be held this month or this year simply because a similar meeting was held last month or last year. Habit and tradition often are the unfortunate, unrecognized, but real reasons for holding some meetings.

2. *Inflexible planning.* An organization, group, or committee has the responsibility for "planning a program" for the coming year or two years. Meetings are blocked into the program calendar on the basis of anticipated needs or interests. The needs or interests change, but the meetings are held as scheduled without alterations in subject or audience composition.

3. *Planners' prestige.* A surprising number of meetings are held to satisfy the interests, prestige, and ego of those planning the meeting or to bolster the reputation of the sponsoring group or organization. Audience wants and needs get second consideration, if, in fact, they get much consideration at all.

4. *Response security.* The presence of an audience at a meeting satisfies the need for response of those planning the meeting as well as those who participate as speakers, panel members, or other resource people. The speaker may be presenting his information to an audience of only 50 or 100 people, and half of those may be truly listening to him. But they are there, and some are responding in various ways—nodding, smiling, laughing at his jokes, and perhaps applauding his key statements. The speaker might reach 5,000 or 50,000 by using a news story

or a radio presentation, but the readers and listeners will not satisfy his need for response.

5. *Competition.* Organization A holds meetings, so Organization B thinks it must hold bigger and better meetings to stay even with or ahead of Organization A.

6. *Familiarity.* From the time we enter first grade until we complete our formal education, we are involved in meeting-type environments. We are completely familiar with the speaker-audience-classroom combination and believe that meetings are "easy" to plan and hold. One only need pick a subject, line up a speaker, and notify the audience. Usually, we are not so familiar with planning and writing news stories, presenting radio programs, and using other channels of communication.

By now you may be wondering why we have included a chapter on meetings at all when we seem so prejudiced against them.

First of all, we are not prejudiced against all meetings—only against those held for the wrong purpose or those so poorly planned and carried out that they fail to achieve a desired purpose.

Second, some meetings, when properly conceived, planned, and conducted, can be the *best* channel for getting certain kinds of information to certain kinds of audiences.

Finally, because meetings are traditional and so much a part of our social customs, all of us are involved at one time or another in planning, conducting, or participating in them. By thinking about meetings in terms of the communication process, perhaps we can reverse the ratio of deadly to desirable meetings. We may not need more meetings, but we do need a higher percentage of effectives ones.

Meetings, like exhibits, come in all shapes and sizes. They can range from a meeting of a three-man committee to a gathering of 3,000 or more people. So we need to establish the framework for our discussion.

In Chapter 5 we discussed the process of communication in a group environment, and many meetings fall into the category of group discussions. A group of people meet to share information, analyze and solve problems, plan programs, or accomplish other objectives. Each member of the group is both a sender and receiver of messages. Such meetings play important roles in our social system, but we need not include them again in this discussion, although some of the principles of communication in a group environment apply to all types of meetings.

Our target here is the traditional, "larger" meeting where one or more persons are clearly identified as the sources and senders of information, and the members of the audience are just as clearly identified as the receivers of the information. Most larger meetings fall into this speaker-audience category.

How, then, can we decide whether or not such meetings should be held, and how can we make them most effective in accomplishing our objectives?

PLACE AND PURPOSE OF MEETINGS

Having considered some of the wrong reasons for holding meetings, we can now look at some of the right reasons. We can examine the place and purpose of meetings in comparison with other channels by posing four questions:

1. *Are the subject-related messages so detailed, complex, or specialized that they must be transmitted via face-to-face channels?*

Complex or specialized subjects usually are related to specialized audiences, and communication is most effective in the environment of face-to-face communication.

There may be many swine producers in a county, for example, but only a relatively small percentage of the total may have the financial resources or management ability to consider a complete confinement system for raising hogs. Mass-media channels are unsuitable for transmitting such highly specialized information to such a small and highly specialized audience. Communication will be more effective if the interested farmers are brought together for a presentation and discussion on the costs and techniques of raising swine in complete confinement.

Few channels would be more appropriate than a meeting for a presentation and discussion on principles of landscape design for an audience of nurserymen, florists, or even homeowners with specialized interests in this field. Landscape design is a complex subject.

It would be logical to arrange a meeting for math teachers in the community's school system to learn about procedures for introducing and teaching "new math" in the elementary grades.

A meeting would be the logical communication channel when the audience is composed of parents of children with learning difficulties and the subject relates to the joint educational responsibilities of the parents and the school system.

Meetings concerned with complex subjects are most effective when physically related to the environment of the subject. The meeting on raising swine in confinement might consist of a tour or field meeting on the farm of a producer who is following the system. The meeting on landscape design might be held at a nursery where plant materials are readily available or near a home or a park where recommended design principles could be pointed out.

2. *Are the immediate actions and reactions of the audience essential for achieving the purpose of the communication effort?*

For each of the examples in the preceding paragraphs, the answer would be "yes." Each swine producer needs to relate the general information on confinement systems to his own particular situation—size of farm, size of enterprise, amount of capital, and so on. Each producer would share common questions with all other producers at the meeting. The meeting provides the most effective communication channel for those questions to be raised, discussed, and answered.

There is a comparable need for audience action and reaction on the subjects of new math, landscape design, and children with learning difficulties.

Audience action and reaction may, in fact, be the expressed purpose of the meeting. The swine producers may meet not only to learn about the confinement system of raising swine but to decide whether to employ a consultant cooperatively to help them design systems for their farms. Math teachers may be meeting to decide whether to introduce the new teaching techniques this year or to delay the introduction for a year.

Many meetings have some form of decision-making as the final objective. The audience is expected to take a stand on a particular issue or to vote "yes" or "no" on possible plans of action. A meeting is the most convenient communication channel and environment for this type of audience action or reaction.

3. *Will the success of communication depend partly upon the contributions of the audience?*

Meetings should be considered whenever the audience does more than serve as the receivers of messages. Even though decision-making is not one of the communication objectives, members of a meeting audience may actually assist with the selection, reception, and interpretation of messages.

The solicitation of pre-meeting questions may provide the framework for subsequent presentation and discussion. Members of the audience may contribute by serving on listening or discussion panels. The discussion period may provide a forum for the experienced to share their views with the inexperienced and thus interpret and clarify the more difficult subject areas.

4. *When factors of time, cost, and achievement are considered, does a meeting offer distinct advantages over other available communication channels for a particular audience?*

The objective is to communicate something to someone in some way for some purpose. The objective is not to hold meetings for the sake of holding meetings. Once we have selected messages and identified target audiences, we should consider all of the alternative channels of communication.

PLANNING THE EFFECTIVE MEETING

The preceding questions all relate to the needs and roles of the audience as key factors in determining whether to hold a meeting. But if those needs and roles are ignored when the meeting is planned, the meeting may still fail to achieve its objective.

Involve the Audience

Unfortunately, most larger meetings—those that don't fall into the group-discussion category—follow a traditional pattern. It is this pattern that makes them deadly.

The meeting planners select a topic which *they* believe will interest a potential audience. They pick the date, time, and place; arrange for a speaker; and notify the audience.

At the given time and place, the speaker and the audience come together, with each having preconceived and preconditioned attitudes concerning what is expected of them.

The speaker accepts his role as an authority on the subject and assumes that the audience is there to learn from him.

The members of the audience, having attended many similar meetings, are fairly sure that their role is to sit and listen to the speaker. The role is familiar and comfortable, and it is confirmed by the physical arrangements of the room and the introduction of the speaker.

The room has a raised platform for the speaker and other program participants and rows of chairs for the listening audience. The introduction stresses the competency of the speaker and *his* interest in the topic *he* will be talking about.

The traditional stage is set, and the speaker presents his speech. He speaks well, demonstrates his knowledge of the subject, and perhaps uses appropriate visual aids.

The audience, in turn, plays its traditional and polite passive role—it listens.

When the speech is over, the chairman thanks the speaker and asks, "Are there any questions?" At the last minute, he finally tries to involve the audience, and the result may be a few minutes of painful silence for himself as well as the speaker and his audience. The silence may be broken by a polite question or two, followed by quick adjournment of the meeting or a call for a break before the next speaker is introduced.

Plan an effective meeting by breaking the traditional implication that all knowledge of the subject resides on the speaker's platform, while the audience is the custodian of all ignorance.

The meeting is held to help the audience solve problems. Those on the platform are there to serve the audience. The audience is not there to honor or pay tribute to the speaker.

As the meeting planner you must find ways to change the passive audience into an active, functioning group, capable of identifying their problems and finding solutions with the help of speakers and other resource experts on the platform. How?

Step 1: Involve the audience when selecting the subject area and the specific messages.

Consult with the audience in advance by asking selected representatives to serve on a planning committee. Make sure the members truly represent the audience, and the audience knows that fellow members had a hand in planning the program.

Involve the audience at the time of the meeting by using the pre-question technique. With this technique, the chairman announces the general topic and gives enough background information to enable the audience to relate the topic to their particular situation. The audience is then asked to suggest specific questions for discussion. The questions can be raised orally or written on cards. They are then listed on a chart or chalkboard, and the speaker or speakers cover the questions during their presentations.

Use of the pre-question technique assumes that the audience has a keen interest in the subject and that the speaker is flexible enough to adjust his material to the questions raised. If you suspect that the audience would not suggest questions, also suspect that the topic is of little interest. If you suspect that the speaker is not flexible enough to adapt his presentation to the questions, also suspect that you have selected the wrong speaker.

Step 2: Provide an environment that encourages two-way communication between platform and audience and among members of the audience.

A meeting has both a physical and a psychological environment. Both should assure the audience that the meeting is theirs —that they had a part in planning it and that their active participation is wanted and needed.

Whenever possible, avoid the "lecture-room" arrangement that features an overly imposing speaker's platform and rigid rows of "listening" seats for the audience. While the speaker and other program participants should be positioned where they can be seen and heard, keep the setting as simple and informal as possible. Remove physical and psychological barriers between platform people and audience people.

If space and facilities permit, use a conference-room setup, with the audience seated at tables. Small tables that seat from four to eight are better than long rows of tables, because the small-table arrangement encourages communication within the group.

Establish the psychological environment for internal communication before the meeting opens. Treat your audience as you would guests in your home. Select a host committee to welcome people as they arrive and to help make them feel welcome in what may be unfamiliar surroundings.

Use the pre-meeting time to start getting people involved in the program. Give those who arrive early something to do. Pre-meeting coffee sessions are good ice-breakers. Pass out background information on the subject of the meeting. Let them start thinking about questions they might like to raise. Distribute pre-meeting true-false quizzes to focus attention on the discussion subject. Show a short film or set of slides on a related subject to stimulate interest and direct attention away from the problems they brought with them to the meeting. Take your cues from the entertainment world, where star performers long ago learned the importance of "warming up" and involving the audience before starting the show.

You are familiar with the variety of ways to encourage two-way communication during the meeting:

Floor questions. When audiences are not unduly large, use the traditional procedure of asking for questions following a presentation, *if* the audience has been involved in the meeting from the beginning, *if* the environment is friendly and informal, and *if* the presentation was structured to provide for a follow-up discussion period. Assure the audience at the start of the meeting that their questions will be welcome. Encourage them to think about questions during the presentation, and provide paper and pencils for those who want to write their questions in advance, even though they may ask them orally.

Listening panel. With larger audiences, a listening panel may establish initial communication between platform and audience. Ask three or four members of the audience in advance to serve on the panel, or call for volunteers at the start of the meeting. The panel members can be seated on the platform or scattered in the audience, but they should be introduced at the start of the meeting. Call for their questions first, following the presentation.

Buzz groups. When the physical setup permits, divide a large audience into a number of small discussion groups following the presentation. Give the groups ten or fifteen minutes to discuss the presentation and to record two or three questions that deserve further amplification or clarification. The buzz-group technique encourages communication within groups and between the audience and the platform.

Regardless of the technique used to encourage audience involvement, always seek ways to use the special knowledge and experience of the audience itself. In almost any meeting on almost any subject, certain members of the audience have unusual and specialized knowledge about one or more areas being discussed. Often they are reluctant to compete with the authorities on the platform, unless the speaker or the meeting chairman provides the opportunity. Whenever possible, give such people advance notice that they may be called on.

There is no "one best" technique for ensuring an interesting and effective meeting. We have reviewed some basic considerations and suggested a variety of techniques, but there are others that we have not discussed. You will find the most effective techniques for the subject and the audience if you sincerely believe that (1) the meeting belongs to the audience and not the speaker or the planners, (2) communication and learning are more effective when the receivers are actively involved in the communication process, and (3) it is your job to provide the environment that encourages audience participation and involvement.

EXTEND AN INVITATION

The best-conceived techniques for involvement at the meeting will fail if only a portion of the intended audience shows up. The meeting plan, therefore, must include the specific steps you will take to invite the audience. The channels used and the invitations themselves will affect attendance and establish an initial psychological setting for the meeting.

If you have the names and addresses of all those who should be interested in the meeting, you can use direct mail most effectively. Consider a series of three direct-mail letters.

The first letter should be brief but should identify the problem or problems in terms of the receiver's interests. Let the person know in the first letter that representatives of *his group* are planning the meeting to help solve *his problems*. Include information on the date, time, and place, so the receiver can mark the date on his calendar. Mail the first letter from four to six weeks ahead of the meeting date.

The second letter, mailed two or three weeks in advance of the meeting, should expand on the reasons for the meeting and include as much program information as possible. Reassure the receiver that the meeting will be worth his time and effort to attend, that the program is designed to help him solve his problems, and that he will have an opportunity to raise questions and take part in the discussion. Repeat the date, time, and place information.

Mail the concluding letter in the series four or five days in advance. Its main purpose is to remind the receiver of the meeting, but it can also include details not available when the second letter was mailed.

Use available mass-media channels to publicize larger meetings or when you don't have the names and addresses of the intended audience. Prepare advance news stories for local newspapers and radio stations, following essentially the same schedule as for direct-mail letters. Use both direct-mail and mass-media channels to ensure maximum coverage.

Regardless of channel, the content of the invitation should reflect sincere interest in the audience and their problems. You are not trying to swell the attendance for the benefit of the speaker or to make your organization look good in the eyes of the public.

Often a few key people deserve special invitations, especially if they can make contributions to the meeting. Agricultural representatives from local banks and other lending agencies might well receive special invitations to attend meetings concerned with farm production and marketing problems, for example, since the adoption of new practices often involves use of credit.

Earlier we reviewed the key roles played by legitimizers and community-opinion leaders. Many of these people may deserve special invitations. If these people are accepted by the group, you might ask them to join the listening panel or lead a buzz-group discussion. Often they contribute to a meeting simply by being there.

CHECK PHYSICAL ARRANGEMENTS

Every meeting plan should include a check list of physical arrangements.

Start with the meeting place itself. The size of the room should fit the size of the audience in an environment that will encourage participation. Small audiences get lost if the room is too big. Large audiences feel confined and restricted if the room is too small. We have mentioned the value of the small-table, conference-room arrangement in encouraging participation.

If lighting is inadequate, provide some means for supplemental lighting. Take advantage of natural light for daytime meetings, but check seating arrangements to ensure that a part of the audience doesn't face window glare. If the program calls for projected visuals such as slides, movies, or overhead projections, make sure the room can be darkened for both day and night meetings. Special supplemental lights may be needed for other types of visuals used by the speaker.

Check all equipment before the meeting starts. Some meetings are remembered more for the equipment failures than for the messages—projectors that wouldn't function, stands that fell over, lights that wouldn't turn on, easels that collapsed, and slides that were projected upside down.

EVALUATE YOUR EFFORTS

Ideally, your meeting plan should include procedures for post-meeting evaluation. By giving the audience an opportunity to tell what they liked and didn't like about the meeting, you have incorporated another technique for audience involvement and provided yourself with cues for improving the next meeting.

You can be misled if you depend upon the volume of applause or polite but hurried exit comments as your evaluation method. You can also be misled if you merely "count the house."

The large attendance may indicate only that advance publicity methods were successful. It does not tell whether the audience benefited from the meeting. The applause may simply register relief that the meeting is over.

Most audiences welcome an opportunity to express their opinions about a meeting. Use a simple questionnaire, requiring only a few check marks to give the needed information, or ask the audience to answer two or three key questions on a slip of paper.

INCLUDE FOLLOW-UP COMMUNICATION

A meeting plan that does not include follow-up communication is much the same as a game plan for a football contest that stops the action on the ten-yard line.

An important part of the meeting *starts* when the chairman announces that the meeting is adjourned. You have an opportunity then to initiate follow-up communication, both with the people who attended the meeting and those who could not or did not attend.

Direct mail may again be the most effective channel for follow-up contact with those who attended the meeting, assuming the meeting plan included arrangements for getting the needed names and addresses. Capitalize on the expressed audience interest by using follow-up communication to summarize and reinforce the information presented at the meeting.

If it may be useful for reference, include a copy, or at least a digest, of the speaker's talk. Ask a member of the planning group to record the key points of the presentation and discussion, and use his material to summarize the key messages in your follow-up letter. You may have leaflets, flyers, and other reference materials on the general subject in which the audience would be interested.

Use the local mass-media channels to report the key information to those who could not attend the meeting, following the suggestions made earlier for writing follow-up news stories.

CHAPTER 27

The Strategy
of Communication

The ability to design an effective strategy of communication is perhaps the most important and demanding of all communication skills.

The dictionary defines strategy as "the science of planning and directing to achieve an objective, that is, as in military strategy."

Communication strategy may be defined as the science or art of planning and using resources to achieve a communication objective with maximum efficiency.

Our objective is to influence receivers in some way through the communication process. Our resources are money and time as related to skills and effort. These resources represent *inputs* in the equation of efficiency.

The other part of the efficiency equation is *output*, and output is represented by the number of people reached who respond as we intend them to respond.

We may roughly measure communication efficiency by dividing output by input—the number of people responding as we intend by the combination of money, time, and effort spent in reaching them.

For any communication effort, inputs are limited. We can afford to spend just so much money, time, and effort on any given communication assignment. Our objective is to achieve the highest possible output per unit of input, and we need a strategy to help us reach this objective.

To design strategy, we use our knowledge of all elements of the communication process and the way in which the elements are affected by different communication environments. To carry out strategy, we use our skills of listening, writing, speaking, and visualizing.

All strategy starts with planning, and planning itself is a process.

FOUR PHASES OF PLANNING

Planning involves the steps that we follow, knowingly or unknowingly, each time we choose a course of action from among several available alternatives. While we may be unaware of the process, we usually go through the steps of (1) investigating, (2) predicting, (3) considering alternatives, and (4) selecting a final plan.

In one way or another, we follow the planning process when we buy a house, a car, or a suit of clothes.

We take the four steps when we select the route we will follow on a long automobile trip. We investigate, predict, consider alternatives, and make a final choice.

We *investigate* by finding answers to key questions—distance, needed time of arrival, condition of automobile, time of year, combinations of highways that can be followed, kind of country we will be going through, number of cities, and so on.

Since we won't have all the facts, we *predict* certain conditions and situations. Based upon general knowledge of the country and previous travel experiences, we predict probable weather conditions, our average driving speed, the condition of the highways, the number of hours we will drive each day, and the availability of hotels and motels.

On the basis of our facts and predictions, we *consider* the advantages and disadvantages of several different routes we might take. The shortest route goes through a number of large cities. A second avoids the cities but involves driving through some mountains. The third alternative route is considerably longer but includes more miles of four-lane interstate highways.

Before making a final selection, we may have to reopen our investigation and seek additional facts specifically related to the three alternatives. We may, for example, check with friends or associates who have recently traveled to our destination over one of the possible routes. We compare their experiences with our facts and predictions. We then take the final step in the planning process and *select* one of the three alternatives as the route we will take.

Communication planning is based upon the same four steps, applied in the following manner:

Investigating

During the investigation phase, we collect and analyze all known facts associated with the elements of the communication process.

Audience. We study all available information related to audience—knowledge of subject, attitudes, wants, needs, and communication behavior. Who are the people we want to reach in terms of numbers, age, sex, education, occupation, and financial situation? What is their social level? What do they read, watch, or listen to?

Message. Is the message simple or complex? Does it intend to change attitudes, skills, or practices? Does response involve minimum, modest, or maximum effort on the part of the audience? What rewards are offered?

Purpose. What is our intention? Do we want to create interest and awareness, change attitudes, or achieve a specified action?

Channel. What channels are potentially available for our use?

Inputs. Our investigation also includes an appraisal of our skills and our resources. What skills do we have, and what skills do we lack? Who else will be involved in our communication effort? How much time can we afford to spend? What is our budget? What facilities do we have?

Predicting

There is no way of knowing in advance how many people will actually come to a meeting we plan. We must predict attendance on the basis of previous experience and our knowledge of the audience and subject. We must also predict probable readership of news stories, audience size for radio programs, number of viewers of a television presentation or an exhibit. We must predict the amount of time needed to hold a meeting, write the news stories, or prepare and present radio and television shows.

We turn to predictions whenever our investigation fails to provide facts needed to make decisions.

Considering Alternatives

With audience and communication purpose identified, we are concerned primarily with alternative combinations of channels and messages that will permit us to communicate most efficiently —to reach the most people most effectively with the resources that we can spend.

While there are no precise formulas for combining channels and messages to reach specific audiences, we can suggest some general guidelines. These guidelines are based upon channel and message characteristics and the relationship of these characteristics to various audiences.

As we have seen, channels fall into one of three broad categories related to audience size: mass-media, group, and person-to-person. Messages can be classified as simple or complex whether the intent is to inform, change attitudes, or alter behavior patterns.

Mass-media channels. We should achieve maximum communication efficiency by using mass-media channels under the following conditions:

1. The audience for the message is large. The mass media, in fact, offer the only practical channels for reaching large, general audiences.

2. The message is simple. This does not mean that the message lacks importance, but the concept should be easy to grasp and understand.

3. The message is timely. There is need to reach audiences quickly.

4. The audience is exposed to the mass-media channels. A large share of the intended audience subscribes to and reads newspapers, or listens to radio, or watches television.

5. Time and money are limited.

Group channels. The following conditions suggest the use of group channels (meetings, conferences, field days, and direct-mail services):

1. The audience is relatively small, specialized, easily identified, and highly motivated.

2. The message is either complex, highly specialized, or both.

3. Communication effectiveness depends in part upon immediate audience response and feedback. The audience does more than receive the message.

4. Message content is more important than timeliness.

5. Time and other resources are available.

Person-to-person channels. The conditions that suggest the use of person-to-person channels are almost self-evident and include the following:

1. The audience is small, and motivation may be slight.

2. The message, simple or complex, must be fitted to the individual needs of the receiver.

3. The timing of the message is not critical.

4. Time and other resources are available.

The exceptions. There are exceptions to all guidelines, of course, and we find many exceptions for those above.

Television, for example, is a mass-media channel, but it satisfies most of the conditions for both mass-media and group channels. Because television carries both visual and verbal messages, it can transmit relatively complex messages for specialized audiences.

In many cases, the person-to-person channel is best suited for communicating with selected receivers who are highly motivated, but the message must still be fitted to their particular needs.

We have placed direct mail in the group-channel category, but many advertisers use direct mail to reach a mass audience. They are willing to pay the cost of direct mail in order to have complete control, or nearly complete control, of the communication process.

Selecting the Final Plan

Once our planning has identified possible alternatives for channel-message-audience combinations, we must match each of the alternatives with available inputs—money, time, effort.

In making our final selection, we ask these questions of each alternative:

1. How many of our intended audience will we contact?

2. Of those contacted, what share will respond in the way we intend for them to respond?

3. How much money and time must we spend?

4. What will be the cost per person reached and per person responding in the intended way?

PUTTING THE PLAN INTO ACTION

Just as there are steps in planning, there are equally important steps in moving the plan into action.

Step 1. Budget time and money for each of the communication activities called for in the plan, and work up a calendar of deadlines for those activities. When will the first news story be written, the first radio program be aired, the first television program be presented? What are the dates for the scheduled meetings, and when must the first planning session be held for each meeting or the series of meetings? When and how will the meetings be publicized?

Step 2. Plan schedules to meet the deadlines. With a realistic time budget, we should be able to estimate the number of hours needed each week to carry out the plan. If the number of required hours is unavailable, we must adjust the plan to fit the hours.

Step 3. Evaluate the plan after each step and make adjustments called for by the evaluation. Our first meeting may have been so successful that subsequent meetings are not needed. Cancel them. We learn that the television station has changed its program schedule, and the show we counted on is unavailable. We must shift resources to other channels. Audience feedback indicates more misunderstanding of the problem than we anticipated. We may need an additional series of news stories.

Step 4. Make a final evaluation and prepare a report on successes and failures for future reference. We can improve our efforts tomorrow only by applying the knowledge gained today.

That thought, perhaps more than any other, guided the preparation of this book.

A Note on the Author

Hadley Read was born and raised on a Hamilton County, Iowa, farm and received his early education in a one-room country school that featured a "library" of 16 books.

He studied journalism and economics at Iowa State University and spent his spare time participating on the University's debating team. He received his B.S. degree in 1939 and his M.S. degree in 1941 from Iowa State.

Before coming to the University of Illinois in 1947 as head of the Office of Agricultural Communications, he worked as an economist-editor for the Ralston Purina Company of St. Louis, spent two years as a daytime farmer and nighttime publisher of a weekly newspaper, and served as an assistant extension editor at Iowa State University.

At the University of Illinois, Read heads a professional staff of 26 writers, editors, broadcasters, teachers, and visual communication specialists.

Throughout his career, Read has been actively involved in the field of international rural communications development. He was on leave from the University in 1952–53 to serve as a U.S. State

Department Communications Consultant for various countries of Western Europe. He has also served as a State Department consultant in Ceylon, India, and Jordan and as a consultant for the Australian Commonwealth Scientific and Industrial Organization.

His guidebook "Getting Information to Farm Families," published in 1955, has been widely used in the United States and overseas.